T0290482

Global Advertising in a Global Culture

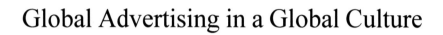

Global Advertising in a Global Culture

Thomas H. P. Gould

ROWMAN & LITTLEFIELD
Lanham • Boulder • New York • London

Published by Rowman & Littlefield
A wholly owned subsidiary of
The Rowman & Littlefield Publishing Group, Inc.
4501 Forbes Boulevard, Suite 200, Lanham, Maryland 20706
www.rowman.com

Unit A, Whitacre Mews, 26-34 Stannary Street, London SE11 4AB, United Kingdom

British Library Cataloguing in Publication Information Available

Library of Congress Cataloging-in-Publication Data
Gould, Thomas H. P., 1953–
Global advertising in a global culture / Thomas H. P. Gould.
pages cm
Includes bibliographical references and index.
ISBN 978-0-8108-8643-8 (cloth : alk. paper) — ISBN 978-0-8108-8644-5 (electronic)
1. Advertising—History. 2. Internet advertising. 3. Globalization—Social aspects. 4. Culture and globalization. I. Title.
HF5811.G68 2016
659.1—dc23
2015031862

Printed in the United States of America

Contents

Preface

I am known as Tom to friends, T.H.P. to fellow academics, and Tommy to old acquaintances, and I have lived in many places in my life. I settled physically some years ago in the middle of Kansas, in the middle of the United States, but live elsewhere mentally. I hope I represent the best example of what I seek to describe in my own research: modern, highly individualized, moderate risk taker, one more interested in the real fate of others than in their immediate, temporal appreciation. Perhaps that last phrase suggests a motivated priest. If born five hundred years ago, I likely would have been just that, if only to access what otherwise would be out of bounds.

I accept that I will never be seen as a Lessig or a Friedman. Yet I believe I have something to add to the discussion of the near- and long-term future of both advertising and journalism: two fields with little in common—or at least no more than do fiction and nonfiction writing. As I spend years mudding around my shared garden, I would prefer that future academic research consider the impact of the reader on what is written, the student on what is taught, the administrator on how information is shared. If we keep these three elements in their unlabeled bottles, we ask not for Kepler or Einstein in our classrooms—however poor they were as teachers—but routine, average, non-researching educators ill prepared for the future but well set for the political mush so popular today. A poor lecture from Kepler seems far more important than the seemingly smooth ABCs from another.

Acknowledgments

I offer my thanks to Bennett Graff and his wonderful associate, Monica Savaglia. The two of them walked patiently with me as I dealt with my medical troubles, waiting patiently for the product to be finished. Andrea O. Kendrick, also at the publisher, has been helpful and understanding in these last few weeks. I also thank my students from the January 2015 Web history class. They put thoughtful words to their considerations, which I placed in various instances herein. But I want to deeply thank the only person who keeps me thinking about writing, living, and dealing with the topic and the sickness in a positive way: Carol, the executive director of a very busy, very demanding learning program, Great Plains Interactive Distance Education Alliance. Responsible for an operation with a name like this, her time is in great demand. Yet she is always present to heal, love, and inspire me. Thank you, Carol.

Introduction

Global Advertising and Global Culture

The stories are old and well told at most agencies interested in globalism (which would be most agencies). Soviet consumers had become wise to the use of advertising by the government to push slow-moving, inferior products. If the product was advertised, it was probably a bad item offered at an outrageous price. These consumers were nothing if not sophisticated. They knew how to detect the best cans of tomato soup, which were all labeled "tomato soup" and rarely, if ever, advertised. They walked the aisles of the store, turning over the cans to read the numbers stamped on the bottom. These numbers were associated with specific factories making tomato soup. Some factories made better soup than others. These consumers were wise to not only the best factory, but to the second best, should number one not be available.

Consider, also, the behavior of Soviet consumers arriving in the United States in the 1970s and early 1980s. They left their Aeroflots at JFK and immediately went to the nearest malls, loaded up on Levi's blue jeans, and planned how and where they would sell them on their return to Moscow. Soviet consumers were keenly aware of Levi's (and its brand values) in a country that did not allow any advertising of the brand. That is, they had created the Levi's brand in their heads. They knew the product details and, more important, its value to other Russian consumers. The exchange of the elements that would complete the brand image was made by word of mouth. Was this slower than what was happening in the United States? Definitely. As Levi's became more and more part of an increasingly crowded blue jean market in the West, they remained the best seller in Moscow.

Times have changed. The acceleration of information flow hasn't changed the average global consumer: it has simply made them more efficient, more rapid, and more in touch with global brands. And, yes, it has made them more powerful. These global consumers exist today in every corner of the planet. Empowered with new tools to reach farther and faster, they are brand savvy, brand aware, and brand motivated. Each is aware of global brands, and each has created a brand image, complete with product values, pricing, and all of the trappings that come along with brand equity. They are—setting aside massive cultural variances—no different from Mom and Pop shopping on Main Street in the United States: they know what they want and where to get it. This is the global consumer, the least restricted, most powerful brand adopter in history.

Consumers have always been branders. Whether sampling the wares brought back from China by Marco Polo or downloading the latest coupon to their mobile phone for a carton of milk, they are brand aware. Whether they are treated to the "Lemon" Volkswagen ad in the 1960s or the online blog pitching the same brand today, they quest for information. And while we as professionals and academics tend to define information somewhat differently and esoterically, these consumers seek it all, use it all, and sift out the useless based on their own individual criteria.

Each global consumer is also a product of a culture. They have their limits. They have their traditions. They are wired differently in how they process information. They are wired differently in how they share that information.

So, what are modern advertising creative directors and media managers to do? How can a media planner actually plan in the Facebook era? How can an account planner represent the mind of a consumer that is defined by behavior, not demographics? And, oh yeah, that behavior is very much culturally driven, culturally defined, and culturally changing.

Experts in global culture such as Geert Hofstede, Milton Rokeach, and Marieke de Mooji have introduced scales of measuring consumers via behavior. They and others consider consumer brand activity in a variety of countries. As is often the case, however, these research findings are not static or rigid. Cultural studies, perhaps more than any other area of research, are ever fluid and ever shifting. Driven largely by changes in information access (as examined later), consumers in different cultures are seeing a wide variety of options, everything from shoe styles to forms of government. The nature of globalism, as defined as a shared set of values and beliefs, as well as shared branding and purchasing, is not standing still. We have few, if any, major brands that are purely local. We have more and more brands that twenty years ago might have been considered local that are now regional, and many that were regional are now multinational. And, of course, a few, such as Coca-Cola and Apple, are global.

Thus, this book will offer a single photograph of where we are in the second decade of the century and suggest where we might be in the next decade and beyond, but with few promises and thin support. The cultural landscape and thus the commercial landscape are changing so fast that the dominant browser of today, for example, will likely become the forgotten browser of tomorrow (e.g., Google vs. Netscape). Equally likely, markets that were once as distant as China from Rome for Marco Polo will become so accessible and immediate that they will appear to be local in both their physical nature and their consumer branding buzz.

As suggested, the driving force responsible for the massive and pervasive shifts in global culture is the Internet. More specifically, I argue that the main future catalyst for brand adoption globally will be (and largely already is) apps. The latest children of the Internet, apps provide a simple and cheap method of providing consumers a way to create their own sites as their own markets, such as Houzz, Pinterest, and others. These relatively new creations have shifted the nature of the traditional information flow described as sender-to-receiver to a far more complex and largely uncontrollable flood of data. What is so irresistible about this new trend may be the richly deep opportunity it offers to have one-to-one conversations with potential consumers anywhere at any time.

Of course, we have some cultural differences to overcome. Culture still defines consumer behavior. Culture still remains the most powerful predictor of communication involvement by potential buyers and brand adopters. The layers of language, tradition, and semantics render most universal efforts at branding difficult at best. The stories abound (some largely urban myths) of Western advertising falling flat in non-Western countries. The cultural chasm that exists between them and us can seem impossible to bridge. And, in some cases, it is. For now.

But we come back to those cute little apps. Easy to install, easy to use, and at times packed with cultural elements that move fluidly from screens through eyes to brains. Only recently have some agencies effectively employed these tools. The possibilities seem endless. For example, why not use an app that allows consumers to compare prices in a store? Oh, they already can do that. Okay, how about one that allows a consumer to buy various Procter & Gamble products, have them delivered to their home (with free shipping), for 60 percent less than what Target, Kmart, or Walmart charges for the same products? That's not possible. Yet. Or is it?

However, it is not a reach to imagine that every grocery chain on the planet knows that direct-to-consumer is moments away and that the entire middle of every Kroger will simply disappear. Consider that it is very likely that, in the near future, large box electronic stores such as Best Buy simply will not be sustainable. Of course, it could be argued that if the Internet was going to lead to the elimination of offline purchasing, it would have happened by now. And, again, this would be the case were it not for the appearance of apps. Future consumers will, no doubt, consider it silly and irresponsible to purchase an electronic device without first checking its brand equity among thousands of prior users via their handheld, personally created, personally responsive, personal advisory app.

The Internet does not invent new opportunities or threats. It makes existing ones better or worse. In the case of globalism, the Internet is the engine. In the case of transglobal cultural change, advertising has been the primary carrier, combining both the Internet with advertising results in a rapidly evolving, rapidly converging platform for political, social, and semantic change.

As we progress through this book, we deal with the easy and the difficult regarding global advertising and culture. Language is easier than semantics, for example. Context is tougher than demographics. Economics are more transparent than brand adoption. Some issues are so in flux that they may defy much more than guesses and supposition. Ultimately, we hope, a perspective on the future of advertising in the heads of future global consumers will become clearer and more precise.

CHAPTER 1: GLOBAL HISTORY OF ADVERTISING: PART 1, BEFORE 1993

Tracks the creation of advertising in the United States and Britain in the late nineteenth century. Of particular interest are famous innovators such as Bill Bernbach and Leo Burnett and the Creative Revolution of the 1960s, whose style of creativity spread to other countries and cultures, spawning new advertising giants.

CHAPTER 2: GLOBAL HISTORY OF ADVERTISING: PART 2, SINCE 1993

Where is advertising going in a totally online, totally fragmented delivery scheme? In a fully "pull" consumer environment, how is and has advertising reinvented itself to meet the new challenges of a fragmented platform?

CHAPTER 3: CULTURE TRANSFER AT WEB SPEED

The speed at which trends and innovations spread in today's environment has created significant impacts on traditional information delivery models. Along with this, the use of the Web as a cultural conduit threatens national identities and cultural microspace.

CHAPTER 4: INDIVIDUALISM IN AN APPS AND CULTURE WORLD

The fastest growing area of the Internet is a world of the small: tiny applications that allow users to skip past the Web to more direct, faster, and more isolated access to games, information, and data sharing. At stake here is the glue that holds offline communities together in a totally ephemeral online world.

CHAPTER 5: APPS AND THE SMALL SCREEN TV

What is television online? Small movies? Image-enhanced audio communications? Something entirely new? How will creativity and imagination be encouraged in an all-online, all-access environment?

CHAPTER 6: INDIVIDUALISM AND THE RISE OF THE GLOBAL CONSUMER

The old insult, "made in China," long ago lost its connotation of cheapness and shoddy manufacture. Today, everything made anywhere is virtually available everywhere—and with free shipping. The economic barriers that served to maintain a degree of difference between cultures are evaporating.

CHAPTER 7: ONLINE ADVERTISING AND RISK, ELITISM, AND GENDER

Does trying a new product come with the same degree of risk that it did twenty years ago? Are advertising messages more keenly created with dialed-in accuracy to match the right message to the right personality, to the right elite, to the right gender?

CHAPTER 8: CHILDREN CONSUMED BY CONVERGENCE VIA APPS

Cultural values are being replaced with global commercial standards. How are children processing information delivered online? More specifically, how are children learning to develop their own values and beliefs within virtual worlds?

CHAPTER 9: EDUCATION AND POROUS CULTURAL BORDERS

If information is the food for cultural change, education is the engine that pushes change forward. What is the role of education in a global university world?

CHAPTER 10: THE FUTURE OF E-ADVERTISING

One message, one consumer, one product delivered at the right time and in the right place. The silver bullet is on the horizon. What 100 percent, consumer-appropriate advertising will mean to future brand adoption.

CHAPTER 11: ONE WORLD AGENCY: GOVERNMENTS AND ADVERTISING, STATES AND CONSUMERISM

Free information sharing among libraries may portend a single global library with varying specialized archives within individual branches. Could such a global trend create the same result within global communities such as nations? As we grow closer in culture, closer in setting a global minimum wage, closer in eliminating trade barriers, will the disappearance of national differences pave the way for a single global advertising agency? We have already seen mergers that pull agencies around the globe into one of a small handful of mega-agencies (WPP, Dentsu, JWT). At what point will all agencies meld into one massive agency holding more than 90 percent of all clients and 95 percent of the global messaging?

Bottom line to all of this is the persistent belief that cultures will remain apart and that advertising will remain differentiated in service to these separate forms of living. But the reality is that nothing remains the same. Everything changes, whether we, like our parents, believe it or our politicians promise otherwise. What is at stake is how things will change. We live in a world that is rapidly becoming more and more the same from neighborhood to neighborhood, from country to country, from culture to culture. The belief that what was true yesterday will be true tomorrow is about belief, not reality.

And that may be what our social scientists face: lots of meaningful, productive research. But our advertising copywriters and art directors, our media planners or social media directors and all the remaining characters within the agency concerned about what tomorrow will look like are far more concerned that the changes might result in shutouts, market shifts, and completely unexpected consumer behavior. Such uncertainty in the future of online advertising, enabled by ever-changing methods of communication—currently apps—makes the world of consumers and advertising both exciting and deadly. Bring it on!

Chapter One

Global History of Advertising: Part 1, before 1993

Q. How did television impact advertising?
A. Probably much the same way the Internet did in the '90s—by putting your ad in front of a large group of people who are curious about and excited about a new media, which is in both cases the best way to market the product at the right time. (Tom 2009)

We are expected to summarize the past before launching into the present and future. We could spend time in this chapter reviewing all that many advertising history books can offer. Trouble is, not much that they contain has much to do with the present or future of advertising. Meaning that we have some discourse to consider, but not much. What we do have to weigh is the impact of past technological advances on advertising as a clever way of positioning our argument for the impact of future inventions.

But let's not start where advertising history too often does: the "lost slave" notices in colonial U.S. newspapers or the flimflammery of late-nineteenth-century advertisements often linked to con artists and cure-alls. Some may trace advertising back to the sixteenth century or earlier. We can even dial back the time machine to a period when all we had was word of mouth or, perhaps more accurately, grunts of mouth. We refer here to the true launching of the history of advertising. Specifically, one is tempted to wonder if cave drawings were promoted on nearby rocks: "This age only! Garl's 'Man Chasing Big Horned Animals: A Study in Red' at the third cave on the right." The message might not have been quite so elegant—probably a few grunts and finger pointing—but the need for those who created a work to share the creation had to involve some form of persuasion. Certainly for some artists and authors, the public's awareness of the art has always been part of the motivation to fashion the work.

Suffice it to suggest that not much changed from the first advertisement, whether outside a cave or in a London circular, until television rocked the world of communication. For here we have a powerful, relatively cheap information-access device. Yes, cheap. A year's subscription to a newspaper is just the first installment in an ongoing purchase to gain access to information. A television, although it costs more initially, is actually far cheaper over the long haul. Information is free on television, free long before the term was used in regard to the Internet. The purchaser shells out a couple of hundred dollars and walks away with an electronic device that provides access to information. And although this transaction has been used to describe a user's relationship with handheld devices, it is just as accurate when used to describe the relationship between a viewer and a television set. Yes, the actual access was limited and the specific information accessed was determined by others, but the access was free—or it was free until the advent of cable.

Yet we spend much more time in our research these days concerned with the impact of newer technologies on mass communication. So what do we make of the impact of more recent new technology on the advertising for products? More specifically, what do we make of the impact on the advertising of products, say, since the birth of the Internet? Given that advertising online has not disappeared (as some predicted) nor created massive problems for agencies (as others predicted), exactly what did happen?

If we were to dial back our time machine to three decades prior to the Internet's arrival, we might have a clue. We take a closer, unique look in this chapter at the ways the work of some very famous advertising giants was affected by new technology in the 1950s and 1960s. This is an argument without much citation. Little, if any, academic research has been done looking at the reverse of what most advertising histories have focused on: the impact of Bernbach, Burnett, Ogilvy, Testa, and others on advertising, specifically television advertising. The argument presented here is that the new technology of the small screen had a liberating impact on these geniuses: it freed them to do what had never been even attempted before—use emotion and motion in advertisements. By doing this, television radically changed advertising for almost fifty years, spawning all manner of icons, from the Jolly Green Giant to hundreds of other iconic images that defined advertising, at least until the turn of the twenty-first century.

HOW STORY PLATFORMS HELP GLOBAL BRANDS GO LOCAL

While the current turmoil in Cairo may obscure the post-revolutionary optimism that pervaded the city last winter, that mood was powerful at the time. Despite the chaos in the virtual absence of government, the metropolitan region of some 14 million was taken over in January by an Arabic pop music video urging people to "go crazy" by committing acts of kindness to spread happiness. The film, produced by Coca-Cola, features street scenes of people being kind and happy in well-known Cairo locations. Locals say it perfectly reflected the hopefulness and optimism of Egypt's people as they embarked on the difficult path of building a new democracy. (Cheyfitz 2013)

The Creative Revolution

They were salesmen; they worked in the mailroom, dabbled in fine arts. They were raised to be actresses. They started as journalists. And, for most of them, advertising wasn't even a blip on the horizon. Bernbach, Wells, Ogilvy, Burnett, and those involved in what came to known as the Creative Revolution in the United States in the late 1950s and 1960s were not the product of university schools of advertising. That would come later for those who followed them into advertising as a profession. These early, soon-to-be icons were streetwise, self-described egomaniacs with little or no school training in advertising or its rules. They charged into a profession defined by the business-focused number crunchers—Reeves, Hopkins, Lasker—without much more than raw talent and outrageous ideas. By the time Bernbach's agency unleashed the now globally famous "Lemon" Volkswagen advertisements, everything had changed, at least in the United States. Globally, it was a slightly different story with very different characters, all equally self-taught, all equally nontraditional. To no small degree, all of those involved in the Creative Revolution—both in the United States and elsewhere—were risk takers, individualistic, and driven mostly by Western beliefs, though a few were more influenced by their native cultures.

Whatever this revolution was, it was not global. The ascendancy of these non-degreed advertising pros would change the profession for an entire generation. Yet the only global quality of advertising fifty years ago was the distinct nationality of the advertising professionals. Cross-cultural appeals were rare and usually restricted to equally cross-cultural product categories, such as fashion. The Creative Revolution was strictly a phenomenon of the United States and to a degree England and parts of Europe. The two parts of this revolution included the more popularly discussed advertising created by Bernbach, Ogilvy, and Burnett. The other part—not as widely discussed—was the almost singular nature of much of the advertising of the era: an appeal to individuality, masculinity, and risk taking.

The Supreme Court of India has overturned a lower court's suspension of a law regulating the promotion of tobacco products and criticized the central government for doing nothing to get the interim order revoked since it was issued in 2005. Parliament passed an anti-tobacco law in 2003, and in the following year it introduced a set of rules that made it mandatory for all shops and kiosks selling tobacco products to display signs that warned about their health risks. The vendors also could not display tobacco advertisements that were bigger than 60 by 45 centimeters (24 by 18 inches). ("Supreme Court Restricts Tobacco Advertising" 2013)

Bernbach and Drama

Bill Bernbach presented far more than a desire to confront consumers with the truth. At least one of the secrets that propelled everything that Bernbach touched into the stratosphere of advertising history was the ability to let the commercial viewer feel a part of an inside joke. Starting with the print ads for Ohrbach's, followed hard by those for Levy's Bakery ("You don't have to be Jewish to love Levy's"), Doyle, Dane, and Bernbach made it clear that the old days of making statistical arguments in ads were over. Freewheeling Bernbach made a strong statement that everything was on the table. What followed were ads for Chivas Regal whisky ("Give dad an expensive belt") and Avis ("We try harder"). Simple, direct imaging matched with strong, persuasive copy. As noted by Mark Tungate in *AdLand*, "The copy was so effective that Avis executives allegedly complained to Bernbach, worrying that they wouldn't be able to live up to the high standards that the ad promised" (Tungate 2007, 278, 53).

But it was television that allowed Bernbach to break away even more dramatically from the analytical. Consider the Volkswagen Fastback commercial that featured a young and largely unknown Dustin Hoffman. Yes, Hoffman walks around the car talking about the vehicle's details. But he does it in an unassuming, almost apologetic style. "Up front where most cars have an engine, we have a trunk. And, in back, where we have a trunk, we have a [pause] trunk. A large trunk." Nothing about this commercial talks about fuel mileage, price, colors, engine size, or any of the mind-numbing details that preceded this era. It was as if the often irritating persuasion that highlighted commercials such as those for Anacin (Fast! Fast! Fast!) had been stripped away and we were left with something that more closely resembled a very short movie. It could be a movie because of the new technology that matched motion with a message, blended expertly with emotion.

Prior television commercials tended to be either powerful (and somewhat obnoxious) arguments, like those for Anacin, or live, in-program spots in shows featuring variety-show hosts, such as Jack Benny. The idea of a television commercial telling a story was unheard of. Commercials of the Reeves era were built to overwhelm the viewer with facts, loading one atop another until the will to resist the advertising product was broken. This technique, which could easily be compared to consumer browbeating, was a function made possible in some ways by the nature of the television set itself. Prior to the advent of cable-delivered channels of the 1980s, the vast majority of television viewers had two or three choices: CBS, NBC, and, in some markets, ABC (usually delivered on UHF [ultrahigh frequency]). The actual television set featured two dials, one providing access to channels one through thirteen. The other dial was a more radio-like channel tuner that provided access to UHF. In neither case was there a need for a remote control. After all, viewers had only two or three choices.

Equally sparse by today's television spectrum was programming. The reality for viewers was that they had no way to avoid being blasted by a commercial, like the obnoxious Anacin with its image of a hammer beating on a skull. And such commercials were guaranteed a substantial share of eyeballs. After all, even with three channels, the average share of the watching market would be one-third. Any programming that earned a 33 percent share today would have newborns named after the producers. It stands to reason: one hundred channels generate an expected share of 1 percent.

In such an environment, all that a media buyer needed to accomplish was to fashion the schedule to somewhat match the intended target: evening programming for families, late night for couples, early morning and afternoons for children, and daytime for housewives. Targeting the actual behavior of the individual viewer was not only ignored, but was considered unnecessary. This was the time of generalities, whether in the tone of evening variety shows or broadsheet magazines such as *Life* and *Look*. The name of the advertising game was to reach the masses with broadly defined and broadly targeted messages.

This is what made the commercials spun out by Bernbach's DDB ad agency so unexpected at the time. Cable and its promise of dozens, if not hundreds, of channels would not appear for two decades. Yet Bernbach chose to target only some commercial viewers. Entertain these few potential buyers. Give them a reason to engage—rather than to suffer through a spot—by making the connection to them. Yes, this was part of the genius of Bernbach's approach. But it was also part of something else.

Television technology in the early 1950s delivered to viewers what looked like low-quality films. The live feature of early television drove the programming. Variety shows populated the schedule in the 1950s, yielding eventually to programming actually produced in advance in the 1960s. The ad-lib nature of shows hosted by Jack Benny and Jack Paar made them platforms that created the expectation in the viewing consumer that the commercial message was just part of the show programming. It was seamless. The routines would blend a skit or interview with a direct pitch by the host for a product or service. Continuity and brand building would come later; at this time, it occurred more by repetition than message or image. Anacin was effective against pain, plain and simple. Making an emotional appeal was not only considered unnecessary in 1950s televisionland, but it would have been an unexpected waste. The mantra of Reeves and Hopkins was repetition and simplicity (and, we presume, irritation).

The technology of television made it possible for Bernbach and others to stretch beyond the earlier bounds. Rather than presenting a factual argument, Bernbach saw the chance to persuade more subtly. The style of that persuasion was made possible by the technology of the viewing platform. Thus, the drama present in television's *Rifle Man* and *Perry Mason* could be carried over to the commercials that supported them.

This new technology initially generated commercials that were largely unavoidable, rough handed, and lacking much finesse. The evolving understanding of advertising pros like Bernbach of what this new technology allowed changed the style of commercials forever.

But how?

The change brought on by Bernbach and others was made possible by the technology. What had changed was more than moving film from the theater to the home. The need for more programming was more a function of the ability to actually produce more programming. The movie-like programming of the 1950s and 1960s presented viewers with shorter stories and a stepwise approach to plots that always led to a completion. Even those programs that left viewers hanging, such as daytime soap operas, wrapped up the plot based on a preset pattern.

Commercials were also established as a stepwise argument: "This is what and why. Buy now." The pattern was simple and direct. Commercials in the Reeves and Lasker era were meant to sell and were created by business school graduates or at least by those who were more concerned with the business side of the argument.

In many ways, this approach was a close approximation of the history of print advertising. Although many advertising textbooks suggest the profession started centuries earlier, the use of print really took off after 1900. It was a form driven by its technology. Initially it was largely black-and-white arguments in a black-and-white format. Color, largely introduced in areas such as fashion and food, expanded the styles of advertising, but the basic format was driven by the technology. Advertising was presented in spaces defined by printing presses: squares and rectangles. Efficiently using the space dictated the right angles of advertising in print.

That degree of efficiency and the sense that every square inch of an ad must convey an argument of consumer persuasion drove the advertising profession. The lack of the multitude of publications that would appear after World War II made the copywriter dominant. Again, form followed function.

What Bernbach boldly proposed was that the form of an argument could be more than that of a copy-heavy print ad. The nature of the commercial could be more subtle, less in the consumer's face. These were softer sells that seemed to want to be friends with the target consumer, to suggest that the advertiser understood what was needed, and were part of why the Creative Revolution was seen as a revolution. That it was made possible by individuals largely self-taught was more of a function of personalities matched to the untapped possibilities of the new technology of television.

> In the past, Style.com has taken a relatively idiosyncratic approach to expansion (remember: this is the fashion website that launched an offline component at a time when most people believed print media was on life support), but its latest venture is solidly attuned to the Internet's driving trends. Style Map, a new channel on the fashion site, launches today with 60 international contributors, ranging from big-name celebrities (Nicole Richie, Courtney Love, Kylie Minogue, Jason Schwartzman) to creative professionals with niche appeal (such as MOCA director Jeffrey Deitch, Stil in Berlin, Mary Scherpe and Ukraine's fashion matriarch, Daria Shapovalova). (Mavrody 2013)

Burnett and Imaginations

Tony the Tiger could only have been created after color television. Ditto for the Jolly Green Giant. Television was a magazine with motion. Television was a movie on a small screen. Television was a family-focused platform that really was created for an individual (at least in the West). The singular nature of one person watching one program from start to finish would rule televisionland for the two decades leading up to the cable world of the 1980s. And few were better at using this storytelling device than Leo Burnett.

Son of a dry-goods store owner, Burnett had watched his father create traditional ads on the dining room table. The technology of printing presses dictated what was creatively possible. And as advertising in the early part of the twentieth century reflects, packing every square inch with information was seen as the only way to reach and persuade consumers. This was the era of product-focused communication. Tell the consumer about what the product can do and make the sell. Little concern was given to whether the consumer wanted or needed the product or whether a message that addressed these needs and wants might make the sell more effective. Consumers in the United States had experienced mass production for a single generation. In many ways, advertising in the early part of the twentieth century was more about explaining what products were, rather than explaining why consumers would find them useful. Advertising in the first half of the century answered "what is it" marketing with details about products over personal persuasion. Following World War II, consumers were wooed by messages that fit into a "what of it" format, followed by "I'll take it." (I should note that Joe Cappo told me in the 1980s that this was the basis of agency/consumer communication. I doubt he thought I would use it, especially in a book.)

Although the dining table experience did not lead Burnett to the advertising industry directly, it certainly must have remained on his list of options. After an initial interest in the printing press itself and then its nearest profession, journalism, Burnett moved to a job with the Cadillac Motor Company in the early part of the century. Over the years Burnett would eventually establish the agency that bore his name and create a series of award-winning advertising images that remain iconic to this day. And almost all of this happened in print, prior to the advent of television.

However, it was television that changed the way Burnett could argue for cereal, frozen vegetables, premade baking dough, and cigarette brands. Avoiding the mountains of information that Burnett saw his father pour into every store ad, Burnett created commercials that made simple appeals, whether for cereal that tasted "Great!" or a cigarette linked to a cowboy. Burnett appealed to the consumer's imagination in a new way, on a new platform. In doing so, it was the technology that allowed for the wide-ranging mini-stories that could be told in sixty seconds.

The resulting images became as much a part of the American culture as apple pie. The icons of a green giant, a cartoon tiger, and a popping-fresh doughboy all were brought to life by television. Yes, they could be promoted via print advertising, but it is difficult to believe that they could ascend to the status they have today: direct connections between the character and the product in the consumer's brand image. What also broke into the field of product promotion was the use of the packaging itself. Rather than simply identifying the product by name, Burnett—again, the son of a dry-goods store owner—used each box as an opportunity to promote an image of the product. Not just a food shot, though almost all packaging these days includes some image of what is actually in the box on the outside of the box. No, this small billboard was an opportunity to grab the attention, and ultimately the imagination, of the consumer. In the case of Pillsbury's Doughboy, the image and icon represented a homemaker's best friend in kitchen. In the case of Tony the Tiger, the box imaging reminded the real target—children—that this very friendly tiger was "Great!" The injection of color into all aspects of product marketing was at the core of Burnett's approach. Of course, it didn't hurt that the use of color in magazines was changing the landscape and fortunes of existing powerhouses, such as *Look* and *Life*.

But the real opportunity to use advertising technology to change an existing product's position in the brand-brain of target consumers would arise with the promotion of a deadly, addictive product. The ethics of such work must be put aside for now, though we revisit this still-relevant issue later in the book.

The Marlboro campaign might be the best example of product repositioning prior to that of Absolut. Here we have a product—a filtered cigarette—that was seen as largely feminine. No real man would bother with a filter. Yet Philip Morris wanted to reposition the product to attract men. The filter was a nod by the manufacturer to rising concerns regarding the health impact of use. Though never explicitly suggested, adding a filter was intended to minimize the consumer's perception of a hazard.

Thus the task was anything but simple: make a product perceived as feminine attractive to men. This was not the first time a product had been repositioned to target a new consumer. However, it might have been the boldest 180-degree departure ever attempted. We are not suggesting that the idea of filtered cigarettes being associated with a less-than-manly man had not been deeply engrained in the American society. We are suggesting that filtering a cigarette was seen as feminine—or at least more "civilized" than the rawness of a Camel. Filterless cigarettes were associated with hand-rolled tobacco, the kind of product only a man could appreciate.

Switching a deeply brand-embedded consumer away from a "raw" cigarette would take a strong message and a strong image. Initial characters used by Burnett were all very masculine, but it was the cowboy that stuck. And although the print campaign created by Burnett in the mid-1950s certainly was a major part of the success of the repositioning, the television ad created an iconic, unforgettable character that became a branding shortcut for male consumers.

In many ways the campaign was a long shot. After all, the cowboy myth that exists even today in the United States is that of a rough-and-ready man who carries his tobacco in a pouch and rolling papers in his pocket. What Burnett presented was a carefully groomed, more mature cowboy with a degree of refinement. Yes, he rode a horse and, yes, he worked cattle (and horses), but he had the crafted image of a retired Wall Street sharpie who knew the business end of a corporation just as well as that of a bull. This was no greenhorn, but he was also no bushwhacking, living-in-the-wild, tough-as-nails cowboy. He was portrayed in the television commercials as a far cleaner, clearly sophisticated, and certainly worldly wise man. He became a mythological icon who could serve whatever purpose the never-seen-a-cowboy consumer could relate to and respect. Launched in 1955, the print ads created by Burnett took the brand from $5 billion in sales to $20 billion in two years.

The television commercial completed what the print ads only started. Featuring non-Hollywood actors, starting with Max Bryan "Turk" Robinson, Wayne McClaren, David McClean, and other working cowboys and rodeo riders, Burnett only cleaned up these men slightly in order to ensure the connection between sophistication and the consumer was maintained. Showing these men actually riding horses, working cattle, and generally assuring the target consumer that they were in-the-flesh cowboys in the many commercials in the 1960s put Marlboro at the top of the heap in sales and branding. Today, the category of filtered cigarettes represents 99 percent of the U.S. market. As a brand, Marlboro has a 41 percent share, with Newport a distant second at 12 percent ("Tobacco Brand Preference" 2014). Annual sales for the most recent available period, ending in June 2015, were well over $100 billion worldwide ("Marlboro Cigarette Sales Volume in Units").

The storytelling ability afforded to Burnett via television allowed the agency to create a myth during a time and in a way that was previously impossible. Television provided what amounted to a mini-movie format, not in a public place, but in private homes. The relationship between the viewer—or the small, related group of viewers (family)—gave the message a more individualized quality. The impact on the viewer was both unique and personal. The singularity of the message was created by the individual (or family) in a solitary or narrowly shared environment. The individuals—a quality of Western culture—created a story line relevant and meaningful to themselves; that is, although the Marlboro Man was portrayed as a rugged cowboy, the myths that were created in the branding actions of the consumers were unique to each viewer. This could not be accomplished to the depth and—perhaps most important—with the speed of any other advertising format. The consumer "bought in" quickly not because the message crafted was a shared myth with others in society (something more likely at a movie theater), but because of the individualized nature of television.

Burnett plugged into this phenomenon. The target consumers—young white males—were able to internalize the Marlboro Man myth more rapidly because of both the shortness of the story and the lack of specifics. Television commercials that followed were more likely to be successful and lauded—such as the Apple "1984" spot—because they neglected, perhaps purposefully, to "explain" themselves. Burnett did not offer the target consumer a life story or a plot line to the created myth. That—whether intended or not—was left to the viewer. The literature of the nineteenth century, specifically romantic literature, might be a prior example to reference. The works of Hawthorne and Poe that failed to provide clear details and that allowed the reader to conjure unique imagery might be a better antecedent of the Marlboro Man than any television commercials that appeared in prior decades. By allowing the viewer to create the story that led up to the commercial and to add to it with each iteration, the Burnett model empowered the viewers to clothe themselves with a uniquely created myth. These myths were created by each viewer, which made them more powerful, more resilient. No previous storytelling platform had ever provided such a thoroughly complete and meaningful experience.

We have with the Marlboro Man a perfect environment for brand creation and adoption. The consumer is presumed to be in total control and, perhaps most important, becomes part of the creative scheme. Burnett created the myth, but each consumer was able to buy in on his or her terms, imbuing the tale with details of such personal meaning and depth that the resulting brand equity resembles an unassailable castle. The resulting brand loyalty was equally unassailable.

How else would a product that is in all ways lethal to the user attain such brand loyalty?

Burnett's series of Marlboro Man commercials was far more than reposi-tioning. The consumer target was shifted from women to men, of course. But the result was something far more powerful than the vast majority of reposi-tioning campaigns. The combination of imagery and sound, as well as mo-tion and emotion, resulted in a new art form not that far removed from fine art. The intent of art taught at universities is one of self-expression, the expression being that of the creator. What a viewer of such art sees varies from what is intended by the artist (this tends to be a classical form) to what is ultimately a collaboration between the artist and the viewer (a more ro-mantic form). In the case of the Marlboro Man, the created work by the creatives at Burnett was certainly a personal statement, but at the same time it was one that was left open to interpretation. It is hard not to admit that this represents a massive departure from the method behind the works of Rosser Reeves, all of which were classical in nature, each intended to generate a specific response to a specific brand statement.

In a way, Burnett's bold and risky approach to branding via storytelling was less about brand attributes than about the story itself. Nowhere in the commercial are any details regarding the product mentioned. In fact, the product itself was both marginalized and simultaneously placed center stage. The Marlboro Man was the central figure. What he did and how he did it was never detailed but left to the imagination of the viewer/consumer. The prod-uct was simply something affiliated with the cowboy image, again with few details.

Some might suggest that the intent on the part of Burnett's creatives was to bind the cowboy image with the product and from there to the consumer. This might be the case among some consumers. But the concrete element within the commercial itself was the willingness to walk away from the message without ensuring any specific intended message (often called a "takeaway").

What we do know about the series of Marlboro Man commercials is the culture that produced it. Burnett's team was probably completely unaware that they had tapped into some primal cultural forces with these commercials. They would have been unaware that such a series of commercials could be analyzed as highly individualistic and appealing to consumers with very low uncertainty-avoidance tendencies. The creatives knew the commercials would appeal to men (this was, after all, part of their marching orders), but how could they have known that their portrayal of the Marlboro Man as a leader, a person in power and control, would result in commercials that would scale high in individualism and low on Hofstede's Uncertainty Avoid-ance Index? Hofstede's scales—individualistic/community, uncertainty avoidance index, power distance index, masculinity/femininity, and long-term/short-term orientation—are part of a cultural matrix that seeks to ex-plain cultural differences. If applied to the Marlboro Man commercials, they would suggest that part of the success of Burnett's approach with this brand was attributable to where it was most successful: Western culture in general and the United States in particular. American men tend to be notably individualistic, masculine risk takers (at least compared to many other cultures). But in terms of elitism (power distance) and time orientation, Americans score on the lower end of the scale (near Germany for elitism and even lower for time orientation).

Yet all five of these indices can be applied to explain the success of the Marlboro Man commercials. Clearly, this cowboy is an individualist, making his own decisions. Clearly, this cowboy is a risk taker, riding and roping with wild abandon. Certainly he is not beholden to follow the lead of another (low power distance). Obviously very masculine, this cowboy makes quick decisions and acts on them immediately. Intended or not, the Marlboro Man is the essential American icon.

But what is most provocative is the willingness of Burnett's team to allow the consumer to arrive at his own specific brand image, complete with a unique story line and brand attributes. This revolutionary move away from control allowed a more thorough and personalized brand adoption within a specific culture seemingly perfectly matched to the intended brand message. This product is for masculine, independent risk takers interested in immediate reward. Period.

> The growing ranks of middle class consumers in emerging markets are increasingly susceptible to Madison Avenue exhortations to open their wallets and shop 'til they drop.
> Except the shrewdest "Mad Men" aren't necessarily based in Manhattan. With headquarters in Paris, the advertising company Publicis Groupe SA is the best positioned among its peers to profit from the buying mood of newly affluent denizens in the developing world
> Publicis provides a range of advertising and marketing services in Europe, North America, Asia, Latin America, and the Middle East. The company offers traditional and online advertising, online marketing, customer relationship management, point of sale marketing, and outdoor display advertising. (Persinos 2013)

Ogilvy: Mythmaking

The heat is obvious: everything is melting. Cars, signs, fountains—everything. One person, a woman, runs to her room seeking a frosty bottle of Perrier. Fumbling the bottle out a high-rise window, she follows it down in a seeming act of suicide, to land comfortably and safely on one of the many melting cars. At the end she is satisfied with a swig of the beverage (Perrier 2009).

Nothing is particularly unique about the commercial, except perhaps that it is produced by a branch of Ogilvy & Mather in Paris and that it contains one line ("love is the way") from a song and only two words: "Ahhh, Perrier." It is perhaps the quintessential global commercial, given that the language barriers—erroneously believed to be the main problem with global advertising—are largely absent and thus neutralized. And it certainly passes a few of Hofstede's marks, but not all. More about that later.

First, let's consider the impact of an Englishman, David Ogilvy, on modern advertising. The self-described daydreaming pragmatist (Tungate 2007, 278) is known for his print advertising more than his television ventures. He created larger-than-life mythical characters, such as the eye-patch-wearing Hathaway Man and bearded Col. Schweppes, both appearing in magazines long before television. But then, so did the Marlboro Man.

Ogilvy, often referred to as the third leg of the tripartite Creative Revolution with Burnett and Bernbach, differed significantly from the other two in the style of his work. But in one important way, he was a match: storytelling. More than either Bernbach or Burnett, Ogilvy loved using story as the message carrier. With the Hathaway Man, he was so successful that later ads ran without copy. Just the man and his eye patch. Immediate recognition, immediate brand adoption.

Very much like Bernbach and Burnett, the stories presented by Ogilvy were left incomplete, giving only the most minimal amount of information. Consumers added the details to complete the narrative. In many ways, Ogilvy's intent was to provoke imagination as much as brand adoption. So powerful were the images of a man with an eye patch and one with a full Scottish beard that the printed advertisements acted as a sort of catalyst, provoking the consumer to fill in the missing details. Much like Isak Dinesen's major character in *Out of Africa*, Ogilvy provided the reader with a gentle shove and allowed each to fill in the rest of the story. Again, although he was equally detailed in his copy for such products as Rolls-Royce, it was the willingness on his part (and that of his clients) to let the target consumer be part of the message that resulted in a uniquely powerful and highly individualized brand image. In a way, Ogilvy created what would later be used by TBWA in their Absolut ads: very little information, trusting that the wise, cool, in-the-know consumer would get it. And, in both cases—the Absolut ad and Ogilvy's work—the power of the story was enhanced by the delivery platform: magazines. Ogilvy's choice of the *New Yorker* for Hathaway was a clear effort to match the product with the perceived elitism of the publication.

Consider the Perrier television advertisement. Not a single attribute of Perrier is expressly mentioned: Not how many calories it contains. Not how it is manufactured. Not the location of the factory. All that the consumer knows is that Perrier is refreshing. But the consumer already knew that as much as the brand itself. In fact, if the consumer is unfamiliar with the brand, the commercial is largely a mystery. Only the already informed, culture-wise know of Perrier. If that sounds elitist, well, that is the soul of Ogilvy. If

Hofstede were to scale the elitism of print advertising, Hathaway, Schweppes, and Perrier would score high. They all appeal to those who seek elite status, while at the same time not offering a single bit of evidence other than that created by the consumer him- or herself.

Ogilvy's approach to advertising is often measured by the characters he created. Yet in some ways, it should be measured more by his willingness to allow the reader to fill in the remainder of the story line. This willingness to let go would have been considered irresponsible by the advertising giants that preceded Ogilvy, giants that he himself believed deeply in. Uncoupling the intended brand message from the resulting brand message was perhaps Ogilvy's greatest accomplishment and his greatest gift to those who would follow. The myths of Hathaway and Schweppes were less about the story details than the story readers. Each consumer was allowed to read into the story line what each saw as logical. The result was a personal brand image.

This personal brand image presumes two very important factors to be true: total market brand adoption is not necessary for a product's success and—in a mature global market—such success relies more on what is not said in a commercial than on what is spelled out. This clearly runs counter to what most advertising textbooks suggest today. Today's advertising agencies are largely about research: know the company, know the product, know the consumer, know the brand, and know the market. The resulting technique would rarely result in either the Hathaway or Absolut ads, since neither suggests any real research went into them or at least that such research played a factor in the resulting commercials.

Yet it is clear that even Ogilvy's ads were culture-centric. Qualities of the messages of both Hathaway and Schweppes suggested a Western, elitist approach. As discussed later, this may not be an important factor if the nature of the elitism is known and if the nature of the market is limited. If you make a million of anything, the globe is not your market. Less than one-tenth of 1 percent of the globe is your market.

> Nielsen has released a new quarterly Global Ad Pulse Report, which shows that although global ad spend continues to rebound, it has only increased by 1.9 percent from Q1 2012.
>
> The report shows that ad spend has dropped in Europe, remained stagnant in North America, and marginally increased in the Middle East, Africa, Latin America, and Asia-Pacific. In the Middle East and Africa spending grew by 2.9 percent during the first quarter of 2013, continuing the recovery from the advertising decline early last year. But the region has also been affected by the political unrest in Egypt, which has always been one of the largest markets for the region. Ad spend has declined by 20 percent in the country.
>
> Latin America saw growth of 11.9 percent during Q1, and spending grew in all countries in the region.

Asia-Pacific also saw growth in ad expenditures, with 5.8 percent in Q1. The top performers in the region were China, Indonesia, and the Philippines, which all saw around 20 percent growth. Japan was the only country in the region where ad spend decreased. (Rossman 2013)

Tragos and TBWA

Whether TBWA was the world's first European agency is certainly up for debate. What is not debated is that TBWA played a key role in a product turnaround. As the old story goes, Vin and Sprit, owner of Absolut Vodka, was considering dumping the brand. Management had sought the opinion of a marketing group, whose research supported a brand kill. After all, the marketing experts noted bluntly, this is a product in an oddly shaped bottle that bartenders hate (because it is an oddly shaped bottle). Add to that that everyone knows that the best vodka comes from a near neighbor of Sweden, definitely not Sweden itself. Other issues involved the name and the readability of the logo on the bottle. Clearly, the best move would be to let this brand, which was pulling in a scant thirty thousand cases a year in the United States in the early 1980s, just die.

Vin and Sprit management liked the brand, however, and wanted another opinion. So as the story goes, TBWA came up with some ideas, including one created by South African art director Geoff Hayes (though some argue a copywriter was involved). Hayes's idea—which arose either in a shower or a bathtub, again depending on who is telling the tale—was the bottle of Absolut with a halo above it. The headline was "Absolut Perfection" (which had evolved via a copywriter from the art director's original idea of "Absolutely Perfect," some say).

The success of this ad and the hundreds that followed resulted in a massive jump in U.S. sales, from thirty thousand cases to more than three million in just a few years.

The question, of course, is why?

Empowering the consumer to complete the story had arisen by way of Bernbach, Burnett, and Ogilvy. Consumers were encouraged to complete their own brand equities of various products via partially told story lines of small cars, green giants, and mysterious gentlemen. Here with TBWA is a bottle of Swedish vodka that challenges the consumer to get the pun served up via the juxtaposition of an image with a headline. Thus, a view of a pool from above showing a swimming pool in the shape of an Absolut bottle with the words "Absolut LA." Or letters being blown off the bottle: "Absolut Chicago." The involvement of artist Andy Warhol, with his various interpretations, may have been the final touch. But consumers were already sending in advertisement ideas by the thousands, dreaming up their own Absolut ads. (I've harbored one of my own for some time: an aerial shot of the desert with a figure drawn in the sand holding an Absolut bottle with the headline "Absolut Civilization.")

Many arguments can be made as to why this campaign worked so well. Most suggested that the consumer was invited to be part of the joke and, by doing so, to be part of an "in crowd" of those who understood the societal factors of each pun. Whatever the underlying cause for the success of the Absolut campaign, it cannot be denied that it required a more sophisticated consumer and the willingness on the part of the advertiser to not fill in all the details for them. In fact, it demanded that the advertising do little more than present the pun, offering nothing by way of product manufacturer or other details that were the hallmark of advertising three decades earlier. As Tungate notes in quoting Maurizio Sala, an associate of TBWA founder Armando Testa, "He [Testa] felt that great advertising should make the viewer a little uncomfortable. If it was designed to please everyone, it wouldn't get noticed; it would just sink into the sea of banality that surrounded it" (Tungate 2007, 278, 141). Perhaps more important, the nature of the Absolut ads and their resulting popularity suggested that the average consumer of advertising in the 1980s was far more worldly than their predecessors. These were consumers who had learned to "read" sophisticated advertising from the teachers of modern advertising. Conversely, these more learned advertising consumers demanded more sophisticated advertising.

The success of the Absolut campaign could be credited to this sophistication, and that sophistication could be traced to the style of television commercials that provoked curiosity rather than drummed a stale message.

> AOL—in the midst of a turnaround but still facing headwinds likely isn't the first place you'd expect one of the digital agency world's leading execs to land, but that's what happened this week when Razorfish CEO Bob Lord jumped ship to run AOL Networks, the group that houses Advertising.com, AdTech and several acquisitions including Pictela.
>
> It's a big hire for a division that is an AOL bright spot—and, from Mr. Lord's point of view, an acknowledgment of how important "the stack" will be to the future of advertising.
>
> What's a stack? A set of technologies that powers online advertising in a series of lightning-fast decisions that occur between the moment a person visits a website and the ads load. When you think of an ad stack, most people think of Google, which started building its platform when it acquired Double-Click. ("How AOL Lured Lord to Lead Networks Division" 2013)

Dentsu and Compressed Imaging

The largest advertising agency in Japan and, at one time, in the world, Dentsu Creative is tied tightly to the media. This bond results in a media department that is more like creative, and creatives who think media. This approach, started decades ago, certainly positions the agency well for the new media age, but equally important, it provides the clients of the agency a bundle of commercials and print ads that takes the greatest advantage of the media in which it appears. This close connection between creative and media was, in many ways, the unstated argument of Bernbach, Burnett, and Ogilvy. The message of any creative team was crafted with an eye toward where it would appear, taking the best advantage offered by the media platform.

This focus on the best use of media within a creative concept allowed for more fifteen-second commercials in Japan decades before they appeared in the West. An example highlighted by Tungate involved a series of fifty Japanese comedians in individual fifteen-second spots (Tungate 2007, 193). The quick mash-up plays off the younger generation's desire to see the message, process it, and move on.

Yet in many ways it reflects a culture that invented compressed thinking in a poetry form still used in advertising textbooks as idea generators: haiku. With its seven-nine-seven syllable construction, haiku resembles both Burma-Shave roadside advertising and the comic poetry of England, limericks. In all three, the advertising ideas are compressed to bare, simple, to-the-point proposals. Used as a way to help copywriters break through creative barriers, these boiled-down thinking exercises result in a message that cuts to the core immediately. These efficient message forms also rely to a great extent on consumers "getting it." Being sufficiently worldly wise to understand a pun or other device requires a consumer educated to at least the world of advertising. Ironically, it is no small indication of Japanese culture and its beliefs about advertising that a popular publication is *CM*, which is wholly dedicated to commercials. As a Japanese advertising executive told Tungate, "Advertising is a form of culture among the younger generation. Today, they barely differentiate it from any other form of entertainment" (Tungate 2007, 193).

Panasonic Corporation today announced at Santos, Brazil, the renewal of its global advertising contract with Brazilian national soccer team and FC Barcelona player, Neymar da Silva Santos Junior. The new contract will last for four years from April 2013. Neymar Jr. will also appear in new advertisements for the company's B2B solutions to be rolled out in 193 countries and regions, starting in Japan from July 22, 2013. By sponsoring Neymar Jr., who is popular all over the world, Panasonic is aiming to develop a youthful, dynamic and swift global brand image for the company. ("Panasonic Renews Global Advertising Contract with Neymar Jr." 2013)

Other Voices, Other Places

With the liberating influence of Bernbach, Burnett, and Ogilvy, dozens of new, refreshing agencies sprang up internationally. And like Testa and Dentsu, each had its own style that reflected its culture. But all were influenced by the creative freedom provided by television. They were not carbon copies of the main characters in the Creative Revolution, but they were all equally freed from the bonds of print by a new technology.

Whether considering Maurice Levy in France, Marcello Serpa in Latin America, John Hegarty in England, or the many other new voices springing up across the globe, advertising was cut loose from the digit counters of the Reeves era. Imagination and romance were injected into campaigns for everything from bottled water to sports cars, from cornflakes to airlines. In the mid-1980s, the advertising industry and its clients received a cold splash of water: the Saatchi brothers moved aggressively and acquired thirty-seven agencies at a cost of $1 billion, almost half of that in swallowing up Ted Bates Advertising. Among the fallout from the deals, agency clients took notice and began to ask a very simple question: "Exactly how much are you guys making from us?" What followed was a series of cuts that ultimately put everything into negotiation, including the sacred 15 percent commission that agencies had traditionally received from media for ad placements. That brief period from the early 1960s to the mid-1980s was a golden era for agencies. After the golden goose was gone, the advertising agencies that had lived off massive media buys lost the independence provided by their financial fiefdoms. They were largely brought back to Earth, with fewer demonstrating the kind of swagger exhibited years earlier.

Television was also affected by technology, with the ease of launching new networks resulting in its own watering down of talent and imagination.

> eMarketer . . . predicts that by 2017, social media ad revenue will hit $35.98 billion, 16.0% of the total global digital ad market. According to eMarketer estimates, the pace of global spending growth is slowing, going from 56.2% in 2014, to 33.5% this year, then dropping to 26.3% in 2016 and 20.3% in 2017.
>
> Advertisers in the United States and Canada will remain the top drivers of the market, boosting ad spending 31.0% this year to pass the $10 billion mark for the first time. The total in the Asia-Pacific region will be $7.4 billion and Western Europe will be $4.74 billion. The North American countries also lead in per user spending, laying out $50.42 in ad dollars for each user, compared to $25.26 for Western Europe and $8.04 for Asia-Pacific.
>
> EMarketer estimates show that the U.S. and China will lead social ad spending for the next few years, making up more than half of the global market throughout the forecast period. Advertisers in the U.S. will spend $9.59 billion on social ads this year, up 31% from 2014 and more than double the amount they spent in 2013. By 2017, eMarketer forecasts the U.S. will hit $14.40 billion, nearly 20% of all U.S. digital ad spending. In China, social ad spending will reach $3.41 billion this year and is expected to be $6.11 billion in 2017, or 12.5% of digital ad spending in the country. (Beck 2015)

THE ROLE OF TELEVISION TECHNOLOGY

The evolving resolution of television monitors is perhaps most obvious in sports broadcasting. Once presented as large block letters on the screen, game scores are far smaller and include far more information. The same is occurring in a more subtle fashion in advertising commercials. The ability to show more detail in the background allows a soda commercial to show two parents gushing over a new soft drink while their bouncing baby boy in the background attempts various feats to gain their attention. This would have been technologically impossible in the 1960s, during the very era discussed in this chapter.

Creative concepts were set free by advances in television in the 1960s, evolving despite limitations in technology. The increasing complexity of commercial messages and imaging continued as television resolution grew. As the picture became more refined, the ideas for commercials could also be more complex, trusting that every detail could be transmitted, every element not only seen but also appreciated by the viewer. Thus, as the science that generated higher resolution within the television monitor industry grew, it provided increased options for the creative groups in advertising agencies. But what did this mean for the average consumer?

What links all of the agencies outlined in this chapter is the ability of each to rely upon a more sophisticated consumer, one ready to absorb a more complex message and to immediately add it to their created, internal product brand equity. But what also links all of these efforts is something rarely discussed: a willingness to let go of the commercial message and its interpretations. Rather than hoping that the consumer recognizes the X factor—a concept present in almost every modern advertising textbook in one form or another—the advertising of the 1960s, whether intended or not, allowed consumers to stray a bit (and perhaps a lot). Rather than ensuring that every consumer got it, the advertising that started in the 1960s made possible by television factored in an element wholly unpredictable and uncontrollable: emotion. This emotional element certainly had been a factor in advertising prior to the 1960s and the Creative Revolution, but never to the extent made possible by television. The movement, speech, color, and drama immediately present and possible in every commercial were far more of a hook than any prior print advertisement.

The target consumer often was presented with statistical information: the product was still a product with depth, width, and height. But what was also present in the commercial was an unpredictable emotional message that could be interpreted by each consumer in his or her own fashion. What might be envy in one consumer could be admiration in another.

This flexible, imprecise interpretation of a message is no small matter: advertising has been considered an element of the marketing plan, with its very precise goals and expectations. Expectations of the success of an advertising campaign were always included in the agency's pitch. And certainly such expectations were included in Burnett's client meetings, as with all others during the years of the Creative Revolution. But what sort of accuracy of market penetration advertising brand adoption could be promised with a campaign that relied upon time and romance as key elements of that adoption? The consumer reaction to the Marlboro Man may have been immediate and powerful, but such strength is rarely promised up front by any advertising agency.

Plus, another factor would have a massive impact on both advertising in general and the nature of the commercials: market penetration.

> Focusing on the culture of these roles, it seems they are generally self-developed, with decent self-esteem—unlike how popular media and general culture like to portray them—and giving to others of their own kind. It doesn't tell us how the roles relate culture-wise beyond others like them, but there is a good basis to see that this isn't something just in the U.S. or Western Europe. Such a culture comes with the role itself. And these are some of the values most companies wish for all their employees.
>
> The stereotypes we often hear about—tech people are argumentative; developers are sullen and lonely; they don't work together; they like specific answers not possibilities—may be because we don't spend enough time thinking in the same way. There will always be differences, but the real value of leadership comes when you try to understand how others actually think. (Shah 2015)

THE RISE OF TELEVISION

On July 30, 1966, more than thirty-two million British viewers watched England defeat Germany in the FIFA World Cup finals on the BBC. This is remarkable, given that the population of the United Kingdom at the time was just over fifty million. Television in Britain could be traced back several decades, but market penetration was boosted by color television in the mid-1960s. Interestingly, the introduction of color to television must have provided advertising agencies with a more powerful medium for persuasion. This was likely especially true for those agencies already using color.

Tracking the adoption of color television by country compared to the rise of new advertising creatives in these countries reveals an interesting relationship. Consider that although color had been fiddled with in the United States going all the way back to the early 1950s, the first television show broadcast in color did not take place until September 1966 (*That Girl* on ABC) ("Timeline of the Introduction of Color Television in Countries" 2007). The ability (or was it willingness?) to use color in broadcasts in other countries, such as the United Kingdom and France, occurred around the same time as in the United States.

According to Wikipedia, of the countries that have adopted color television, twenty-nine had done so by 1969. The vast majority of these were in Europe and North America. As has been suggested, the rise in use of television in the 1950s opened up the creativity of advertising within a more emotional and powerful medium. The addition of color must have been seen as a powerful boost, if used wisely. Though, no doubt, early color commercials were likely simply reshot black-and-white spots, creative directors at agencies from New York to London to Paris and beyond must have seen this new technology as an advantage in promoting brands. In many ways, this transition from black and white to color must have been similar to the challenges facing actors when sound was introduced to movies. For advertising agencies in the 1960s, an entire world of new possibilities and requirements put them back on square one: they could either understand how to use color effectively or face losing clients.

Adopting new technology has always been a challenge, whether it is color television or the new media of today. The ability to understand how a message can be altered to take best advantage of a changing medium has spelled the difference between success and failure. Resisting or ignoring these new technologies relegates agencies and their clients to second place or lower.

Adding color would require that agency creatives consider how to best use this new tool. Commercials would have to be changed from their black-and-white nature to something that included color as a central role. The target message or X factor was still paramount, but the best spots would use color strategically to improve targeting adoption. As television manufacturers added more lines of resolution to television screens, the ability (and responsibility) of the agency creatives to add more detail to each commercial also grew. The issue of whether television technology made Bernbach, Burnett, Ogilvy, and others necessary or simply made what they created possible is irrelevant. What is important here is that no successful advertising agency creative director could ignore these new technological advances. They had to change with the technology.

It is often part of mass communication introductory classes to track the speed at which various media platforms evolved in the last century. One measure is the time it would take each form to achieve market penetration; that is, when a vast majority—usually more than 90 percent—had adopted a new communication technology. Radio took longer to reach market saturation than broadcast television, which, in turn, took longer than cable television. New media attained market saturation even more quickly. Instead of measuring the adoption of new media by consumers in years, as was the case with television, it was measured in months. In the world of new apps—small, non-Web-based applications—the rate is measured in *weeks*.

What is not discussed, however, is the impact on advertising creatives of the speed at which market penetration of color television occurred. For the Creative Revolution giants of the 1960s, they had years to make the switch. The pressure on these same advertising agencies in the world of new media would be greater, given that market saturation globally has taken much less time.

And what I consider here is much more global. Color television would take decades to simply appear globally. Some countries, notably those within South America, Eastern Europe, and sub-Saharan Africa, would not see color television until the early 1980s. Just as interesting, the actual introduction of these color televisions was measured country by country. The political barriers—whether in South Africa or Eastern Europe—defined consumer access. The technology existed literally next door—in Japan and China or Italy and Albania—but would take more than a decade to spread from one to the other. This was not an issue of technology as much as it was politics, though, notably, color television was introduced in North Korea three years before it would appear in its neighbor to the south.

> Derreck Kayongo, entrepreneur, Top 10 CNN Hero and creator of the Global Soap Project, stepped onto the Templeton-Blackburn Alumni Memorial Auditorium stage Wednesday in his white seersucker suit and brightly colored tie to tell Ohio University students the power of American competition.
>
> Kayongo, who is from Uganda, said the strategy to achieve the American dream is no secret.
>
> "It's about taking small ideas to the land of giants," he said. "A powerful event in your life can inspire you to do something remarkable."
>
> Kayongo's idea came to him in Philadelphia, where he stayed in a hotel that provided him with three different kinds of soap. He decided to use one and then put the other two in his bag for later, only to find they were replaced the next day.
>
> But later on, he began to think the hotel would soon begin to charge for the soap, and he took them back to a concierge who laughed in his face and told him the hotel would have thrown the soap away regardless.
>
> "Three bars of soap, who does that?" he said while laughing. "Two million children die every year from sanitation and hygiene illnesses, and this soap is being thrown into the environment."
>
> Kayongo said there are 2.6 million bars of soap thrown away by hotels across the United States a day, totaling 800 million bars each year. This waste has become a cultural norm in America, and he recognized the problem.
>
> "When there's that assumption something cannot be done, that's where the business opportunities are," Kayongo said. (Fernandez 2015)

THE NEEDS OF GLOBAL COMMUNICATION

One requirement for global communications is some agreed-upon standard. That is, for television programs to spread globally, all carriers of the signal must agree upon some protocols and standards. Otherwise, what we have is a hodgepodge of programming, and, for advertising agencies, a nightmare of differing requirements. Interestingly, given that a true global advertising commercial has yet to appear (despite the possibilities), the possibility of just such an event has been tossed about the water coolers in the hallways of multinational advertising agencies for years. It seems that the barriers are too great. For some time, the thinking among advertising pros, as reflected in various articles in *Advertising Age* and *AdWeek*, has been that all that is needed to make a commercial work globally are varying politics, language (and its attending semantics), and gender. That's not quite the situation.

For a television commercial to go global, far more complex cultural differences must be considered. Yes, we have issues of language and gender among varying cultures, but we also have all the others dealt with by sociologist Hofstede. As we move forward to discuss advertising going global, we must understand that it simply cannot be successful without taking into account such factors as the willingness of consumers within a culture to take risks, to disagree with opinion leaders, or to make decisions more quickly. These challenges as now presented are skewed to a Western (largely American) point of view. Western consumers tend to be more risk taking and individualistic, less elitist, and more rapid brand adopters that those in other cultures, such as those in areas of Asia. Repositioning a brand, for example, requires far less heavy lifting in Britain than it does in Japan.

But will such differences remain? Unlikely. Ask any Chinese student attending a university in the United States or Britain. The differences between those students after one week, four weeks, and a year are remarkable. But more on that later.

REFERENCES

Beck, Martin. 2015. "eMarketer: Social Ad Spending Will Hit $23.68 Billion Globally This Year." *eMarketer*. April 16. http://marketingland.com/emarketer-social-ad-spending-will-hit-23-68-billion-globally-this-year-125410.

Cheyfitz, Kirk. 2013. "How Story Platforms Help Global Brands Go Local." *Harvard Business Review*. http://blogs.hbr.org/cs/2013/07/how_story_platforms_help_globa.html.

Fernandez, Marisa. 2015. "Founder of Global Soap Project Shares Entrepreneurial Advice." *The Post*. April 15. http://www.thepostathens.com/culture/founder-of-global-soap-project-shares-entrepreneurial-advice/article_6a8a5e6a-e3a5-11e4-aee7-4b6fe922a417.html.

Hofstede. G. W. "An Engineer's Odyssey Trailer." http://www.geerthofstede.nl/index.

"How AOL Lured Lord to Lead Networks Division." 2013. *Digital Business Social Marketing Services*. July 20. http://digital.socialbusinessmarketingservices.com/how-aol-lured-lord-to-lead-networks-division.

"Marlboro Cigarette Sales Volume in Units." *CSI Market.* http://csimarket.com/stocks/operatingstat_single.php?code=MO&statistika=stat1.

Mavrody, Nika. 2013. "Style.com's EIC Tells Us Why the Fashion Website Just Launched a New Global Channel." *The Fashion Spot.* http://www.thefashionspot.com/buzz-news/latest-news/314451-style-coms-eic-tells-us-why-the-fashion-website-just-launched-a-new-global-lifestyle-channel.

"Panasonic Renews Global Advertising Contract with Neymar Jr." 2013. *MarketWatch.* July 22. http://www.marketwatch.com/story/panasonic-renews-global-advertising-contract-with-neymar-jr-2013-07-22.

Perrier. 2009. "Melting." Commercial. Ogilvy & Mather. http://www.youtube.com/watch?v=msBQR-Cml2E.

Persinos, John. 2013. "Madison Avenue on the Seine." *InvestingDaily.* July 22. http://www.investingdaily.com/17927/madison-avenue-on-the-seine.

Rossman, Caitlan. 2013. "Nielsen: Global Ad Spend Slowly Rebounding." *ClickZ.com.* July 19. http://www.clickz.com/clickz/news/2283701/nielsen-global-ad-spend-slowly-rebounding.

Shah, Rawn. 2015. "Software Developers Overflow with a Helpfulness Culture." *Forbes.* April 16. http://www.forbes.com/sites/rawnshah/2015/04/16/software-developers-overflow-with-a-helpfulness-culture.

"Supreme Court Restricts Tobacco Advertising." 2013. *New York Times.* July 23. http://india.blogs.nytimes.com/2013/07/23/supreme-court-restricts-tobacco-advertising.

"Timeline of the Introduction of Color Television in Countries." 2007. *Wikipedia.* Last updated 2015. http://en.wikipedia.org/wiki/Timeline_of_the_introduction_of_color_television_in_countries.

"Tobacco Brand Preference." 2014. *Centers for Disease Control.* http://www.cdc.gov/tobacco/data_statistics/fact_sheets/tobacco_industry/brand_preference.

Tom. 2009. "How Did the Internet Affect Television in the 1950s?" *Answer Bag.* http://www.answerbag.com/q_view/1596661.

Tungate, Mark. 2007. *Adland: A Global History of Advertising.* London: Kogan Page.

Chapter Two

Global History of Advertising: Part 2, since 1993

Honestly, I think the Internet advertising is very nagging and quite annoying. For example, it seems like every single YouTube video I watch has a very lengthy ad before it. Yet, it may be effective because people are rather forced to watch it; it makes you almost not want to use YouTube. The Internet ads are not very effective because whenever they come on I try to ignore them or preoccupy myself with something else. Pandora is another example of ads that do not have much effect on me because when I go from listening to music to listening to an ad, I turn down the volume and do not listen to it. I believe that TV has far better advertising that can hit your emotions. Such as the commercials for the beaten and abused animals cause you to appreciate the animals and [they] create a sad emotion. —Ryan [1]

It seemed a golden solution never imagined possible. In the early 1990s, a relatively new communication was seen as a perfect solution to reaching and motivating consumers. E-mail. Two decades ago, the buzz in the advertising industry was focused on a single, simple solution: e-mail potential target consumers, give them some special nugget of information, and simply invite them to go to the product Web site for answers. Simple, clean, direct. Those who were not interested could simply ignore the e-mail and move on. Those who were interested could be "sold" the brand on a Web site teeming with as much information required to make the brand adoption complete.

So simple. Some pundits even suggested that e-mail would replace television.

---

1. Ryan is a student I taught in a recent online class about, oddly enough, online material: The Web and Culture. Other students are quoted in this and later chapters.

It, of course, didn't exactly turn out that way. Lacking in the calculations was an activity that was wholly unpredicted. The overly optimistic idea was that targeted e-mail would be just that: targeted. If consumers were not seen as potential buyers, they would not receive the e-mail. Targeting to ensure the best match would not overwhelm those consumers not seen as a good match for the product. This naive thinking left out an important element of human behavior. Laziness. Within days of e-mail being created, massive e-mails would appear in millions of mailboxes as Internet service providers (ISPs) sold their client addresses to direct marketing groups. A couple in Florida took the lists to an extreme. They started sending out e-mails to everyone on the millions-plus lists, leading to outrage, congressional hearings, and complete consumer pushback. The couple's defense was simple and, moreover, unassailable. They were exercising free speech, much as anyone on a street corner could pontificate about whatever crossed his or her mind. The couple rapidly became a footnote as e-mail spread globally, and the ability to stop anyone from sending anything was rendered impossible. What could be (and was) accomplished was the deflection of unwanted e-mail by browsers and ISPs.

But this was not the first case of massive e-mail dumps that would come to be called "spam." Two decades earlier, in the mid-1970s, a salesman used ARPANET (Advanced Research Projects Agency Network, the predecessor to the Internet) to reach a few hundred potential clients. The ARPANET list was small (six hundred e-mails), and the "mass" mailings were only a fraction of this. But the action of sending out one message to multiple recipients so inflamed emotions within the online community that the "offender" was ultimately banned (Quigley 2010).

By the turn of the last century, a pattern emerged that has been repeated many times since. An individual or individuals use a telecommunications device inappropriately—at least in the eyes of those targeted—which results in demands for regulation, restrictions, and elimination of the offending activity. To be accurate, the first of these actions focused on postal junk mail, the incessant flow of flyers and brochures to potential client mailboxes through the U.S. Postal Service. Following the largely ineffective attempts to restrict postal "spam"—which would anticipate the same frustrations regarding online spam—laws were passed restricting similar use of telephones, thus the birth of no-call lists in every state. Though not complete, no-call lists have given consumers the opportunity to block computer-generated telephone calls and faxes, at least those from for-profit entities. Nonprofits still have a pass.

> I absolutely believe we need the Web and are entirely dependent on it. I sometimes wonder how my parents were able to find out random tidbits of information or other things such as how to tie a tie (sounds pathetic but true). I

for one use it almost every day or in a crunch when I need to find out something fast. Without the Web, I would probably have a much lower GPA than I do now. We take it for granted every single day, and if it were to suddenly disappear forever, we would all be in for some trouble. This sounds like a first-world problem but it honestly would turn the world around for all of those with access to the Web. No longer could we be stuck on the side of the road and google how to change a tire, and we would actually have to go to stores and buy what we wanted instead of ordering from Amazon and having it arrive on our front doorstep in two days. Yes, these are two examples of a lazy society, but yet it would still affect us greatly. The Web is a huge part of our life and I don't see, at this point, how it could ever be gotten rid of due to its convenience and the near-infinite opportunities it possesses. —Connor

E-MAIL AND INDIVIDUALISM

For the first time in human history, one person could communicate with an unlimited number of readers immediately at light speed (or at least quickly). Here we have a simple, no-frills application that allows the user to type on a keyboard and share ideas, feelings, imagination, fears, or a passing thought. The transportation mechanism, Internet Protocol, made possible the sharing of a message that could be so trivial as to be of literally no value—certainly not the value usually contained within handwritten or typed letters shared with others via the postal system. The use of e-mail eliminated the need to attach value to the missive. Anything, any thought, any occurrence of any day could be shared globally at little or no cost. This devaluation of human communication—so easy and so cheap—has rendered needless the requirement to "commit thought to paper," a phrase often used in the past to suggest a very real investment of time and resources into the act of thinking and sharing thoughts. We have made sharing so very simple that we give little attention to what we write or read. E-mail by its very nature is a valueless product that has become so much a part of our lives that it is presumed unending.

We need to consider for a moment a bit of technology that preceded e-mail and allowed for information sharing: Usenet. One of the oldest information sharing platforms still in use, Usenet was created in 1979 and came into general use at Duke University and the University of North Carolina at Chapel Hill the following year. It contains groups divided by subject areas—called newsgroups—established and controlled by the creators. In fact, Usenet allowed the creators of these groups to set standards, including banning posters who were determined to be "off subject" to the group. Spamming by posting across multiple newsgroups would result in a fierce online conversation and ultimate banning of the offender (who could, of course, merely rejoin under a new name and continue spamming). Although still used today, the Usenet population is far smaller than that of e-mail users, perhaps because of the structured nature of subject areas.

E-mail is an integrated, presumed part of our daily activities. In fact, it is so ingrained in our lives that the idea of setting it aside for any amount of time becomes an example of personal strength, something so important that to do without checking our e-mail is a show of personal restraint, a sign of maturity.

Historically, writing down our thoughts has been judged as different than speaking our ideas, with the latter typically easier than the former. E-mail confounds this thinking by allowing the most simplistic thinking, most commonly associated with speaking, to become written words with little or no involvement of high-thinking skills. Early e-mail included users scolding each other for typos. In those days, much angst was expressed in whether e-mail should be spelled "email" or "e-mail," with hundreds, perhaps thousands, of users arguing emotionally as if the future of the English language hung on the outcome. Today, with the casual use of acronyms to cover everything from an emotional outburst (LOL) to common phrasing (BTW), e-mail is seen more as a verbal conversation in style and demeanor.

For advertising, the rise in e-mail use rendered reaching the consumer more challenging, as each became isolated via e-mail. So even though the thinking has been that more consumer contact would be possible, e-mail empowered the potential buyer by launching a significant surge in individualistic behavior that in turn resulted in more and more withdrawal from traditional communication channels. This move toward individualism was global, with cultures that were very traditionally collectivist in nature showing signs of more personal decision making outside the community structure. Although collective cultures still exist and still exhibit a reliance on tradition and elders, the personal desires of individuals within these cultures to make decisions outside the group—such as attending college outside of their native countries—are indicative of a more personal awareness based on their own collection of values.

E-mail encourages individuality. Very few e-mail addresses are shared accounts by more than one person. So while the comments of one can still adhere to the thinking of the many, it is still the action of one that results in these facile communication artifacts. I am not suggesting the end is near for those cultures based on collectivistic thinking. I am suggesting that the degree of this thinking is shifting, largely because of e-mail and all the easy communication applications that have appeared. Again, e-mail encourages individualism. It allows a person, without permission or identity, to speak (and listen) to the masses. It enables expression without criticism, especially prior criticism. And it seems to be without any element of danger or risk. Removing identity, allowing anonymity emboldens those who might have had concerns regarding being identified with their "free" speech. Remove punishment and grant rewards for communicating with friends, acquaintances, and perfect strangers, and you have the perfect recipe for individualism. Reckless individualism, in fact.

Yet, group participation was considered an important enough function of e-mail that the ability to send a message to more than one person—in fact, an unlimited number of persons—was built into the original e-mail software, even though the activity in the 1960s and 1970s of sending messages back and forth was possible only within a single server network. The transition of enabling the sending of e-mail messages to multiple individuals across multiple networks was a clear predecessor to the sharing abilities of modern blogs, such as Facebook. These groups, however—typically early user-known recipients within a shared job environment—were far more substantial than the relationships exhibited by more modern online sharing sites today. After all, the invention of the verb "to friend" is an artifact of today's superficial and wholly imaginary online groups.

As e-mail grew in popularity, the ability to commercialize what was considered "free space" generated two definitions: those who practiced mass mailings considered it marketing and many of those who received the unwanted mail would label it spam. Whatever the nomenclature, the resulting activity of marketing/spam generated significant pushback. Software manufacturers quickly responded to the demand for spam blockers by manufacturing simple-to-install and inexpensive tools that would identify spam by tracking how many recipients had been included in the "to" line of the message. Thousands of e-mails clearly indicated spam and allowed the software user to shuffle the message away. Ultimately the browsers themselves would provide the ability for users to define spam, effectively block spam, and end e-mail as an effective tool for advertising. Some spam manages to get past the software—much as new pathogens "learn" resistance to drugs intended to kill them—but the vast majority of spam is blocked and eliminated without the user ever actually seeing it. In fact, now seemingly undelivered e-mail that is now part of our lexicon might be in the spam folder of the browser: "Have you checked your spam?"

Spam is dead.

At the same time, the long-term use of e-mail itself is in question. I consider that later.

> Yes, we need the Web in this new age. And it's *not* like TV where you don't particularly have control over what's rendered for viewing but a few selected TV channels with filtered content. In which one might possibly still have to deal with random ads because these companies advertising their products or services through the TV media basically fund the media. I'd say [a] very good number of the world if not all of it needs the Web in this age we are in. One just has to sit back and figure out how much advantage the Internet has to offer him or her, talking about living and learning to get through everyday life rather

than minor disadvantages. I believe this Internet thing is bigger than what we think it is. —Tosan

THE INDIVIDUAL AND INFORMATION (PRODUCT) SEARCHING (ADVERTISING)

In 1993, I was busy selling my services as a hand-coder of Web sites for corporate types who had no idea what to do with their sites. They were just told that everyone would have one, so they needed one, too. These were the years of a new language, both within hypertext, but also within the world of corporate techies: breadcrumbs, alt text, ADA-friendly sites, and others. These new elements of the Web sprang up within years of the first site going online (one created and placed by the father of the Web, Tim Berners-Lee). Each new function or requirement of the Web also demanded a new cottage industry that generated dozens, if not hundreds, of so-called professional site developers, along with the silliest, most egotistical, and most overused moniker, "webmaster."

As mentioned earlier, the idea was simple: create a Web site and consumers could learn all they wanted to know about your products and services. They could also opt out of the Web site when they had made a decision. A significant difference from television, the consumer watches only what is provided at this one "station"; the consumer seemingly lacks any options other than to view or not to view. Yet the Web site provides the consumer with a degree of control unavailable in any prior advertising platform: the decision to look or leave, to ask questions, to sign up for future information, and to ultimately block those future messages all were granted to the user of the browser. None of these is available on a television screen.

Even more interesting, perhaps, is that each consumer who ends up directed to a Web site has the ability to browse the site on his or her own pathway, opening whatever link he or she chooses—not what the site creator (or the company sponsoring the site) might have wished. This individualized learning model does not presume that only one pathway exists to a final decision. At the same time, those early sites were not actually created with the idea that consumers would collect data in their own way. Individual consumer decision making was like so many elements of this new media: a behavior learned after the fact, after millions of consumers made it clear that they would use their own learning patterns to gather information in their own stepwise scheme.

This certainly must have frustrated—and still frustrates—some site builders and marketing managers, but it must also frustrate those who believe such static patterns of leading are morally wrong. In cultures where decisions are arrived at via group decision making and careful reference to identified experts or elites, the ability of a potential consumer to navigate to whatever information was sought was more than simply troublesome, it represented a corruption that threatened commercial society. I am not referring to pornography here, though I must admit that builders of such Web sites were (and still are) at the cutting edge of new technologies, however ironic that may be. For example, pornographers were the ones who pushed site builders to create ways to deliver streaming video online, long before traditional marketers ever considered using such technology on their commercial Web sites. They were also the early creators and users of instant messaging and live "conversations."

But I digress.

New surfers of the Web established their own standards of decision making, what data they required and from what source. Individuals, not some group (or family) or reference to past beliefs, would determine the degree to which they chose to believe the information they were gathering. This impact on decision making reinforced individualistic thinking in the United States, for good or ill. It also did much the same elsewhere. Unfortunately, as many researchers, including this one, have pointed out, new learners—whether in high school, college, or beyond—believe what they find in the top 3 percent of the Web to be all that is available. For them, if what they are seeking is not on the first page of a browser's search, the information simply does not exist. Clearly, this represents a serious threat to education. But that is a discussion for another place and another time.

What the Web ultimately created was tiers of seekers: those very committed to finding *the* answer, those who simply wanted *an* answer, and those who just wanted anything that popped up with no concern for accuracy or value. The amount of commitment, in terms of time, runs from high to low among these three types of Web users. Again, technology shaped consumer behavior. But what did the rise of Web sites as a marketing tool do to the advertising industry?

With the demise of e-mail as a reliable consumer outreach and director tool, advertisers started looking elsewhere within the Web for places to find consumers and "push" them to their Web site. The sites themselves largely targeted users in North America in the 1990s, though the creation of these new information platforms was certainly robust in parts of Europe. But one has only to consider the nomenclature used in naming sites to appreciate that the new communication channel was essentially designed for users in the United States. The Uniform Resource Locators (URLs) that were created for domains in Europe and elsewhere contained a country code, letters that do not appear for Web site addresses hosted in the United States.

At the turn of the century, as e-mail strategy was fouled and rendered useless by spammers, another possible channel of information arose: other Web sites. Most prominent would be search sites that connected online surfers to other sites. One of the first of these, Netscape, offered few services other than a search function early on. These early searches relied upon "engines," often spiders, which also browsed the Web looking for words and then counting them. When found, the word (information) would be catalogued based most often on the actual words being used. This crude word counter provided users with an opportunity to find Web sites corresponding to the terms used to initiate the search. Of course, such early searches were often foiled by semantics and completely frustrated by language barriers. Over the years, words (called "tags") were hidden in the HTML coding of the site. Web builders created these "meta-statements" to reflect the content of sites, thus making possible more accurate searches. Searches were still crude, and semantics still thwarted many a searcher's success.

To a great deal, the success of each search rested upon the ability of users to apply the appropriate terms. As the number of sites grew into the billions, the reliability of these simplistic searchers was overwhelmed. Enter Google. The Google browser, unveiled in 1998, had catalogued more than three billion Web documents within three years ("Google History" 2014). Using more than unreliable word counting, Google actually incorporated the search habits of Web users to build better search results. That is, rather than counting, the Google browser *learned*. It also represented an interesting evolution from mainframes serving dumb terminals, to personal computers remote from servers, to (finally?) "cloud" computing serving smart terminals (mainly iPads). This first stage tethered the user to a terminal that had to be within the vicinity of the main server. It also made it clear that the user at the end of the connection from the main server had limited access to limited areas and certainly little if any ability to personalize the workspace. Phase two, the personal computer, cut the user free of the main server, essentially making the user an independent agent. Of course, storage space of gathered information by the user was forever limited and a serious issue at every turn. Gather too much, share too much, and the personal computer would cease to operate. Phase three still allowed the user to act independently but also eliminated space limitations. Cloud technology eliminates the need to store information locally but ensures access to that information from any device at any location.

Google also, starting in 2006, allowed users of the search engine to create their own environment, complete with various small computing applications, which would come to be called "apps." This is significant for advertisers, though, no doubt, few took note. By allowing users to create uniquely different "skins" for their access devices, Google enables each user to create his or her own interface with the Internet. Each user created his or her own space that reflected his or her own values, personality, and priorities. Each of these interfaces was a sort of fingerprint, a uniquely personal statement.

Google also was responsible for taking online advertising to a new sphere, starting with the creation of AdWords. But this skips an important step that got to AdWords: banner ads.

> I think we have definitely taken the Web for granted. Just as a classmate mentioned, I would be so lost if it weren't for the Web to teach/remind me how to fix a flat on the side of the road in the middle of nowhere. An app can't do that; it would have to be specifically tailored for mechanic information. That is, assuming I had already taken interest in downloading that app. What if I don't have the tools I need; it's the Web that will give me an array of different ideas or ways to do something. To think of the Web and Internet separate helps me see the difference between apps and the Web. For example, if my app quits working or I run out of memory on my device, I can still go to a specific Web site and receive the same information if not more. I don't think the Web is going anywhere; it will just evolve. —Erin

THE WEBSITE AND ADVERTISING

One of the earliest online sites to post forms of advertising was now-defunct Prodigy, a content-delivery Web site owned by IBM. The first client was Sears, which posted a non-clickable ad. Clickable ads would follow, with the first, Coors, using Hotwire to promote Zima. The form of these advertisements was standardized over just a few years, with all conforming to the online format of Web sites, which—after some very bizarre site designs by those inclined to think of self-expression over readability—tended to settle on a 500 to 700 pixel width, reflecting the standard monitor size and resolution.

Hotwire.com was one of the first platforms to offer large quantities of advertising on its home page. The strategy was simple: exposure. The actual ad was usually language driven, thus largely restricted to one culture/region (Western and bicoastal). This remains true even today, as advertising strategies think global but act local. Rather than targeting a person who actually has a headache, these advertisements simply pushed the aspirin on everyone. The logic is scattershot, employed with the hope that someone with a headache is actually out there and actually looking at the advertisement. If this sounds familiar, it should. The basic advertising strategy of the mass market has been shared globally for more than a century. It requires little research, little creativity, and almost no strategic planning. It is not just a hook with bait on every fishing pole in every lake and stream; it is that selfsame fishing pole in every street, driveway, and garage, even though the hoped-for target rarely appears in those locations. Early online advertising employed the same approach that had been used for decades in print and broadcasting platforms and generated much the same returns: next to nothing.

Banner ads themselves evolved as the browser technology they used became more sophisticated and HTML code added new Web functionality. Moving from static banner advertisements to animated imaging, banner ads offered more colorful options for the same unchanging mass communication model: sender—message—receiver. As agencies clung to what they knew well—putting commercial and print advertising in front of largely poorly defined viewers and readers—the landscape of mass communication shifted. Rather than being passive receivers of messages, the millennial consumer became more engaged in choosing not just the information to be consumed, but how, where, and when it would be digested. The awakened in-control consumer, also far more individualized regardless of culture, moved to not just block unwanted messages, but to choose the messages they wanted. The shift was subtle but powerful. No longer would the target consumer be in one place at one particular time, but what this consumer would actually be doing would be of far more importance than ever before.

Banner advertising, no matter how colorful, animated, or interesting, would produce the same returns all advertising had during the prior century. The push model of taking information and shoving it at the intended target was based on communication devices that either did not have the form or function they had in the past (newspapers) or were in the early stages of evolving into something very different (television and radio). The period after 1993, especially after 2000, revealed an asynchronous world of audio and video watched purely when, where, and how the target consumer wished. And no matter how much the existing agency mentality and that of their clients wished it not to be, the time line predictability of information exposure and processing was over. Each consumer would choose the time and place for information transfer. This extended en masse to entertainment material such as television programs after 2010, opening up the possibility that a century of a creator-to-studio-to-network-to-viewer model would be simplified in just a few years to a two-step model: creator to viewer. The ability to deliver content without any cost associated with the traditional channels of television and theaters renders each artist a producer and every consumer a network creator. That is, without the historic pathway that controlled content from the top down, the ability to deliver information when, where, and how is set up by the consumer of that information. Again, the rule of the individual over all content creation and its delivery is present, if in rudimentary form. It does not require magical thinking to see the direction that online content is moving.

But what of advertising?

One of the more provocative elements of this new advertising world order was the ability for consumers in the United States to adopt the same attitude toward commercials that their counterparts in Japan have had for decades: twenty-something consumers in Tokyo see little difference between commercials and programming. Both are forms of entertainment. Judged by this standard, commercials and print advertisements that are poorly made and poorly scripted would be doomed to the same fate as equally flawed television programming. In both cases, an important factor is present: the evolution of the consumer from passive absorber of advertising to active seeker of information. In many ways, these consumers are much like the Internet itself. They see no difference among all forms of information, whether it be music, movies, news, television programs, or advertising. All are judged by an individual who is cut free from group standards and social chronology. The particulars of when, where, and how, which have dominated the world of information flow, have been replaced by the singular behavior of the consumer, which turns all traditional media planning and its associated message delivery strategies on their heads.

As the consumer rapidly used new technologies to take control of the information landscape, a key new component entered the battle: clickable banner ads. Actually, the ability to link banner advertisements to the manufacturer's Web site started almost immediately with the first banners. What changed was the methods of payment. Advertisers could pay just for the appearance of the banner advertising on a particular information site, such as a new online site. Other options evolved, including what came to be known as click-throughs. These rewarded the Web site that ran a banner ad with a higher fee. In some cases, an even higher fee was paid for an actual sale that was initiated at a particular Web site. In some ways, this reward-for-success model was seen as a good idea in an environment where some information platforms were suspected of paying individuals to click on banner advertisements to juice the system.

> The Internet is a network of networks that links computers together so that they can "talk" to each other and share info. The Web is just one of the layers on top of the Internet (one of the "languages" or types of communication). So, my simpleton assumption would be that the Internet would essentially stay as is (the foundation). The Web, however, will probably morph into a bigger, better, badder version as our technology continues to evolve. Our society, like other societies before us, will create new languages and new ways of communicating that are more evolved and mature. In terms of what this will look like, my brain just cannot imagine big enough. I'm still stuck on flying skateboards from *Back to the Future*. —Crystal

MORE REFINED WEB ADVERTISING

What emerged in the first decade of the century was a new form of advertising that seemed less like advertising and more like consumer behavior targeting. Launched by several Web sites in and around 2000, the ability to link advertisements to the words used by Web users conducting searches represented one of the first instances of aspirin advertisers actually reaching that elusive headache sufferer. The words purchased by advertisers were those that might be used by a user. For example, if a consumer used "headache" in a search, Anacin could post a few words, usually either within the first few search results or within the column at the right of the results. Payment methods evolved as banner advertising had evolved. Options were available. Generally, if a consumer clicked on the search terms, the search engine owner charged the brand a fee. Some search terms were more valuable than others. For example, it would be far more expensive to purchase search terms related to a recent movie smash hit than those that might be related to an obscure academic research article. And, as in the case of Leonardo DiCaprio, advertisers could purchase even the various errant spellings of a particular famous person's name.

The key here is that, for the first time in history, the consumer has been granted the ability to literally conjure up a commercial message based on her or his behavior, not on the much-used demographics or vague psychographics. The consumer's actual behavior was judged to be more important than any other factor present. This renders the entire planet a target market for every search, no matter the language. Of course, the linked consumer's reaction to the delivered Web site would continue to be based on the many factors that have ruled information processing since the dawn of sentient ability, including cultural factors that have been previously discussed. But that initial response, the moment at which the consumer, presumably in a searching mode of thinking, has chosen to check out a suggested source of pertinent information, is both anticipatory and behavior driven. The advertiser presumes the searching consumer is actually searching, and the consumer assumes the link will result in a successful information find. In both cases, these presumptions are based on actual consumer behavior at the moment of choice. Given that the days of charging consumers for the time that they are linked to the Internet are long over (e.g., AOL), the cost to the consumer to find this link is nil, except for the desire to find the appropriate information (and, therefore, the appropriate solution) as quickly as possible.

Perhaps even more significant here is that the consumer is in charge of the environment in and around the actual information search itself. Compare the environment of watching television to that of searching for information online. Both are opportunities for the consumer to learn, and both presumably have an equal opportunity for success. Yet, because the consumer is in control of the searching, the appearance of the appropriate "message" is not in the control of the advertiser. Additionally, the long-honored practice of using the time at which the commercial is shown to dictate the content of the commercial is out the window. All online searches are asynchronous. All control is placed in the hands of the consumer. All that remains is making an argument to a motivated information seeker. In the world of salesmanship, this is the moment of truth. If the message presented cannot convince the consumer who is seeking the information at the optimal time and place (as defined by the consumer), then the conclusion is that the product itself is either flawed or inappropriately presented.

Of course, the argument that the advertising at the beginning of online videos will continue is a strong one. However, that these messages are particularly efficient compared to the advertising sought out by consumers is unlikely. Placing advertising ahead of content online is more than ever likely to result in the consumer seeking a "skip" button. Consumers, empowered by their ability to control the time and place functions of advertising delivery, are less likely than ever before to welcome unwanted messages (aka "spam"), no matter how much they wish to watch or read the information secreted behind the advertising curtain.

Tools to manage spam e-mail have already been created and have proliferated. It will not take long for technological solutions to provide the information seeker (consumer) ways around the seemingly pervasive and ill-received push videos preceding such sought-for items as online videos. Although the argument can be made (and has been made) that such videos are a revenue stream that costs the consumer nothing, such logic ignores the simple reality that the times in which we live demand that the control of information flow be in the hands of the consumer. When it is not, we have an angry, poorly motivated potential consumer. Put bluntly, the consumer will control the conversation or will reject the message, no matter how timely or appropriate the information may be.

We have left the era of group thinking controlling individual actions. As the vernacular would describe it: the toothpaste is out of the tube. Never again will there be a time when obnoxious, irritating commercials and print ads accomplish much more than a consumer desire to skip, ignore, and delete. Not only must advertisers consider the appropriateness of the message, but they must allow consumers the right to watch commercials on their own terms. This requires far less push and much more pull. Consumers, if considered and respected as the seekers of information, must be convinced that they are not being "sold"—and thus probably being lied to—but rather informed.

> The Web is something that I do take for granted often, but when I think about it, I love the access that I have to almost any information I want at any moment! It is incredible thinking what I have been able to accomplish with the use of hundreds of Web sites, not just apps and different streamlined sources for my own personal education. I have taught myself how to play multiple instruments, how to cook different things, discover new music and art that I never would have without it, and see and hear people's valuable opinions on things that I never would have without the use of the Web and its many different angles on almost every subject imaginable. I have learned so much

through my use of the Web and have loved it. I hope to only continue to use it
more and more for education down the road as well. —Ryan

REACHING THE NEW CONSUMER VIA MYFACE: EGOTISM, NAÏVETÉ, AND "FRIENDING"

Sometime within the last decade a new word appeared. Well, actually it is an old word used in a new way: the verb "to friend." The action is to announce to the universe that you "like" someone else and would like to "friend" them. Keep in mind that the meaning of "like" and "friend" has little to do with the traditional definitions of the words from which they were jauntily derived. In the content of Facebook and Myspace, these terms refer to the ability to add people—some of whom truly are your friends and some of whom are no more your "friends" than a star in a remote constellation—to your "circle." These "friends" are just people (one assumes) who, for whatever reason, signify they want to "follow" you online.

Both of these platforms (and others), which I've combined into "MyFace" to shorten the reference, offer varying levels of friends, including the usual "family," no doubt also vaguely defined. These online posting areas provide the illusion of belonging, a complete fiction of community that is easily modified and even eliminated. The glue of traditional relationships, be they positive or negative, is absent. And, in so many ways, MyFace represents a shortcut for individuals to *act* social without actually having to *be* social. And, yes, my name for them seems iconoclastically appropriate.

The software prods users to easily add "friends" to various areas within MyFace. The ability to delete a friend is not so obvious. Clearly, the software manufacturers want users to have lots of friends and would prefer that these same users not "defriend" existing contacts. Rationale? Advertising. Although still a small portion of the half a trillion dollars spent on advertising worldwide (Orr 2013), online sites such as Facebook are attracting a larger share of that total each year. In 2009, Facebook attracted almost half a billion dollars in advertising. By 2012, that total neared $3 billion, a significant share of the nearly $15 billion gathered by all online media (Cohen 2011).

On the other hand, visiting a MyFace platform lacks precision. The posting of seemingly disconnected and random information by "friends" hardly offers any degree of targeting to advertisers. No, MyFace is merely a consumer-created news arena with a variety of poorly defined reader-friends.

But stepping away from the more generalist MyFace, we might consider the future of the blog itself. Take, for example, a blog site whose creator comments on being a bicyclist in New York City. Bike Snob NYC (Weiss 2007) is dedicated to all things related to bikes in New York. The site is tastefully filled with various banner ads down the right side of the page, all related to bicycling. Presumably, readers are interested in bikes. But are they exclusively interested in bikes? Couldn't someone be interested in the city? Or in snobbery? Certainly. This renders even a seemingly well-defined blog as this into a more general news source. Not as general as the *New York Times*, but certainly no more narrowly defined than the *New York Times* Sunday fashion magazine.

What this seems to suggest is that even in the short term, advertisers will have platforms to communicate with potential consumers. What it does not address is the direction, except in vague terms, of advertising online. No matter how the use of online search terms is tracked, no matter how carefully blogs are chosen to target potential information seekers, advertising agencies are left wondering: is this the right tool, at the right time, to reach the right consumer?

> People indeed do take the Web for granted. . . . If it just disappeared even for twenty-four hours people would go crazy. Needless to say we all once in this world survived without these things, but we have got too addicted and abusive with these things that there is no way it will be going away anytime soon. TV and Internet can kill so much of our time, which is a good things but often a bad thing. I do not know why I am so fascinated with television and the Web. . . . Well, maybe I do. I am so fascinated with the deeper physical buildup of it all. I find it fascinating how producers edit TV shows and the animations and extra things that come with movies. I am fascinated with how a computer works and where it came from. So I am that 1 percent who actually appreciates technology not because it gives me something to do but [because of] how genius it is. I would never want it to go away especially since I am a MIS major and I need these things to get my job career field booming. — Aaron

APPS AND ISOLATION

With the birth of the World Wide Web, new attempts to reach consumers arose, each met with derision, each generating a market for software designed to thwart the activities of the generalists. After the turn of the century, a new form of information transfer presented new challenges and opportunities: apps. As noted by Chris Anderson and Michael Wolff in "The Web Is Dead," the appearance of these new apps, which run primarily through the Internet and not the Web, presented some interesting options and community stratification (Anderson and Wolff 2010). It also completed the consumer circle, moving from giving consumers what advertisers think consumers want to giving the consumers what the consumers themselves think they want. Control of the commercial conversation moved completely into the hands of the consumer with perhaps the exception of irritating, poorly targeted push messages in pop-up windows and banner ads. Just as was the case with remote control and mute buttons and the more recent ability to block e-mail judged to be spam, new software will arise to deflect easy-to-create push messages propagated by those targeting the service to the lazy and unimaginative.

In many ways, the creation of apps, intentionally or otherwise, can be linked to less and less thoughtful involvement of members of the society with society itself. More alarming, the mind-numbing nature of these apps bears no relation to anything that might even in a general way be considered progress. Yes, some apps are intended to provoke thinking and perhaps even make us smarter. But those are rare compared to the hundreds, thousands, and hundreds of thousands that are simply games like Angry Birds. Perhaps the role of apps is not to actually do much beyond distracting us from our largely humdrum and unproductive lives, much as the ancient Roman coliseums were intended to keep the masses of the day happy. A distracted citizen is a citizen much less likely to look for a more progressive, healthier, and predictable life. One wonders whether countries that ban things like Facebook might find the Internet more valuable by allowing their citizens access to mind-numbing app games. Very little progress or change is argued within Angry Birds, and the value of small victories within the game no doubt creates a sense of personal success for the user. It is an old story (and I wonder if it is true), but as a student in science in my early days, I was told of a rat that was placed in a cage that allowed for the self-administration of a narcotic. The rat self-administered itself into oblivion, choosing the drug over food or water. Is that then the role—intended or otherwise—of these simple, easy-to-use and easy-to-understand games?

Whatever the ultimate impact of apps on society, what cannot be denied is their reinforcement of the sense of individuality within the user. Very few apps are intended to be true group activities, even though some provide for a competitive environment. These role games—usually involving battle or racing—are still almost entirely individualistic. All that has happened is a replacement of the computer with a human or humans. In all other respects, the experience of the user remains solitary: me against the universe. Apps are not team builders, and those that seem to suggest that they are, like Facebook or Twitter, are simply self-aggrandizing platforms that reinforce singular action.

For example, decisions to post or not to post are not rendered to a group vote. The role of the user within apps is to act entirely on his or her own, with the ultimate power of sharing or not sharing, "friending" or "defriending" completely up to the individual. These apps are not similar in any way to a group activity, such as a meeting. At a meeting, any member of the group can be called on to offer his or her opinion. Even the decision not to share in a meeting setting involves a clear and direct action. This does not happen with apps, even those proposing to be social platforms.

Apps are created for individuals, used by individuals, and purposed by individuals. They may be the most powerful antisocial tools yet created.

Each user is able to see him- or herself as in complete and total control of all outcomes. It is as if we are creating millions of small tyrants, each provided the tool to modify, improve, or delete anything within a largely self-created fictitious world. At no point is the individual engaged in self-betterment, much less in generating anything that might lead to the betterment of others (society?). Progress simply isn't an intended outcome. That might be acceptable for a society that relies on progress for the general good. But it is even more troubling that this new form of individualism is not particularly interested in education. One of the oldest saws is that experience is what results from trying and failing. What useful education (vis-à-vis experience or outcome) is gained by failing (or succeeding) to kill all the pigs in Angry Birds?

I suppose the use of new technology for intentionally unproductive activity is hardly new. Consider the value of an automobile as an ambulance versus as a NASCAR vehicle. One saves lives. The other entertains people with the possibility of costing lives (some believe the major attraction of a race car event is the chance of seeing an accident). We are acting as individuals, specifically individuals who have no interest in even accidentally moving the group forward. Self-aggrandizing? Of course!

Rainie and Wellman imagine that what I have described is not traditional individualism per se, but rather "networked" individualism. The argument is that rather than being isolationist, new media, specifically apps, create a new sort of community: "They have become increasingly networked as individuals, rather than embedded in groups. In the world of networked individuals, it is the person who is the focus: more than the family, the work unit, the neighborhood, and the social group" (Rainie and Wellman 2012). They go on to describe what they consider a "community" comprised of new individuals. Of course, this community has been set aside by the individual: "Unlike the days of village life when everyone knew everyone else's affairs, people in the high-tech age are more liberated now to act on their own or with various segments of their network." This is hardly a community by any imaginative stretching of the term. It is pure individualism. The challenge for those wishing to see a bright light behind all the clouds, I suppose, is to calculate a way in which the new individual can be seen as some form of improvement. Rainie and Wellman ask: "Is Facebook making you lonely or [making you] feel more connected?" (2012). They might better put the question: is Facebook tricking you into thinking that you are not alone, surrounded by your fake friends?

Whatever the real situation, the app world consumer is a very different one than what we encountered even twenty years ago. This new consumer is degrees more distant, less likely to stomach a traditional advertisement, and worlds more cynical (perhaps better put as "worldly"). They can spot a pitch light years away. But more interesting, they are defining their world of information flow. Moving beyond even the previously considered echo chamber, consumers are crafting their own browsers tracking their own created set of sites, using their own selected apps that reinforce their worlds apart from each other both physically and mentally.

The challenge is not somehow slipping an advertisement within a Mario Brothers app or offering options for information (commercials) to consumers using a particular set of search terms. That we can do now. What we face is an isolated consumer who reaches out for information, blocks all "accidental" encounters with commercial information, and sets rules to avoid what might even slightly smack of commercial information. The mind-set of advertisers must change from merely selling the virtues of a product to somehow presenting the values the consumer seeks—and only that information, as if the actual creation of the commercial message is in the hands of the information seeker, not the agency. This is being done today. We call it buzz.

> Digitally tricked-out vending machines keep popping up around the globe, surprising and delighting consumers with new gimmicks and free samples. Local goodwill is the endgame if you take the activations at face value. But in truth, they're plays for views on YouTube. Coca-Cola is the standard-bearer. Its videos of machines like the one trading free sodas for hugs in Singapore were widely viewed. A Coke Zero video of a machine sending consumers running through a James Bond-style gauntlet in Belgium for free movie tickets to *Skyfall* has racked up 10 million views since October. It also has had nearly a million Facebook and Twitter shares, per video tracker Unruly Media. (Beltrone 2013)

CREATING BUZZ GLOBALLY

It starts with a balance between the creativity of thought and expectations of consumers/readers. Smart, interesting, well-targeted messages/events/stunts are picked up by avid readers and spread via a multitude of apps. The rapid spread of the message is a factor of a couple of variables: the interest in what is being posted and the number of "friends" the information spreader has. Both of these must be high to give the information a chance to buzz.

One an agency can control. The other it can't. And when we consider how a message might be equally as likely to be sarcastic, the agency may not have much control over the former. If it is of any consolation, ideas that are considered mildly silly or stupid rarely reach buzz status. They are mentioned and the herd moves on.

Buzz-worthy events or ideas are

- provocative: a shock or unexpected idea or proposal;
- hilarious: a message within an action that is extremely humorous;
- amazing: an activity that seems almost impossible or at least very unlikely;

- emotional/joyful: a message that tugs hard at the heart of even the most cynical, until the cynic decides to mock the event or message;
- scary: a message or event that generates the secretion of hormones associated with a fight-or-flight reaction.

And probably a few other emotional responses, as well. Bottom line: whatever is being presented must be more than just interesting. For example, the Coca-Cola commercial message alluded to at the start of this section presents the reactions of people in two locations to one common device. The viewer of the commercial certainly sees what is happening and may share the commercial. But the actual individuals involved with the event itself probably took pictures and videos and shared them with friends who in turn shared them with other friends. Classic buzz. What is perhaps most interesting here is that the typical event that provokes buzz may not involve much expense. Certainly many of Coca-Cola's previous and future commercials cost (and will cost) far more than the two-minute message created here. The technology was simple, and though not cheap, certainly not in the six figures.

As to the actual spread of the message, there are two steps: the initial spread of individuals reporting on the event as it happened and those watching the commercial online. Neither involved much expense, if any at all. And yet the message was carried forward via both pathways.

So what must also be included in these types of buzz creators is a degree of control and predictability. A poorly managed and poorly defined message can generate negative buzz that can damage brand equity far more than the worst traditional commercial. Without a degree of certainty about how the message will be received, the event/message that generates the buzz becomes a potentially expensive mistake, one that can take years to heal. It is an old belief in advertising that there are three types of consumers: those who know your brand and love it; those who know nothing about your brand; and those who know your brand and hate it. The latter group is the most expensive to recapture, costing more than the reinforcement of the brand to the first consumer and introduction of the brand to the second.

As advertisers of the future add buzz creation into their media plans (something that undoubtedly will consume more and more attention from planners over time), the nature of the event or message will require more and more imagination. It will also require that media planners understand their target consumers. As has been noted, if I have only three hundred thousand Jaguars, I need to talk to only the three hundred thousand consumers who might be interested in (and able to actually afford) a purchase. At the same time, leaving untouched the consumers who know nothing about Jaguars and who are not interested in purchasing one at the present time is also a good idea. Even the Coca-Cola India-Pakistan sharing commercial/event has possible downsides, though it is hard to identify them, beyond the fact that the commercial is in English. The product is understated but at the same time presented as a connector of peoples. What more could an advertiser ask for?

REACHING THE MILLENNIAL INDIVIDUAL WITH A SINGULAR MESSAGE

The challenge for advertisers starts with fully understanding exactly what the consumer is doing at any given moment, but most especially at that moment when the need matches access. Spillage—the wasted effort of advertising on those who are not ready to purchase, not ready to consider, or simply not interested in the message—is the enemy of all advertising agencies. Spillage can appear as a consumer ignoring the message or, perhaps far worse, a consumer hating the message. The latter of these two possible outcomes generates a consumer who becomes the most expensive future convert to the brand. The negative consumer has a negative brand image and, unless approached in a particular way, the negative brand image is simply reinforced every time any message is received. In fact, it is better to not advertise at all than to advertise an unwanted, nonworking message to a consumer who holds a negative brand image.

Yet in a mature market—which the entire world is rapidly becoming—it is unlikely that many consumers fall into the "I don't know the brand" category. Like world politics, few are undecided; many more are deeply vested into one camp or another: you either love Coca-Cola or Pepsi.

Clearly this does not include emerging markets in regions where autocratic rule has suppressed Western consumerism. Nor does it include countries amid civic war or areas experiencing a rise of individualism. These regions and countries are markets that Western corporations are keenly interested in reaching, if only because the new consumers are likely ignorant of global brands.

But are they? Consider that during the 1970s, when Russian consumers associated advertising with poor products, these same consumers were keenly aware of Western brands. In fact, Joe Cappo, a longtime advertising professional, related to me a story regarding Russian consumers when I was conducting research as a graduate student in the early 1990s. Russian consumers, Cappo noted, who flew to New York or other American cities, often got off the planes and rushed to the nearest mall to stock up on Levi's blue jeans, both for personal use, but also to sell on the streets of Moscow. The awareness of a brand, the creation of a brand image in a seemingly noncommercial world was more than obvious. How did these consumers even know about Levi's, much less have created a strong positive brand image of the product?

It seems that consumerism is an inherent part of the human experience. That is, one of the most common human behaviors is the desire to identify good from bad. This can occur in almost any culture, acting as an independent value based on trial and error. Consumers, regardless of their economic standing, make some decisions that always involve quality. The equation invariably present in choices (and branding) by consumers includes quality. It also involves value, and, of course, cost. Put simply, every consumer makes a decision, rational or emotional, that weighs the product's quality and its cost to determine its value. Not everyone can afford a Jaguar, but everyone can make a decision regarding an automobile purchase based on the quality of the vehicle compared to its price.

Consider those same Russian consumers walking the grocery store looking for tomato soup, another story passed on to me from Cappo. Understand first that at the time, all cans of tomato soup were simply labeled "tomato soup." The Cyrillic lettering included no hint as to a brand or brands based on which factory produced which cans. However, they did bear a number on the bottom of the can associated with the factory that made that can of soup. Consumers learned which series of numbers was associated with the best cans of tomato soup. In fact, Cappo related, when their favorite was not available, they knew of the second-best manufacturer.

This is branding at its crudest and most individualized form.

It is also a singular message being processed by a singular person.

We cannot step past the cultural barriers and opportunities that face every commercial, political, or social campaign. Culture will persist, just as brands do. In fact, in some ways, brands and cultures are one and the same. They both are closely held beliefs. They both are shortcuts for the individual: they are a roadmap of how to choose or behave, how to value or reward, how to like or love. The main difference may be that while cultures seem to be moving toward each other, brands are intentionally kept apart. No brand wishes to be confused with another (at least not those acting legally). And where brands are legally separated from each other, cultures seem to be racing toward each other at light speed—quite literally.

Reaching that millennial individual with that individualized message is obviously not easy. The individual is a moving, changing target, which can be influenced by friends, random information, social (cultural) rules, and one's own trial and error, either of the product or of one that they have deemed similar. Perhaps the most powerful of these is culture, which the individual uses to set the rules and degrees of influence of the others.

REFERENCES

Anderson, Chris, and Michael Wolff. 2010. "The Web Is Dead: Long Live the Internet." *Wired.* August 17. http://www.wired.com/2010/08/ff_webrip.

Beltrone, Gabriel. 2013. "Brands Find the Link between Viral Videos and Vending Machines: Marketers from Belgium to Singapore." *AdWeek*. August 5.

Cohen, Jackie. 2011. "Report: Facebook Leads in 2011 Online Display Ad Sales." *SocialTimes*. June 20. http://www.adweek.com/socialtimes/report-facebook-leads-2011-online-display-ad-sales/350767?red=af.

"Google History." 2014. *Google*. http://www.google.com/about/company/history.

Orr, Casey. 2013. "Ad Spending Expected to Grow to Half a Trillion Dollars." *FoxBusiness*. June 18. http://www.foxbusiness.com/industries/2013/06/18/ad-spending-expected-to-grow-to-half-trillion-dollars.

Quigley, Robert. 2010. "Today in History: The First Spam Email Ever Sent." *The Mary Sue*. May 3. http://www.themarysue.com/first-spam-email.

Rainie, Lee, and Barry Wellman. 2012. "Networked Individualism: What in the World Is That?" *Networked*. May 24. http://networked.pewinternet.org/2012/05/24/networked-individualism-what-in-the-world-is-that-2/.

Weiss, Eben. 2007. "Bike Snob NYC." http://bikesnobnyc.blogspot.com.

Chapter Three

Culture Transfer at Web Speed

I was walking down the main street in Plainville, Kansas, on a spring day in 2003. I was consulting at the time with the local school system about introducing Internet learning and online resources, specifically Web site construction and evaluation. I had just had a close encounter with a class of eighth graders and had decided to spend a few minutes sampling the local cuisine. As I was walking, an F150 pickup sailed by with the latest—like released the previous day—rap song blasting out of the rolled-down windows. I was struck by the fact that the song had made it all the way into the boonies of Kansas in just twenty-four hours. No way this would have happened prior to the Internet. Cultural transference in the form of a non-radio-transmitted rap song from Detroit to Plainville, Kansas, in twenty-four hours? No way. —Thomas Gould

Culture abides. Culture moves slowly as it adds and subtracts, refines and eliminates. It took decades for the style of music enjoyed in central Europe in the fifteenth century to transform into something different. It took centuries for that same music to morph into the soundtrack of *Run Lola Run*, a heart-pounding, drum-driven theme song for a very Germanic film.

But the transformation was hardly smooth or systematic. Nor was it entirely Germanic at the end, at least compared to the almost certainly "local" music of 1450. Ideas, in the form of music, books, paintings, and other cultural art forms, were shared via horseback and carriages six centuries ago. A work by Mozart might take months to progress (if it did at all) from one end of Europe to the other. This was due not just to the geographic challenges, whether mountains or rivers, but also to political intervention. Information itself was guarded and valued by monarchs, especially those in the small city-states and provinces that were scattered across Eastern Europe. They valued knowledge as a weapon of war, a means to eventually dominate a neighbor or defeat an enemy. The university system in place at the time was more about hoarding than sharing, as if education itself was an asset, a part of its economic system. It is not too much of a stretch to imagine the universities in Paris and Bologna using their educators as a form of advertising or public relations. Even then, students were a source of monetary advantage.

Some cultural sharing did occur at the time, generally among the elites, the very rich, and the very well connected few. And with the technological advance of the movable-type press, ideas could be shared in more than one approved cross-cultural language (Latin) and across national boundaries in the form of relatively cheap books. Books, and the ideas they contained, became a threat to or cure for cultural isolation. More thoughts could be packed into three hundred pages of a book than could ever have been shared using traditional handwritten scrolls and wood-carved pressings.

In fact, when the cost of creating a Gutenberg bible was compared at the time to the monk-illuminated bibles, the cheapness of the former made the most valuable data (ideas) available to an entire class of individuals largely shut out by the latter. Yes, individuals had possessed their own bibles prior to Gutenberg but only those in the richest locales. The average citizen of Utrecht might still find owning a personal bible a bit of a stretch. But it would be possible, and it would be in German.

This singular event represents more than just a major shift away from church control of information. Placing into the hands of the individual ideas in a known language is more than simply educating the individual. Providing the individual the sense of the ownership of ideas encourages not just more learning, it creates a sense of separateness from others. Each individual then becomes a gatherer of knowledge, of course, but they also become a unique gatherer, each with their own interpretation of the ideas they seemingly uniquely possess. We become more unique individuals with every new book, with every new idea.

The acting of sharing ideas with others, even if carefully controlled by the use of bonds to control printers, was still far more than had occurred even a century earlier. Yes, this sharing of ideas generated new ideas and led to many new inventions. It also led to a new religious sect. But relative to what is happening today, the invention of an idea-sharing tool, whether in Europe in the fifteenth century or four hundred years earlier in China and Korea, allowed people to define themselves by what they knew more than by what they did. The earthy tradition of being known by a combination of a name and a profession, such as Arthur the Blacksmith, would fall by the wayside, just as the role of the monk in small city-states and communities at the turn of the first millennium would shift from jack-of-all-trades to solely clerical. That is, even within the church itself, the canonical tradesman—that is, the monk—would become more stylized, more singular in practice.

The exchange of information became less of an issue of language or custom than it was of efficiency. One book from a printer in Berlin could be carried to London, translated, and made available to the English. This ability to share across cultures generated not just an age of scholars and thinkers, but also an age of unique scholars and thinkers, each with his followers. While their numbers were limited and their followers few, these scholars worked within a competitive environment.

Over time, new generations of readers and thinkers became known by what they read. Kant stood separate from Hume, of course. But those who involved either or both in describing their own world of thought themselves created an individualistic existence. Ardent followers became their own thinkers, using some of a predecessor and adding their own touch.

Still, the ideas generated in Europe were hardly shared at light speed. Scientists were notorious in coveting and not sharing gathered data, whether of chemical measures or astrological findings. Scientific minds often found themselves relying on the uniqueness of their data as a means to an end, the favor of monarchs. They could be forgiven if they were less than anxious to share their best information with those who might eclipse them. It was simply a matter of self-preservation. No one got very far up the social ladder with information commonly known by all. Unique data, unique findings on the part of what would then be considered a unique individual, was the cache that ensured a warm bed and routine meals. Being judged as average at that time was as it is today. Standing out, carrying a reputation, acting as an individual through the accumulation of unique or rare information—both secondary research published by others and primary data gathered by the individual—all factor into the social capital that drives status and progress in the modern world.

> For this future class I think it'd be really cool to implement something about sports. I say that because I play football here at K-State, and just learning about sports in general is really cool. You can teach something about the history of sports and when it started and where it is going. There's always a ton of topics you can come up with on sports. You could talk about should college athletes get paid or not. It's a really sensitive topic but it's always interesting to get others' feedback and thoughts on it. I believe talking about sports would also be a good one to talk about. Because it'd keep conversations going and someone will always have an opinion on something about it. Also food is a really huge one to talk about. I say that because you can see what's traditional for some people and how their family has meals on certain holidays. I think it'd also keep the conversation going because people would get ideas on a good idea and keep going on and on about how something can be good or change the food that a person cooks, et cetera. . . . So sports and food are a really important role in my life, haha. —Connor

CULTURAL TRANSFER VIA EDUCATIONAL EXCHANGE

For some societies, culture is worth fighting for. This warfare rarely involves cultural elements such as art but often is hyperbolic when it touches on religion. This strife has never been so apparent as we see today, as factions within religions fight not only those of another belief but just as often those of another sect within the same religion. Much of the bloodshed can be traced back to colonialism in the nineteenth century and earlier. European countries drew lines on a map creating false national boundaries that had not existed in Africa, the Middle East, South America, and Asia. The creators of these nations ignored cultural schisms, assuming that just as European countries allow differences within their own societies, so would these new countries. To ensure that the new societies would remain peaceful (and supportive of the colonial power), dictatorships were encouraged or at least tolerated. Yes, this is a simplification of what was a far more complicated process. Yet the product was a Sudan with two very different cultures jammed into one country. It resulted in a Syria with a multitude of religions and sects within religions forced together and held together by a dictatorship of fifty years. It resulted in the disintegration of a single India into three countries, two of which have remained on a war footing since the middle of the previous century.

But something is happening today that may result in levels of bloodshed not seen in sixty years.

Keep in mind that the natural tendency for some is to ensure their own cultural survival by eliminating the cultures of all others. The fuel for this is often religion, but there are other factors as well, such as gender roles, social behavior, and ageism. Bottom line, though, is that as two cultures grow closer together, both in geography and their own distinctions, the desire of some within each is to push back. Some of this pushback comes in the form of protecting cultural identities, a task cast as noble and vital. In some ways, this often-emotional plea for cultural protection seems similar to environmental measures taken to save rare organisms, as if the existing culture will fade and disappear, resulting in the denigration of an entire society. Ironically, however, few cultures that exist today can claim purity. Almost all reflect a replacement of a previous culture.

But let us set aside the issue of whether the culture to be saved is anything more than a culture that has already replaced another and consider what is actually happening on the ground. Cultural erosion can be seen every time one culture is introduced in another culture. That is, cultural transfer takes place automatically, transparently, and rapidly at the moment that one culture is introduced into another. This action of introducing one culture to another is actually encouraged by educational institutions in a number of countries in order to fulfill goals of encouraging diversity, cultural exchange, and international learning. That is, we actively, through our institutions, create cultural exchange that leads to the transformation of culture within both societies. This educational scheme rests on the belief that cultural exchange is part of the fuel that creates progress. New ideas, new ways of thinking, and new ways of looking at challenges can be enhanced via cultural exchange.

But the process is not without its side effects. As one culture—perhaps that of South Sudan—is introduced into another—let's say in an anthropology class within a Stateside university—the culture of the American students is changed, perhaps only slightly, but changed nonetheless. For the citizen of Sudan, that person is changed, perhaps even more than the students in the class. This change is then carried back to Sudan and shared there.

In 2013, I had the pleasure of working with a graduate student from China, specifically from a small town outside Beijing. During the two years I helped him complete his thesis, he noticed that the subjects of his study— fellow students from China—exhibited their cultural attitudes based on how long they had actually been in the United States. Those Chinese students who were recently enrolled in the university held different attitudes than those who had been here longer, with the change starting within months of arrival. My student remarked that this seemed surprising to him, given that the cultures stood so far apart from each other. Over time, notably, this student's own attitudes changed, so much that he believed that he could not return to China: "I won't fit in anymore. I have changed."

His interaction with other graduate students no doubt resulted in some cultural transference from him to them. More important, the change he expressed was not a cultural shift, but rather a personality modification. He believed that his own personality, a culture expressed at the individual level, had changed because of his exposure to Kansas culture. This included several aspects of culture, some obvious, such as music, some not so obvious, such as personality traits. Rather than the shy graduate student I knew in the first month I worked with him, he was far more outgoing and opinionated, going so far as to disagree with those older and far more educated than he. This willingness to stand his ground was attributed by him to his fellow graduate students.

At the same time, this student noted that students from other countries tended to "clump" together, regardless of their schools of study. And, when together, they spoke their native languages. I had noticed that students from abroad who were learning English as a second language also spoke to each other in their native languages as they walked out of class. I had also noted that faculty from other countries tended to clump together in public.

Cultural modifications are not complete, nor are they instantaneous. But they are present, especially within our universities. And they are rarely correctly interpreted. One has only to visit a food court within a student union at any university to see items presented as "Chinese" or "Mexican" or "Italian" to understand. None of these is an accurate representation, for starters because there is no such singular thing as "Chinese" or "Mexican" or "Italian" food (any more than there is "American" food), and also because what is presented is a far cry from authentic regional food.

Yet the actual presence of food that purports to be non-American represents contact with a non-American cultural artifact. The mere awareness of another culture reflects back on the experience of the one. The irony is that while we strive to provide a multicultural experience for students (and, to some extent, nonstudents), we experience a fierce sense of cultural clarity, as if we all know what represents our national identity. Just as we are not the country we were in 1783, we are not the culture present at that time. And as we join with others in other places to educate the planet, we are bound to change even more. Whether it is a study-abroad program offered by a university, an international student center on campus, or a robust interlibrary loan system, we are exchanging cultural elements in a sort of free-for-all, with little care for the outcomes or the consequences.

> I think the Internet makes advertising more prevalent or more of a commodity but not worse because the Internet allows you to skip ads. With the addition that they have become more annoying and in your face, many people are prepared to ignore them. I don't feel I'm being manipulated because I still have choice. I don't think a majority of ads directly affect me unless I'm already in position to buy into whatever it is they are trying to sell (example: me being hungry seeing a food commercial). But I believe that the advertising world does nothing by accident but people choose how they want to be affected. Not every emotional commercial makes me cry or feel for the object of empathy. —Tim

CULTURAL TRANSFER AT THE SPEED OF LIGHT

In the opening scenes of *Blade Runner*, advertising is shown on the sides of blimps floating just above crowded streets. One such ad shows an Asian woman taking a pill and then smiling. No words. Just taking a pill and smiling. Without any reference checking in the book that spawned the movie, the viewer can surmise that the pill has something to do with the smile. Hardly rocket science. In a world filled with a wide variety of cultures blended into one, who needs language to carry an advertisement? Even in a future depiction of Los Angeles, the concept is simple, direct, and easy to follow. The pill equals happiness. Take the pill and be happy. Both the act of using a pill and the state of happiness are culturally bound. Only in a world with one singular culture would the masses get the point. Is this where we are headed? One world culture?

Whatever is happening, it is happening at the speed of light. Ideas, whether spawned in the mountains of Tibet or the backwoods of Appalachia, are shared instantaneously worldwide. Yet the ideas themselves are filtered by the culture doing the transferring. We do not—yet—have immediate event-to-viewer information platforms. In almost all cases, an intermediary offers an interpretive view of the event at hand. The cultures that are present still have the ability to present the same event to various peoples and generate various responses based on a cultural foundation of ethics, beliefs, tradition, and linguistic semantics. We have no universal translator that offers much accuracy. And yet we have never been closer to a single world culture than we are today.

When I was a graduate student at the University of North Carolina at Chapel Hill, I shared many an ale with a department technical assistant from India, somewhere near New Delhi. He noted that on his way back home each year he would take a bus on the last leg, passing numerous shops, each with its own handmade sign. On a more recent trip home, however, all the hand-made signs had been replaced by Coca-Cola or Pepsi signs. He was mildly upset by this, suggesting that something had been lost. And perhaps it had. But clearly the change in the signage made for a more readable business name, a more modern communication with potential customers, and a more "mature" presentation of vital data. The culture that was lost, that of hand-made business signs, had been replaced by something far more standard and undeniably more sterile. A plain sign is called plain because it lacks any distinguishable culture elements.

The same is true for clothing. Often accompanying a local disaster are the images of individuals—perhaps teenagers—walking down a blasted street. Those teenagers in this century are as likely to be wearing a Nike or Pepsi T-shirt as they are some tie-dyed tee. Neither of these has anything to do with the traditional culture of the community. They have everything to do with the current culture of that community. It is far too easy to pass this off as an accident or convenience offered by an aid worker. It is far more likely that the person wearing the Western-influenced T-shirt is fully aware of the brand and in fact has a fully developed brand image in his or her head. The market-ing of America worldwide is carried by a variety of objects beyond advertis-ing. Again, Russians knew of Levi's blue jeans long before they saw a single commercial for the product.

We, as fairly intelligent bipeds, thirst for information. We tear down metaphorical walls to get at it. We seek out what is new perhaps more than we value what is old. After all, no one wants to be known as an old fuddy-duddy. Making sure we remain relevant means making sure we know what is happening. In fact, being the first to know that something has happened is as valuable—perhaps even more valuable—as it was five thousand years ago. And the tool we use today to ensure we are—if not first, pretty close to first—to know something is all about bandwidth, the measure of how fast information moves online.

Information is moved in a variety of ways, using everything from traditional copper wire to fiber. The former is so slow compared to the latter that they are rarely spoken of in the same breath. Information transfer in the early years of the twenty-first century involves two distinct options: cable or fiber. Yes, wireless is forever present, but it is sensitive to user loads and weather, far too sensitive to overloads and the likelihood of complete failure for elite information seekers to trust or tolerate. Fiber actually carries information as light and represents a vast improvement over cable, with capacities fifty times larger. Its use in the United States as of 2014 remains thin compared to Europe, if only because we have few competitive markets that would cause providers to actually offer the option.

The communities with fiber options enjoy a significant advantage over those who "just" have cable. The advantage follows along Thomas Friedman's flat earth arguments that fast connections are the "steroids" of information sharing. "Never before in the history of the planet have so many people—on their own—had the ability to find so much information about so many things and about so many other people." Part of that "information" being shared is culture. Again, a culture shared is a culture changed.

> "The Steroids": Wireless, Voice over Internet, and file sharing. Personal digital devices like mobile phones, iPods, personal digital assistants, instant messaging, and voice over Internet Protocol (VoIP). Digital, Mobile, Personal and Virtual—all analog content and processes (from entertainment to photography to word processing) can be digitized and therefore shaped, manipulated and transmitted; virtual—these processes can be done at high speed with total ease; mobile—can be done anywhere, anytime by anyone; and personal—can be done by you. ("The World Is Flat" 2005)

CULTURE AND ECONOMIC DISINCENTIVES

Consider for a moment the prime incentive for a person in Country A to jump over a fence to work in Country B. Wage differential. Politics. Transmigration of entire populations, whether in the southwest United States or on the borders of India or Europe, is propelled by two possible incentives: political freedom or increased wages. Setting aside the former for now, I would suggest that the greater the differential between the wages in Country A compared to B, the greater the likelihood people will jump the fence. In fact, the greater the wage differential, the greater the willingness of those fence jumpers to take greater risks. This may be an aberration of Hofstede's *Dimensions of Culture*: traditional low risk takers are incentivized to take greater chances if the economic imperatives are significant enough and if their and their family's physical survival hangs in the balance. The significance here is that those seeking the higher economic status on the other side of the fence carry with them their culture.

Garden City and Hutchison are two rapidly growing communities in southwest and central Kansas. Both of these cities have seen their school populations shift in the past decade with the inclusion of far more Latino students. In fact, the populations of these Kansas communities are almost half or more Latino. The answer to the shift in culture is obvious: higher wages are available in Kansas than in those countries south of the Rio Grande.

But what if there were a global minimum wage? What if one standard existed to ensure that all workers received at least as much as the workers across the border? Would fence jumping continue? And how would this impact cultural exchange?

Clearly, if those seeking higher wages remained in their homes, the transference of culture would diminish. Given that there are more reasons for transmigration than higher wages alone, the movement of people from one country—and one culture—to another would not cease completely, but the primary incentive for those on the other side of the fence to jump would suppress the majority of those who do.

Thus, perversely, the leveling of wages among cultures would likely lead to less cultural transfer. This is, no doubt, an underlining reason why, as pointed out by Friedman, no two countries that both have a McDonald's have ever waged war against each other. Equal enough wages between two countries would reduce the sharing of cultural artifacts.

But such wage leveling is more likely to follow cultural leveling than to lead it. That is, it is more likely that two countries will see wage parity after their cultures have grown closer. Consider Germany in 1989, the year before East and West again became one. Wage differentials were very high between the two countries, which, in almost all other respects, had very similar cultures. The disparity obviously lessened after reunification.

Consider cultural differences much as the fence along the Rio Grande or the Berlin Wall in Germany. Consider each cultural difference as a way for one culture to misunderstand another. Wars have been fought over less.

> I was on eBay the other day looking at something and I logged out of eBay and went to a completely different Web site and was browsing and the ads on that page were geared toward what I had been searching for on eBay. I'm not sure if they used my browser history or if the page was linked to eBay (I doubt it), but it is creepy. These marketing and advertising people are good. What else do they know about me? —Erin

NATIONAL BARRIERS FLATTENED AT THE SPEED OF LIGHT

Media provides only a portion of content in the twenty-first century. Consumers fill in the gaps, build new walls, and draw in new users. Consumers judge and then notify all other possible future consumers. Consumers are the holders of the brand and sharers of the actual real-world use of the product behind the brand.

How some consumers are different today from most of our predecessors is our willingness to share new ideas. Even those who purport to represent the traditions of the past cannot help but share any new information they find. New information is the best coin of the realm, of course. But information not widely known—even if relatively old—has value to the consumer. Sharing information with others becomes a status symbol for worthiness. For consumers, the information may be about an innovative brand or brand improvements via line extensions. For the politically active, the information may be anything that supports one's position or denigrates the opposing position.

But that's for sharers, who are not the majority of any population. Most of us are lurkers or perhaps more gently described as gatherers. We seek information not to share, but to understand, to feel more aware of our environment, to feel safer in our decisions. Even many sharers are often lurkers. To some extent this is a factor related to the overwhelming amount of information available. More is posted than can be digested and sent out to our own "friends" within our own "circles."

The danger of all of this sharing may be that it is done without national distinctions. The disconnection of the individual from that individual's country via information sharing online can threaten national identity. A country is only the sum of its citizens (that is, individuals acting as members of a country). Part of the experience of a being a citizen is a sense of belonging to a citizenry, a country.

Sharing information with anyone, without regard to whether he or she is a citizen, can lead to a disconnection of an individual from the status of citizen. If that information sharing becomes so quick and so fluid, what is the need for a nation?

Of course, communities will continue to be required: someone has to make sure the water is running and the lights come on. But nations are about something else, something more than the needs of a very large community. Consider the university as a small nation. It has its residential areas, its working areas, its dining areas. It even has its own information-gathering area: the library.

During the past fifty years, libraries globally have worked out ways to share information smoothly, rapidly, and fluidly. Interlibrary loan standards have opened up the holdings of libraries in faraway places to one and all. The rules associated with these loan practices are generally globally accepted.

The addition of new libraries to the umbrella of these loan practices occurs daily. Users of any one library can see the holdings of all other libraries with few, if any, geographic barriers. Found material is simply scanned and forwarded, usually within hours of the request. The distinction that once separated top universities—the holdings within their libraries—is largely moot. If I can access all the holdings within Harvard via interlibrary loan, how does it matter that the work is at that Harvard University library?

Does this mean that we are witnessing the creation of a single global library? Possibly. One single library with hundreds of branches. Perhaps each branch would come to be specialized in some way: Kansas State's Hale Library might be the holder of all information on the Great Plains. Or, more likely, each library might develop a crew of specialists who know where the information regarding a particular topic could be found globally. This does not begin to consider the issue of cloud technology and its ability to hold all human information. Again, the ability to locate information within a massive, universally available cloud database will be more than merely vital. It will establish winners and losers in every area of human commerce. It will be the gauge for measuring social capital.

In a way, this gathering of all libraries into one system of information gathering and sharing is already under way. The distinction of being a library in Kansas would be of little interest to users. What would matter is that the information is available, no matter the geographic locale of the source.

Thus may be the future course of nations. Setting aside issues of security, which may be a more global than a local issue in terms of standing armies, nations have little function when information can flow smoothly among interested parties in a discussion. As we witness the rise of the individual, we must consider the fading of nations. As information runs smoothly—regardless of national standards, laws, or treaties—those in control of that information, millennial individuals, will dictate what is appropriate, what is of special value. It will not be the legislature, no matter how this group is defined or elected, that sets the rules of information sharing. It will be the individual, also known as the consumer.

The user of information will set the boundaries, define the rules of engagement, and modify those rules as necessary. We have few international laws (note the term *international*); we have even fewer effective international laws controlling information transfer. As seen lately with the theft of hundreds of thousands of documents by an individual with security clearance, the rules for sharing are not effectively set by nations, but rather by those who actually are in control of the data landscape. Whether the information seeker is in Siberia or New York City, if all other factors are equal (access, speed, etc.), the status of the two will remain the same. National status is irrelevant online. Yes, hot spots of speed will always be a feature of an economic system that favors the elites. But the difference between very, very fast connections and very, very, very fast ones will be nil. At some point speed will no longer be the defining measure. Access will be the only important measure.

> Yes, the advertising makes the Internet worse. This is because of all the personal information it stores. People tend to believe that with the correct privacy setting, they are beating the system. I constantly update my privacy settings on my computer for various uses. The fact is that the Internet remembers what I've looked into or just stumbled upon in an advertisement and directed to me on Facebook. Sometimes these advertisements can be offending or straight-up irrelevant to my life. This is frustrating and as you said can mess with my emotions. I can't stand that the Internet saves info just to advertise and manipulate their users. —Chante

TONY THE TIGER IN SUDAN

One of the most interesting elements of culture is consumerism. This may reflect a personal bias on my part, but the choices of consumers often drive changes in culture faster than education. And choices by consumers overwhelm or simply ignore efforts by social groups, usually comprised of legislators, to slow change. However, we cannot draw a direct line between consumerism and progress, given that so many of the desires of consumers have little or nothing to do with the beneficial elements of the latter. Consumerism is largely about economic factors, but it contains a real interest in change. The idea of "new and improved" being of interest to shoppers is based on the consumer's belief that the two words represent some beneficial element to them. Perhaps the mere existence of such a term as "new and improved" is proof enough that advertising agencies believe that consumers care about such things.

Yes, romance is important. Yes, peace and comfort are qualities most humans value. But none of these can be attained via economics. Even the Beatles discovered this with their tune "Can't Buy Me Love." Living as a monk with little interest in consumer items or creature comforts may be the choice of some, but the numbers of those who choose to do so will forever remain small. We can, as individuals, sustain ourselves with only access to consumer goods—food, clothing, shelter—far better than we can with access to only other cultural elements of life. Maslow's hierarchy of needs pretty much covered this issue. The basics come first.

In such a world as this, what factor does technology play?

Consider your local supermarket or grocery store. In general, the layout in one is very similar to all others: perishable items line the edges of the store. Nonperishable and frozen foods are placed in aisles in the center of the store. Employees are mostly concerned with refreshing the larder of fresh vegetables, meats, dairy, and breads. Cans require little attention, except to make sure the shelves remain filled.

Now consider the manufacturers of those items in the center of the store. For example, Procter & Gamble is probably the largest manufacturer of all things nonperishable. P&G, which spends billions of dollars a year in the United States in advertising alone, is continually attempting to connect with the consumer who walks these product-loaded aisles. These consumers are not just potential buyers, they are the keepers of the brands that have made P&G such a global force. Failure to ensure that consumers are thinking of a P&G brand first as they walk aisles filled with competitors would be a disaster for the Cincinnati, Ohio, corporation.

But why should P&G rely on a grocery store to deliver its goods?

After all, P&G has at least one other option, one that it has already adopted: direct to consumer. Consumers can go to P&G's Web site, shop from a vast majority of the products offered, and receive them all for just $5 in shipping. Who wouldn't prefer to receive twenty-four rolls of Charmin toilet paper delivered directly to their homes with no traveling to a local grocery store, no negotiating for parking, no walking the entire store, no standing in line to check out, no drive home? Convenient? Yes, and especially when the shipping is free, which it has been as of 2013. The corporation Web site claims it is not truly committed to direct-to-consumer sales, but rather engaging in a "living learning lab" that tracks consumer interests. I suspect this interesting nomenclature has more to do with avoiding causing an immediate spat with Walmart and Target. At the same time, however, the wording used here, especially the term "learning lab," may have a lot to do with future P&G plans. After all, if P&G were interested in launching a direct-to-consumer platform, little would stand in its way, not even Walmart. Of course, a great deal of planning would be required, planning no doubt based on data collected from, perhaps, a test-drive Web site offering consumers a chance to purchase directly with no shipping fees. The global possibilities are gigantic. At some point, direct-to-consumer could connect Cincinnati to Moscow, New Delhi, and Nairobi. Of course, other cultural issues remain in the path of a global consumer marketplace, which are addressed later.

For now, let's consider other examples of direct-to-consumer models that may be new to a company like P&G, but certainly not to corporations in other commercial areas, such as Amazon.com.

Like the rest of those who commented, I find online advertising to be more annoying than anything. Does it work? I'm not sure that it works any better/ worse than advertising done on television. Yes, the online advertising seems to be "smarter" and hones in on personal wants/"needs" (in a word, "creepy" seems to be an appropriate response), but generally we just immediately close

out the dialog box, stop the play on the video or ignore the pop-up altogeth-
er . . . similar to what we have always done with television commercials.

Nonetheless, commercials toy with our emotions and do so on purpose:
insert any holiday commercial, soldier coming home from war, Sarah
McLachlan and her animals in need of rescue, and here come the water works.
Are these a bit emotionally manipulative? Perhaps. Nonetheless, I don't mind
this type of "manipulation"—I guess I'm a sucker for the sappy advertising.
—Tim

ONLINE SELLING OF CULTURE

Make no mistake, Amazon.com is a powerful force in cultural change.

Born in a garage in Bellevue, Washington—what is it about garages that
seem to be so fertile for new technology ideas?—Amazon.com offers global
consumers online what amounts to a Harrods on steroids. Amazon.com
started as a sort of bookstore Web site. Jeff Bezos looked to leverage the
universal access features of the Web to put his resell operation at the finger-
tips of consumers worldwide. Within months of its launch, Amazon.com
sales were taking place in all fifty states and more than forty-five countries.
The logic was obvious: pull all possible consumer products into what
amounted to concrete warehouses scattered worldwide, connect to other possible product providers, and sell not only new, but also used products without
the need for a storefront. In a way, Bezos had created a Walmart without the
need for consumers to visit a store. The products offered were able to stand
on their own branding. For instance, Progresso soup was already an established brand; all that Amazon.com offered was an efficient, low-cost channel
to access existing, well-established brands.

The success of this approach hinges on a few elements: simple Internet
connection, the ability for the consumer to control the interaction, and the
willingness to offer anything to anyone, anywhere. Is Amazon.com a bookstore? No doubt millions of consumers would say so. But Amazon.com also
offers an incredible variety of other consumer goods, from mp3 and cloud
players, to beauty, health, and grocery items, to clothing, shoes, jewelry,
sports clothing and exercise equipment, to home and garden tools, to electronics and computers, to movies, music, and games, and automotive and
industrial goods. No, you cannot get fresh lettuce from Amazon.com, but
virtually the rest of the traditional grocery store is covered.

Included in the sales model is an automatic shipping plan that automatically sends consumers a consistent list of goods on a buyer-established
schedule. Thus, toilet paper, cans of soup, soap, and whatever the consumer
defines as necessary is automatically shipped on a defined regular basis. In
the Los Angeles, San Francisco, and Seattle areas, fresh vegetables and other
perishable goods are included on the Amazon.com site for local delivery.

Amazon.com represents a singular Web site platform that offers all consumers access to a complete line of products. In a very real way, the Web site represents everything Walmart can do at a lower price, a more convenient delivery system, and a far easier method of shopping. It also spreads worldwide brands, everything from Revlon to Apple to Philips. In a very real way, Amazon.com has become a pathway for cultural exchange, cultural adoption, cultural absorption.

This does not mean that consumers shopping India's Amazon.com Web site are not exposed to different brands from those available on the Web site serving French consumers. They certainly are. But the very existence of a single overarching Web site umbrella opens the pathway to more sharing of goods and services on a global basis. Consider that the French Amazon.com site (amazon.com.fr) not only offers high-tech products that are uniquely French, but also Samsung, Apple, Nokia, and other global brands.

Amazon.com is more than just an online store selling books, computers, cans of soup, and a variety of other consumer goods. It is selling culture, marketing culture, and spreading culture via a simple, global model that makes everything available everywhere. And, yes, some shipping is free. But more important, the Amazon.com business model presumes global demand while adding in local brands. Without engaging in marketing anything other than its Kindle Reader, Amazon.com connects consumers to brands through a cheaper, more convenient format.

The impact on culture is obvious. For centuries, one of the elements that protected cultures from assimilation into others has been geography. To some extent this remains: brands available on India's Amazon.com site are largely unknown to consumers in the United States. But their very presence and accessibility online to consumers in other countries raises the possibility that these brands will spread. In fact, prior to the Internet, such transcultural transmission simply did not exist in large numbers. It goes back to that example of Russians grabbing Levi's blue jeans in the United States and selling them on the streets of Moscow. With online retailers such as Amazon.com, such activity is rendered unnecessary. Consumers in Moscow can simply purchase whatever jeans they want, no matter where they are made, no matter the brand.

Amazon.com is literally a culture destroyer, if only because culture relies on some degree of isolation, and such isolation simply does not exist online. Rather than awaiting some isolated Marco Polo to wander in from one region to another, consumers within any culture can purchase any product made anywhere on the planet, or they will be able to in the near future. Part of any culture is the uniqueness of its music, its dress, its scents, its art, and a host of other physical items that are unique to one region of the globe. Lacking that uniqueness, the culture of Bombay becomes very similar to the culture of Los

Angeles, as do the cultures of Korea and China grow similar to that of Plainville, Kansas.

The driving impetus that makes Amazon.com such a success is not culture but consumerism. Amazon.com assumes that consumers already know the brands, and if they do not, they will do the necessary research—also online—to become familiar with them. The international, largely noncultural information bank presumes consumers are the defining element, the unit of cultural preservation or modification. The reality that cultures globally are melting into one is exemplified by the dire efforts of some to preserve their own seemingly unique culture. Again, as more global cultural flattening takes place, the more likely that consumers wanting to experience a British pub will be able to do so at Epcot in Orlando, Florida.

Amazon.com is the conduit that allows for not only the spread of culture by making what is created in one area of the world available in all areas of the world, but it renders the sharp differences in these very same cultures less distinct, less obvious. It also makes clear that cultural assimilation is a two-way street, with one side a bit wider than the other. That is, Western culture powerfully absorbs new ideas, new products, new thinking, and all other foreign cultural aspects faster than smaller, more isolated cultures can. This might be a function of the status of Western technology. It may be a function of language. But, most assuredly, it is a transient phenomenon: more consumers in a larger global marketplace are more rapidly assimilating new cultural artifacts. That is, change has always been an aspect of the meeting of two divergent cultures. The absorption of different cultural aspects by previously isolated cultures has been a function of all aspects of human activity. Some argue that the nature of the English language itself is a function of cultural exchange via the invasion of the British Isles by the Norse, Germans, French, and others.

What we are experiencing today via the Web is a commercially driven cultural exchange and absorption. The ability of a consumer on one side of the planet to access a brand on another side is no longer an aspect of geography but rather of awareness. That is, unique brands exist in India that are not common in the United States. The mere fact that consumers can actually access those India-based brands, no matter where they are, is a clear sign that whatever cultural differences that exist within the economic systems on this planet are not long for this world. Yes, the risk taking so ably described by Hofstede will persist, but it will do so on a global basis. Early adopters described by Rogers will continue to be the ones who pull in new products from great distances (with free shipping). But the newness of consumerism will not stop with risk takers and early adopters. As consumer activity moves across previous cultural boundaries, the exchange will result in a change in both, seamlessly, with little thought or intent. Consumerism within a world of fewer other barriers may arise to be the most powerful modifier of culture.

That is, Amazon.com now operates many Web sites globally, each offering global brands and local ones. Over time, the distinctions between Amazon.com.fr and Amazon.com will lessen, as more consumers pay little or no attention to where a product comes from, but rather to what it is, what it is made of, how much it costs, and its availability (with free shipping, of course).

In many ways, the sharing of culture via books, food, and other tangible artifacts has been taking place for centuries. All that we see today is a lessening of the traditional barriers—largely geographic—that have always allowed some cultures to remain at an arm's distance from others. Amazon.com is a concept driven purely on access: any consumer anywhere can purchase anything at any time. In the crosshairs of such a business model are the easily ignored cultural distinctions that make India uniquely India and France uniquely France. We cannot have it both ways. We cannot, as consumers, demand access to brands uniquely French and at the same time suggest that our own culture is not affected. It may cause discomfort among the French to think that their language and differences may fade into a global language with few differences, yet the likelihood is quite obvious, starting with Julia Child's tome on French cooking. We cannot expect cultures to remain different when all the tools necessary to blend, adopt, and absorb are readily at hand.

> Pinterest allows you to post content, including photos, comments, links, and other materials. Anything that you post or otherwise make available on our Products is referred to as "User Content." You retain all rights in, and are solely responsible for, the User Content you post to Pinterest.
>
> More simply put: If you post your content on Pinterest, it still belongs to you but we can show it to people and others can re-pin it. ("About Pinterest" 2015)

EVERY IMAGE IS WORTH A MILLION WORDS: PINTEREST, HOUZZ, AND OTHER SHARING PLATFORMS

Ask a student about Pinterest and you'll likely hear about cool posts and great images. Pinterest is an online sharing Web site that allows users to build what amounts to a personal journal of photos regarding (as of January 2014) decorating, crafts, fashion, and food. Created by Ben Silbermann in 2009, the site rapidly grew to become the third largest social network by March 2011. Experian reported in 2013 that Pinterest had become the largest re-director of users to retailer sites (*PR Newswire* 2014). The concept is relatively simple: retailers and users take photos of their landscape project, furniture, fashion, and foods, then post them to a searchable database operated by Pinterest. Sharing is a key element here. In fact, users are encouraged to repost or "pin" images they find on other sites. What is created is at once a personal site that contains images created by the owner, as well as images grabbed from other sites.

But what is the motivator here? Why would this attract more than eleven million users just a few months after launch?

We can start with inflated egos, of course, something along the lines of "look, see what I have done/own/created/have that you don't have." But the tone of the platform seems not so much braggadocio, as it is a statement of personal likes. That is, Tom creates a Pinterest page to gather ideas in the form of photos and shares them with others. Okay, Tom is a more unlikely user than Susan (58 percent female to 42 percent male, at last report in 2013), but you get the point. The personal likes of Tom or Susan become a source for others, who are also sharing their personal images. Yes, this is a pure idea-sharing site, with little or no real sense of ownership of images (or interests). In most cases it seems that the imaging comes from elsewhere, seemingly initially from manufacturers, before being shared over and over again, without citing where the shared image originated. These are just ideas, unfettered by ownership, unwarranted by status, unedited by new users. The ultimate idea-sharing site with no interest in the source of the pins.

This would seem to fly in the face of individuality that has so dominated this chapter. But does it? Each user of Pinterest can visit any other image-packed page via a traditional search function. For instance, plug "composite decks" into the search function of pinterest.com, and you'll receive an endless variety of images, each with a brief description. Scrolling down the page, the imaging includes everything from photos of decks and homes to plans for building and finishing. Reach the bottom of the page and more images are added automatically. No end, it would seem, in sight.

But the saving of these images is the act of an individual, yes, grabbing the works of others, but reusing them with little or no consideration of the original creator. Ah, the land of copyright-free images, taken from one Web site and put into another with little or no sourcing. The point of the collecting is not just to create a personal diary of what you find most interesting, but to share it with others, clearly the act of individuality. The user is both sharer and personal promoter. In fact, the number of times images are shared by others is included in the data under each search result, as is the number of people reporting a "like" by way of a posted image of a small heart with the number next to it.

The site has some oversight, largely done by the users themselves. The Pinterest user information area includes a request that creators of images be properly credited and that users should report both incorrect usage and pages that include images that users consider "porn, hateful stuff, or anything that encourages people to hurt themselves." The former seems to be more of a request that users notify posters who might be giving incorrect credit for something. The latter asks users to forward information about objectionable images via the "Report Pin" button. This clear dichotomy seems more focused on keeping the Web site "clean" than terribly obsessed with who "owns" what. In fact, tracing ownership seems of far less interest than the actual image itself. Ideas are shared so freely that it seems that the original creator of the image (and therefore the idea) is just an afterthought. In fact, users are "encouraged," not required, to offer the creators of great ideas credit for their work.

In the end, the Pinterest concept feeds the individual's ability to create their own world, share it, and take credit for it with little more than a click of the mouse. The function of creativity is rendered to the ability to wield that mouse, over, say, the image of the original photograph and, with it, the original idea. We have what amounts to the perfect sandbox for the self-possessed individualist: "See what I have found (created)! Aren't I clever (imaginative)?"

Houzz, which emerged online sometime shortly before Pinterest but grew far more slowly, is marketed as a crossroads for architects, interior designers, landscapers, and those sharing home improvement ideas. Bottom line: it is very similar in format, with photographs provided by professionals intended to not only offer ideas, but also to drive sales. Unlike Pinterest, the actual professionally created content is far more select. Also unlike Pinterest, the ultimate goal seems to be less about sharing ideas than it is about retail sales.

And this may be why it has grown so much more slowly. Pinterest is a site created by the "average" individual with only one desire: to share ideas. Houzz is also dependent on photographs submitted by others, but the professional mercantile nature of the site is always present. What Houzz is missing is the open participation by those who are not sales focused, but rather idea-sharing focused.

What is happening on both sites, however, is culture transfer, perhaps best described as culture "averaging." With the ability to share cultural ideas in the form of photographs and images with no language barriers, both sites provide users from other cultures an exposure to new ideas, new styles, and new solutions for something basic to all: home design. Impediments that twenty years ago would have been complete barriers to culture averaging—everything from language to publishers to physical bookstores—are all rendered secondary. We still have language barriers, but we stress imaging in our idea exchange (and, thus, our culture exchange). We still have publishers (such as Web site owners), but their roles are minimized from editing and selecting to promoting and supporting cultural averaging. And we still have physical bookstores, but they have faded into the landscape as Amazon.com support devices.

We have no real need for language when it comes to photography. And we have no real need for classes about how to use a camera—something any freshman at a university might have encountered—including instructions on how to develop film. In fact, the complications of photography that weeded out the less than committed are all but gone. What we have in place is the instant, point-and-shoot culture grabber: the digital camera.

> Digital photography and camera classes are available through Ridgefield Continuing Education. Beginning Photography (meets Thursdays, Feb. 27; Mar. 6, 13 and 20; 7 to 9 p.m.; Veterans Park School; $86) is for people with a camera that allows some manual control over exposure (look for controls labeled [M], manual, aperture priority or shutter priority). Photography: Your Point and Shoot Camera Exposed is a two session workshop (Thursdays, Feb. 13 and 20; 7 to 9 p.m.; $49) that demystifies the basics of photography. Instructor Michael Serao holds a master's in fine arts and has been employed in art and photography and teaching for over 20 years. —*Ridgefield (CT) Press*, February 10, 2014

EVERY IMAGE IS SHOT, SAVED, AND SHARED BY AN INDIVIDUAL

Photography has forever been the act of an individual. Very few group photography situations occur on the camera holder's side. Taking a picture—whether of a group, a mountain, or a lit candle—is an act of a singular person acting almost entirely on his or her own. It is also a languageless act, freeing the communicator wielding the camera from the bonds of words, syntax, and semantics. Imagery—from the photography we are discussing to fine art and ink—while certainly an artifact of culture, is less difficult to share across culture borders than works of writing. What we have seen in recent years is a shift of photography away from fine arts to common art, from a required profession built on years of experience, trial and error, and books of technique. We are in a point-and-click world, where the technology covers up everything it can. And that technology—whether a Nikon Coolpix or an iPhone built-in camera—is so much easier to use now than was a comparable device from 1990. Consider than in the age of film, each shot was carefully framed, carefully planned. After all, you had at most thirty-six shots per roll, and each roll had to be developed, either by the photographer or a camera shop. Being a photographer in 1990 was far different than being one today.

My friends who are photographers—especially those who are professionals working with publications—balk at the idea that a point-and-shoot cameraperson can create anything truly creative. It takes training and an eye for the shot, they argue. This is very true, at least to some degree. But an individual with a camera who has little or no training can take hundreds, perhaps thousands of shots with little or no planning, talent, or even technique. Among those thousands, one single image may approach professionalism. Again, in 1990, thousands of frames on hundreds of rolls of film would present an economic barrier. And the time required to load the rolls of film would in no way model what is possible today.

What is the point here? Perhaps that an art form that captures a culture is rendered common, so common that it is hardly an art form but rather a mechanical device as unique as a car and certainly not as artistic as an oil painting. Add to this the ease with which imagery is shared globally, again with few words, and what is rendered is a smoothing of cultural differences. An image is worth more than a thousand words: it is worth thousands of ideas disconnected from the ties to language for understanding. This represents a cultural transfer, a cultural averaging requiring little or no effort. Those wishing to share ideas with others who do not share a language can do so via images. More than a convenience; we face an open door to the elimination of culture itself.

Modern photography—print or film—is just one tool that can be used to bridge a gap between cultures. Not only is the imagery simple to capture, the simplicity of that capture renders an object of more honesty, more directness. Such direct presentation of an object is far from the presentation of that same object as an art form. It may not be fair to suggest that such works are more "honest," but it can be argued that they are less a presentation of an individual as unique. It is the curse of amateurism that the works are not an expression of something artfully different. We can carry this very thought back to the blogs and other communication forms discussed in this chapter. Blogs are not Hemingway. Blogs are not the Bhagavad Gita. Blogs are not great works of individualism that can be identified by critics as having been created by a particular author. Bloggers are individuals acting so much within their own individualistic world that they are far less interested in fame than in their own individuality. In fact, it is the drive to simply state things with little no interest in the judgment of others that separates an individual and an artist. Even the most independent of artists seek some comment, some interpretation. Some, such as existentialists, may seem to be uninterested in the reaction of the world to their works, but, at the very same time, they create works to be judged within that same world. Is this really the case within the blogging environment?

Consider that some bloggers are self-driven, seeking the least amount of feedback possible. A simple "thumbs-up" image button is sufficient. Anything more than that is overkill, ignored by the blogger, who, no doubt, has moved on to his or her next announcement. Actual critical analysis of what has been said—as little of it as there is—is not what is sought. Bloggers simply feel a need to express whatever thought they feel they need to state while offering little or no context.

As we witness a world where everyone has the ability to blog, even those who just lurk are drawn into this throwaway cultural averaging. Before we think this averaging is not happening, consider that blogging is an activity practiced only for months, not decades or even years. Already the posts are measured in the billions. In a world where value to attached to rarity, anything that is measured in the billions offers little in the way of actual worth. We post on a blog and move on. The "conversation" has cultural elements, of course. Even images carry some cultural elements.

And this is the point: simple, valueless exchanges of personal information via the Web are already resulting in the mixing of differences, smoothing out elements that could once have been used to define one culture as standing apart from another. We stand as witnesses to a blending of cultures that will result in a cultureless society, perhaps within our lifetime. The impact of such an averaging certainly has some negative outcomes. But let's be honest: some elements of culture ignite war and carnage. Given that we cannot prevent cultural averaging, we are likely to suffer some of the losses and benefit from the loss of others. Having our children experience an English pub at Epcot is sad. Not having them be caught in a war over cultural differences is certainly far more beneficial.

REFERENCES

"About Pinterest." 2015. *Pinterest*. http://about.pinterest.com/terms.

PR Newswire. 2014. "Experian Marketing Services' 2014 Digital Marketer Report," http://www.prnewswire.com/news-releases/experian-marketing-services-2014-digital-marketer-report-shows-that-social-media-continues-to-grow-as-an-influential-source-of-traffic-for-retail-and-other-social-sites-252700121.html.

"The World Is Flat." 2005. *Wikipedia*. http://en.wikipedia.org/wiki/The_World_Is_Flat.

Chapter Four

Individualism in an Apps and Culture World

Tocqueville unintentionally popularized the signifier "individualism" with the publication of *Democracy in America*. He used a French term that had no counterpart in English. Translators of Tocqueville labored over this French term because its signification wasn't part of the English lexicon. Emerson's first mention of "individualism" was not until 1843.
(Mendenhall 2011)

We live in an age of individuality. That is, we live in an age of people thinking that they are individuals acting in individual ways. Few, if any, think that they are part of a group first, and few, if any, products or brands want you to think that you are part of a group. After all, the sale is one to one, not one to part of the many. The idea of being clumped together with a herd of like-minded consumers (even though that is largely what is happening) is contrary to what each ovine would like to think. I am *baaaa*, separate, *baaaa*, unique, *baaaa*.

On the other side of the coin from individuality is isolation. We are keenly aware of what it means to be culled from the herd and isolated. Even though we like the sense of uniqueness that comes with individuality, we are not anxious to assume the condition of being cut off from all others, neither physically nor mentally. The research abounds: a well-balanced human wants to be around other well-balanced humans. Isolation leads to depression, not an optimal state.

However, isolation and individuality should not be confused. They are not one and the same. They have some attributes in common, including a single person acting within him- or herself. However, the former—isolation—needs no one else, while the latter—individuality—is defined by the potential presence of others. We are isolated without the need of another person. We are individualistic only within the concept of another person. One is an absolute (one cannot be "somewhat isolated"). The other is variable: we have degrees of individuality. Shall we have one "friend," or several, or many, or so many that we really, by definition, have only a few? Individuality is a far more mushy word than isolation. We know when we are alone. Being an individual is a far more varied concept.

Nothing better exemplifies individuality in the first quarter of this century than the use of online applications or apps. Yes, we use e-mail and other traditional ways to connect and share ourselves and our ideas, but apps are special and what we do with them is also special. They are both servants of our own egos and self-imaging, as well as sharers of these images with those who care to look. More important, however, is that they track our own shifts of belief, largely with little or no involvement from others. But I'm getting ahead of myself. I'll deal with that later. First, let's delve into these applications with some degree of specificity in terms of subject matter and use. After all, they have been around now for what, almost a decade? That's a generous amount of time online (measured in dog years). Much can happen in ten years online. Much needs tracking and explaining in a decade online. Each category has had its own impact, each drawing out its own "culture," its own population, its own tribe of users. It seems, almost, that the use of an app defines the user more than the television channels they watch or the radio stations they listen to. This may be because each app comes with its own set of options. That is, each Angry Birds app has dozens of versions, allowing the users to choose the ones that they prefer. How does it go, twelve things taken eight ways . . . a little calculus generates a seemingly unique user. Of course, we have no "unique" users. We just *seem* to have them. But we live in the universe of very large numbers that renders any calculi common. Multiply ninety-nine cents times ten million buyers and you have a multimillionaire. This isn't new math. It is new marketing. New distribution.

ANGRY GAMES

For starters, what is an app?

> Application software is a set of one or more programs designed to carry out operations for a specific application. Application software cannot run on itself but it is dependent on system software to execute. For example: MS Word, MS Excel, Tally software, library management system, billing system, etc. The term is used to contrast such software with another type of computer program referred to as system software, which manages and integrates a computer's capabilities but does not directly perform tasks that benefit the user. The system software serves the application, which in turn serves the user. Exam-

ples include accounting software, enterprise software, graphics software, media players, and office suites. Many application programs deal principally with documents. Applications may be bundled with the computer and its system software or published separately, and can be coded as university projects. ("Application Software," *Wikipedia*)

An important element was left out of the above excerpt: the app is defined by the user. Without the user, the app is nothing but a standard bit of software. In fact, it is the involvement of the user that makes the app so uniquely important to our discussion. Apps—whether puzzles used by friends or security-penetrating devices used by gamers-turned-criminals—are not complete without an actual user.

Civilization V is a nice game, at least for those who like such games. Fans claim it allows them to build, fight, collaborate, and, in general, rule a world, for better or worse. In some ways, Civilization provides us with a simple example of how online app game users are like all other online app users: they like control, they like interaction, they like positive outcomes. But they mainly like control. That is, they like to win. Few play to lose, or, for that matter, to learn, and many of us are aware that failure is how most of us actually learn. Failure teaches us more than success. Experience, as they say, is what happens when you fail at something else. Winning, with all of its good feelings, works well with the lone online user. Let's profile this user as an average sort, at least according to the current myth: a thirteen-year-old, white, English-speaking male with little interest in doing much beyond conquering the online universe. In reality, app users are pretty much everyone. Consider that the latest figures for users place the numbers for 2012 a bit over a billion.

No doubt we are standing significantly over two billion in 2014, and well on our way to the projected 4.4 billion by 2017. A couple of things to note about table 4.1 and its data: note the trend in users in North America actually drops as a percentage of total users between 2012 and 2017. Actual users,

Table 4.1.   Users of Mobile Apps Worldwide by Region, 2012–2017

	2012	*2013*	*2017*
Worldwide	1.2 billion	n/a	4.4 billion
Asia Pacific	30%	32%	47%
Europe	29%	28%	21%
North America	18%	17%	10%
Middle East and Africa	14%	13%	12%
Latin America	9%	10%	10%

which are predicted to run around 440 million in 2017, are not indicated here. The 2017 estimate of 440 million is roughly twice the users in 2012 and represents about 80 percent of the total population. Compare that with Asia Pacific, which will see its usage jump from 30 percent to 47 percent of total users between 2012 and 2017. Compared to overall users, that is an increase from 360 million in 2012 to 2.2 billion in 2017. Sounds like a huge jump, and it is. But as a percentage of population, it still leaves Asia far behind. With estimates of 4.2 billion in 2010 (United Nations Economic and Social Commission for Asia and the Pacific 2011), Asia Pacific users represented less than 10 percent of the population. Even by 2017, with the massive increase in both users and population, it is unlikely that overall usage as a percentage of the population will be much higher than half.

The difference here is not a function of economics: Asians are not poorer, nor are they less connected. Something else is present that makes app usage so much more popular in Western culture than in Asian culture. Consider the actual app itself. As noted by many reviewers, though we may see downloads of apps topping three hundred billion shortly, such numbers do not reflect actual usage. Many apps are downloaded, fooled around with, and then simply dumped. After all, building a castle can become more work than it is worth, and games that feature shared worlds, such as Celtic Tribes or Tower Madness, can come to feel more like middle school every day (remember that thirteen-year-old male?).

The actual integration of an app is still—for a large portion of users—in the entertainment stage. Yes, we have Houzz and Pinterest, both useful tools for those who are either considering building a new home or seeking to build their own reputations. But in total use, such tools pale in comparison to games. Western societies still see apps largely as entertainment tools, something that distracts us from our current state. This reminds me of an old AOL commercial from the 1980s that featured a scan down a row of cubicles to an employee who looks over his shoulder at the camera and proclaims that his boss thinks he's working but "actually, I'm just goofing off." The message was clear: online gaming was not intended to be productive or to add anything to the economic output. So it was in the 1980s, and it remains a personal entertainment tool today ("Most Popular Apple App Store Categories in June 2014, by Share of Available Apps" 2014). It can be argued, of course, that a large percentage of users have not seen apps as anything but a tool for entertainment, even though the category spans more than a dozen other areas, such as business, education, health, and news.

But take into consideration that apps, at least those used in North America, seem to be built for individual use within an individual world. Yes, you can build an empire with other individuals (you can even have them e-mail you on occasion to remind you that they need your help). But the actual involvement of you is not you any more than the involvement of others as actually "real" individuals. This is where things go off into online la-la land. This is where the *New Yorker* dog cartoon is so applicable. Not only do you have no idea who your close ally, Carbon154, actually is, but the same is true for all who play with you.

Now, it would be easy to suggest that those who post to Houzz and Pinterest are "real" people with "real" interests. But why? Where is it written that I must be true with Pinterest any more than I am with Gods of War? Keep in mind the cultural landscape we are wandering through: North America is a place that is becoming more individualistic, more self-defining (Goswami 2011; Rainie and Wellman 2012; Roster 2014, 321; Whitley 1997, 147–63). We have more options to satisfy our individualism, starting with anonymity. We can be whoever we care to be, in whatever landscape, playing whatever role. The result is less about what might be termed deception than it is about what Suler termed "online disinhibition": "Rather than thinking of disinhibition as the revealing of an underlying 'true self,' we can conceptualize it as a shift to a constellation within self-structure, involving clusters of affect and cognition that differ from the in-person constellation" (Suler 2004, 321).

This may seem a complicated way of defining a rather simple outcome. Users of apps in North America simply check their "true selves" at the edge of the click, taking with them only what is considered necessary or impossible to shed. They enter into their app land as whatever they care to be, with the carefree knowledge that what happens in Civilization 5, stays in Civilization 5.

So why are such entertainment apps not as popular in Asia as they clearly are in North America? For starters, are we sure they are not? Actually, plenty of research can be found that supports such a conclusion, though the findings are rarely termed in such a blunt fashion (Goswami 2011; Maghnati and Ling 2013, 1–9; Peabody 2012; Sharpe, Yao, and Liao 2012, 156–66; Wang, Liao, and Yang 2013, 11–22).

Let's consider one form of art that has evolved online in Asia (and has spread globally): anime. Anime as a form of imagery was created in Japan almost a century ago. Its popularity as an entertainment platform exploded in the 1980s on television in Japan and rapidly spread online. Its use within apps today stretches from Animania, Toonmania, Dramania, and Mangania to the more than two thousand platforms available (mostly free) via Amazon.com. In some ways, the story lines within these anime reveal the essence of Asian culture: groups, families, friendship, community, collaboration. Story lines are about how individuals work within a group to accomplish sought-for victories.

What makes this stand apart from what we see in North American app behavior (again, in a very general sense) is that lack of individual action without an accounting for group outcomes first. That is, the individual may act alone, but he or she does so with the good of the group at the center of the goals. This sense of the group good is, by the way, what often baffles the Western legalist who sees many Asians as common copyright violators. The reality, in many cases, is that the Asian perspective is that what is good for the many precludes the rights of the individual. In fact, ensuring that the individual is acting for the group ensures the individual is doing the right thing, being ethical, being correct and fair to all.

In some ways this is the behavior we see in Asian online app users. They may play a game of Angry Birds, but it is not a given that they seek to tally the highest individual score or even that such an outcome is a significantly important part of the game. The impetus to play may seem to be very simple—play and win—but winning may not be the goal so much as the action that takes place along the way for Asian users. If the focus of the North American individual app user is to win, the focus of the Asian app user may be simply to play.

But is this a static phenomenon? Unlikely. Conversations with Asian graduate students in recent years have made it clear to me that they are being "infected" by Western culture. Their views of what is important shift, the outcomes that are important seem to be more about the results achieved than the process involved. It almost seems as if their culture is being compromised. That, of course, is a naive perspective. They are merely reacting to the world around them. But why is it that the reverse does not seem to occur? Why is it that Western graduate students at universities in Eastern cultures do not shift away from individuality?

> When I am at home, I watch TV and do not watch shows and movies on the Internet like most people do now. I prefer a TV to a computer because of the larger screen and because I can record the shows I want to watch and watch them at a later time, which is the same concept of watching shows and movies on the Internet. However, when I am at school I only watch shows and movies on the Internet because I do not have a TV in my dorm room. The Internet does put control in your hand that a TV cannot in the sense that it allows you to watch shows that are no longer available on the TV, which I will admit is a plus! The Internet also does not have commercials, so you do not have to sit there and wait for your show to come back on. There is a downfall to watching shows and movies on the Internet (at least while at school). Due to the Wi-Fi issues in the dorm rooms, while I am watching my shows, it buffers a lot throughout the show, which is really annoying. I prefer to watch the TV though because of its bigger screen and no buffering time. —Mackenzie

ISOLATION IN PUBLIC

Consider the users of Facebook and Twitter. Call it a billion, call it a hundred billion. Let's start with the isolated souls who reach out to the nothingness that greets them daily. Some massive number of blogs (Facebooks and Twitters) that have no visitors except their authors. Posts are dutifully logged, but no one reads them. So why are they posted in the first place? Why do so many individuals put their innermost thoughts (or shallow throwaways) online, only to note (or ignore?) that no one reads them and no one responds to them? This might be easy enough to pass off as idle narcissism: some people like to write about their feelings circling highly personal events, much as teenagers keep diaries. But these are potential public ramblings, not secrets locked away in adolescent notebooks. Call it just another unexpected side effect of online economics. But the net effect is far reaching and far more profound.

The unread postings of the thoughts of millions, perhaps billions, of people into the Internet void may suggest a ramping up of a pattern of behavior that has been forming more slowly for centuries. This penchant for expression may constitute the highest plateau yet by the I-individual: a curious, fairly recent phenomenon born of higher degrees of education, a sense of security, and an abundance of communication options, most of them used by the masses at little or no cost. The rise in global education levels occurs despite efforts to avoid them, prevent them, and, at times ban them on religious, economic, or other politically created standards. The rationale to avoid a more educated public is obvious: such a populace is a bit harder to manage, a bit harder to control, and a good deal harder to suppress. Smart voters are hard to manipulate. Smart shoppers are harder to mislead. Smart readers/ viewers are hard to sell on bad ideas and lousy writing. The demand for education could not be clearer, with one estimate projecting the global need for a new university every month (Fisch 2012) and others suggesting a more global push even as countries build more universities within their borders (Ruby 2013, 1).

The sense of wanting to be safe is not a throwaway sale item at Walmart, yet feeling safe comes and goes. That is, if you are wandering the wilds of Scotland in 1300 AD, the chances of losing your head, literally, were certainly a great deal higher than they are today. That hardly requires a scholarly citation, does it? The very real sense that, overall, the world is a safer place today than it was when the Khan visited Rome hardly requires a Google search. What should be taken into account and tracked with some detail is the fluctuation in this sense of security. As discussed later, the sense of the world as a dangerous place is largely driven by how information is shared about what is happening in the world. It is a blend of context and sales.

Let's all agree that the New England poet philosopher was right: if you understand the concept of one murder, then the details of all others that follow are nothing but gossip. So much of what we agree to declare "news" is really just gossip. I feel I can declare this since I teach in a school of journalism. We watch local news on television and get the "if it bleeds, it leads" thinking every night at 6 pm. Nothing in context, nothing provided in the "big picture." Consider that forty-four thousand or so people die on U.S. highways every year. Compare the reaction of this to that of the loss of less than a tenth of that number in three attacks on September 11, 2001. The former is a lackluster acceptance of what must be, living as part of a modern, moderately dangerous society, which requires getting from point A to point B in a limited amount time. The latter represents a reaction against a society that accepts the first hazard but not the second. Anarchy is never welcome except by the anarchists, and even they have a hard time after they have won the day.

Thus, what seems "news" is really just information that has next to nothing to do with you, is used rarely to improve your life, and is forgotten hours later. Test yourself: who was the last person murdered in your city? Setting aside whether you knew the victim or the accused personally, what impact did this event have on you? It was an individual act, perpetrated by an individual, on an individual. In a short period of (titillating) time, it will be forgotten. Yes, sad. But this is how we are built. Even more so with apps that render all information into bite-size chunks that can be consumed, digested, and ejected in minutes. It is no accident that we are called "consumers" of information. Rarely do we consider the entire process of consumption.

The way information regarding the murder of John Doe is passed to you has changed since 1990. The use of devices to communicate with others has lessened the need for face-to-face and thus human-to-human conversations. Whether in business (the impact of which was highlighted in a 1980s United Airlines commercial) or in private, actually sharing time with others has become so rare and unnecessary that it is now the subject of messages dealing with the lack thereof. But what is lost in all of this is the context, the stress, the emphasis, the tone that makes what is said so very different than what is read. Ah, but that may be largely allowed for, as we replace text with video, moving from Facebook to an easily produced, easily posted, easily downloaded, and easily watched message that even comes (for a brief period needed as we morph into a *Blade Runner* "street language") with subtitles. This expansion occurs not by our own conscious effort. It will simply happen as certainly as Western soft drinks will replace local products and local ales will spread into regional and, eventually, global markets, and new ones will appear in local markets. New words will appear. New objects will be created. Everything starts locally. It is how fast it becomes global that measures where we are in the cosmic world.

This chapter attempts to trace the history and future of individualism, the rise in the sense of personal safety, and the long-term possibilities of both within the hypersolitary, global cultureless world of the Internet, best exemplified by the appearance of thousands, perhaps millions of small, self-contained mini-computer applications simply referred to as "apps." I offer no long-term predictions, nor am I suggesting that apps will (or will not) be replaced by some other online invention. I leave the hyper-predicting to the futurists. They are, after all, much better at either getting it right or having a great cover story when they don't.

I am suggesting that life at two possible levels is at real risk: individual culture itself and individual societies. I freely admit that one exists only within the existence of the other: one cannot have a unique culture without first having a unique society, and all societies then exhibit unique cultures. Thus, as long as we have a distinction of societies, we would expect a distinction in cultures. And as long as we see cultural differences expressed, we should expect distinct societies (some might even call these societies "nations"). But the global trends are in two seemingly opposing directions: more nations seem to lead to more globally distinct cultures. So why does it seem to be heading in the other direction, with one global culture overrunning local (aka, national) standards, very much to the alarm of many political and religious leaders? Good question.

> You can be an absolute idiot with the Internet by posting personal information on public forums and your banking information on sketchy Web sites; this is a sure recipe for identity theft, which would be cause for worry. However, I am not an idiot online. I don't include personal information on my social media sites, I won't enter my credit card information unless I know it is a trusted site (I typically look for the stamps of approval that say this site is certified to handle money transactions). I don't feel like the Internet is invasive because I don't let it become invasive, nevertheless it holds great potential to. The worst problem I feel like is how people use their smartphones. They are on them for *everything*! It is sad because people are losing the art of communication and trading it for a cheap substitute. This fact is not worth it. —Zachary

We are sharing more culture icons and beliefs while at the same time demanding a separate existence, including life at the tribal level (for now). As noted by Anderson,

> Many have pointed to our society's options for privacy to the point of isolation, for example, or preference for the private automobile over mass transit, the privacy of personal TV's and computers over public squares, halls, and theaters, the privacy/isolation of suburbia with its separate homes, enclosed yards and increasingly fenced in and gated neighborhoods. Needless to say, the ultimate in privacy and isolation will occur when each home, or better each person in each home, has his and her individual goggles with video monitors, headphones, gloves and body suit hooked to computes enabling them to access or create their own visual, audio and tactile virtual worlds and communities. (2000, 153–58)

Anderson has it well defined until the very last word, I would suggest, and even then it is open for a Lynne Truss-esque interpretation. Did Anderson mean "communities" or "virtual communities"? The sentence structure leaves both interpretations possible. In terms of which might be most viable, the former may simply not be necessary. After all, are we not moving toward all communities being more virtual than "real" (and why am I finding the need to put "real" in quotation marks?). That is, I guess, the whole point of my argument. Yes, we still hang out with friends, but we have far more "friends" on Facebook. Yes, we still have friends over for dinner, but we still post to far more "friends" on Twitter. That is, which is more the community? The dinner crowd or the online crowd?

For example, Hawe offers us a way of looking at communities in four ways: (1) as population, (2) as a physical setting, (3) as a social system, and (4) as a psychological status (Hawe 1994, 199–210). Several researchers in the latter part of the previous century offered us descriptions of three basic types of communities: (1) geographic community—a group of people living in a nearby area, (2) function or attribute community—a group of individuals sharing common values, and (3) interest community—a group of individuals working toward or engaged in a common goal (Crow and Allan 1994, 229; Lee and Newby 1983; Willmont 1986). All quite useful, these fail to track what is actually happening online. The "community" as defined by Facebook has none of what Hawe would define as a real population, given that people come and go as they wish with little or no tracking (or "stickiness"). The physical setting is nonexistent and the social system is in one direction, which hardly describes a social group. As to the psychological events within Facebook, that's a good question for others at another time and place. The researchers—Lee and Newby, Willmont, and Crow and Allen—offer us little more. What is happening within the Facebook "community" is not what we traditionally associate with a community by any prior definition of the word, mainly because it involves very little actual "social" back and forth beyond the most superficial information, such as "what I did today."

This is not to suggest that more traditional exchanges do not occur. But they are not necessary to the progress, survival, or success of society. The main task, the defining moment is the post. Whatever happens after the post is superfluous, unnecessary, just so much "whatever." The main and only real communication message might as well have gone into the void as far as the poster is truly concerned. These are blind posts that generate blind, or at least unimportant, responses. We might as well be conversing with each other in a pitch-black room using voice maskers. The idea that a "real" person is behind each post is as valid as the idea that communities are necessary online.

Consider one J. F. Sebastian, genius creator in Ridley Scott's *Blade Runner*. Sebastian created his own "community," his own world of artificial intelligence beings that populated his self-manufactured world. None of his "people" is much different (except in size) than those who ultimately arrive to kill him. They also are artificial and a replacement for what we might consider the "real" thing. But that's the rub, isn't it? What constitutes real and unreal when it comes to humans versus artificial intelligence is as much of an issue as what constitutes a traditional ("real"?) community versus Facebook. Facebook creates artificial communities, artificial societies, artificial conversations between artificial beings that might as well be machines generating automated responses. You type, "Hi." It responds, "Hi! Whatsup?" How would you know it is a machine you just had a (okay, very brief) conversation with? You know this isn't already happening because you are that smart, right? Would it matter? After all, I can imagine some machines would be far more interesting than some of my friends (real or pseudo). Somehow this reminds me of a certain very wise and somewhat small person commenting that "I don't know half of you half as well as I should like, and I like less than half of you half as well as you deserve." I've always wanted to be able to work that quote into something I published. There, I've done it.

I suppose the bottom line is that at least one consequence of losing the personal, human-to-human (as now defined, and let's hang on to that for a second) touch in communication is losing the sense of community that drives our sense of society. But we as individuals are less needful of a traditional group-defined, group-created society, it seems. And, no, I am not suggesting Facebook-created society substitutes. I think, rather, we are moving toward a society we ourselves create, modify, and even destroy and rebuild. I guess the big question that sits at the core of this book (and many others struggling with this) is, will the self-created society actually work?

Before we launch into the entire idea of individualism as a rising tide (and the concurrent consequences), let's consider the distant shore, when being a community mattered. We need not go into great detail here: we all know the points between then and now. Let's just cast our thoughts back a few centuries.

> Could I "live" without the Internet—certainly (no doubt we are a spoiled society, but I am old enough to remember the days without Internet—gasp! — and I seemed to have survived just fine). However, could I live as comfortably and with as much ease as I am currently—no. There are definitely concerns with people getting ahold of various account information, banking statements, credit cards (I have had my number stolen twice) and the very real threat of identity theft. I am sure most of us have had a financial cyberattack of some kind and have recovered mostly unscathed (irritated, but fine nonetheless). After it happens we get new account numbers, new credit cards, and continue to use the Internet for financial transactions; the ease with which we can do these types of dealings typically equates to a higher reward than the risk associated with them. However, I believe the more dangerous threat to our

privacy hinges on how we use the Internet to connect personally: Facebook, match.com, Twitter, et cetera. Yes, these sites allow friends and families to connect/reconnect, but at the cost of having perfect strangers see who you are, who your kids are, where you live, where you work, et cetera (even down to the GPS coordinates!). It is a stalker's paradise and people are being much too lax and foolish with what information they post for the world to see. I believe the risks to our privacy are much too high to make it worth it. For the most part the ease of use is worth the risk (and fairly easy to bounce back from if your information does get stolen). I am a regular customer of Amazon and other online shopping. My concern mostly lies in the risk of personal information (where I live, work, where my kids go to school, etc.) on social network sites such as Facebook. There is an unrest knowing that people are so flippant with this information and may not fully appreciate the risks involved. —Crystal

THE VILLAGE

First, let us accept a definition of "village":

A village is a clustered human settlement or community, larger than a hamlet but smaller than a town, with a population ranging from a few hundred to a few thousand (sometimes tens of thousands). Though often located in rural areas, the term urban village is also applied to certain urban neighborhoods. Villages are normally permanent, with fixed dwellings; however, transient villages can occur. Further, the dwellings of a village are fairly close to one another, not scattered broadly over the landscape, as a dispersed settlement. ("Village," *Wikipedia*)

What is left out of this definition is the need for the village in the first place: safety. Given the likelihood of rubbing elbows with those whom one might find less acceptable than desired, some powerful motive must be present to overcome the tendency to avoid the undesirable neighbor. Danger would certainly be a significant rationale, as would commercial convenience. The danger would be lessened by the grouping together of many of those who are interested in peace and quiet. The commercial convenience would be enhanced by the nearness of others. But for now, let's consider the dangers involved in wandering the countryside of a wild Britain in the fourteenth century.

But wait: a simpler way to consider this fits well with our task in this work. Let's revisit the app Civilization, now in its fifth iteration, outlining the progression of a society from 4000 BC to the present and beyond. It contains many interesting details, such as requiring the construction of a library in a community before a university can be built there. But what is most useful for us is the way it deals with workers outside of the protection of towns: the farther they are from the town center, the more dangerous their lives become. This, in many ways, has been inverted in recent years in the "real world," with metro centers being considered far more dangerous than rural land-scapes. But in centuries past, the presence of robbers and thieves was largely based on their ability to avoid armies and legal officers, whose presence was mainly centered in towns. Going to town meant going to the legal heart of a community. Hanging out in the "wilds" literally meant just that: things got a little wild.

Tracked over time, wandering outside a town's walls was dangerous 24/7, then it became progressively safer so that working in the fields during the day was okay but strolling through the forest at night was not. The act of being in the forest was an act of being alone, and such a decision to be alone was the critical act. That is, it was not just the locale, but the choice to be in the "dangerous" locale in a solitary fashion, without the company of others, that in fact made the locale so dangerous. It was not that individuals did not desire the company of friends. Instead, it was that individuals sought to define the rules of the engagement, the presence of friends, and, by way of doing this, to define themselves.

Controlling who we want to be our friends and those we consider our enemies is as old a measure of personal freedom as might exist. Being about to express this judgment is a measure of the progress of freedom within our society. As described by McKenna (2009, 203–21), Schultze (2014, 84–95), Roster (2014, 321), Kafai, Fields, and Cook (2010, 23–42), Suler (2004, 321–26), Talamo and Ligorio (2001, 109–22), Ikäheimo (2007, 224–47), and Ikegami (2011, 1155–84), the growing individuation of the self allowed for the evolution of the persona that started as a creature of a town community to become a solitary, self-defined, self-satisfying individual whose existence was self-sustaining. This is not some sort of quasi-psychoshop descriptor of an egotistical ideal. It is, instead, the logical evolution of a persona from safety focused to individual focused, increased incrementally by the sense of online safety that simply did not exist prior to the latter part of the last century. We progressed from sharing our lives, whether we wished to or not, with those we called our friends, on a sliding scale of friendship from the traditional close friend, to acquaintance, to the post-Facebook era of "friend-ing" individuals we never met and defriending those we never cared to en-counter.

Part of this sense of safety outside the village today is the certainty that we are able to cloak ourselves behind anonymous names that mean little and are hard to trace. After all, everyone knew that Robin Hood was, in fact, Robin of Loxley—or was it Hobbehod or Wetherby? Mox nix. As noted by Talamo and Ligorio (2001, 109–22), the ability to take on this anonymity, also referred to as an "avatar," allows for the person to be whoever he or she wishes, a sort of heroic mask or demonic license. It is more than the oft-cited *New Yorker* cartoon of two dogs and an Internet-connected computer. It is the ability to redefine the very core of a person's being to the point that he or she no longer considers the entity that is online to be the same biped as he or she is offline. This is so far removed from the village of the twelfth century that one might be excused for suggesting that a single, unbroken line connecting the two cannot exist.

But it does.

Information sharing lies at the core of the transition of that very real village of York into the New York that exists purely online within Second Life or Civilization V. What has radically changed is the incidental conjunction of commerce and culture that has in the past accompanied such information exchanges. The total disconnect that occurs within the online information transfer world eliminates the chance telling of stories, the one-in-a-million meeting of what becomes great friends, or the deep mistrust that sometimes arises without personal interactions. The information transfer is not disinfected, for it was never infected at the start. The information was entirely nonhuman, bionic, and in many ways purely incidental and accidental. The data contained was simply gathered and transferred with little or no traditional context included in one-to-one conversations within both spoken language inflections and unspoken gestures and actions. The result is information that carries little, if any, cultural context, a pile of data that lacks what some researchers would regard as key to a full understanding: a cultural overlay.

That is, without context, how do we understand even the most basic concepts within a language? This is something perhaps best handled by Lynne Truss in *Eats, Shoots and Leaves.* We have, until now, handled context—at least in part—via language and stress. That is, where the stress is put, as Truss puts it, is at least one argument between what makes a Catholic different from a Protestant. But in all of her writings, one feels a sense of the group, not the individual, trying to understand the writings of the individual. Here lies the problem (or at least a big part of it).

Online platforms like Facebook allow the offline truth teller to act, well, like something that in all other respects looks a lot like a bald-faced liar. A person who we think we know in all respects is sweet and adorable is a vicious, nasty little cat online. What is happening here?

Suler defines this—users with benign tendencies, including becoming more affectionate, or those with increasingly bad behavior, saying what they wish without fear of reprisal—as the disinhibition effect. So what can we derive from the disinhibition effect referred to by Suler (2004, 321–26)? That the acts of those online vary wildly from the same offline? As Suler argues, the fantasy online entity is not that far from the fantasy offline individual: we are honest with few if any of even our closest "real" friends.

But this is not the argument here. We accept that if we are liars offline, we may perhaps even be more vividly so online. After all, it is at least as old as the Internet itself to believe that nothing is made evil online: what is already evil is simply made more so. We accept the hyperbolic affect of the Internet on all actions and outcomes, both good and bad. Even these actions presume the involvement of more than one person. Few act out negative (or, frankly, positive) acts without some expectation that others will be made aware of these actions and be made to feel good or bad. The question, at least here, is whether the Internet and its vassals—apps—render the need for any involvement with others. These need not be witches primed to be burned at the stake (news creators or otherwise). Nor are they angels perfectly prepped for heavenly status. Completely disconnected, socially unaware, these individuals are less non-engagers than simply nonplayers in any sort of real world. Maybe their world is the world that will be. Whatever it is, it has some elements in common, not the least of which is the likelihood that it will create one global singular culture, which, by definition, represents no culture at all. But more on that later.

> I believe it does give you more control and freedom to watch as you please, but it does have the drawback of advertisers starting to adjust to this shift to online streaming services, so now even sites like Hulu have annoying ads that you are forced to watch. I have found that I am using more online services to watch my favorite sports teams, whether it be through NHL Gamecenter Live online or using NBC's Sports Live Streams, and the amount of options that these services provide allow for a better user experience. For example, NHL Gamecenter Live allows you to choose what camera angle you would like to watch the game with and even [allows] you to follow your favorite player using the star camera angle. I think with this switch to watching TV online through streams and Web sites, we are starting to see more interactivity with users and the creators so now TV is starting to become a two-way street. Rather than just watching TV, we now have the ability to interact with it, and with this emphasis on listening to the consumer, TV is becoming smarter and more responsive. —Andrew

FACEBOOK AND THE WORLD REDEFINED

Facebook—seemingly at the center of much of what we have discussed thus far but certainly not all that we will explore in the next few paragraphs—was created in 2003 or 2004, depending on how you want to define "created." The initial idea was driven by—what else?—sex: a request that viewers determine which image of a person was "hotter." It evolved quickly over the next month into a personal posting area, but it became more than that. We already had e-mail. We already had Usenet (though, admittedly, in FTP alone and used by few somewhat techie types). Facebook managed to touch a very personal need that Myspace, a similar concept, had failed to address. It became something more than a shared diary, something more than a place to exchange information. In fact, the idea of exchange was not part of the equation. This may be the largest and most important part of the new structure offered by Facebook. Here we are offered the largest divergence from prior online activity that intended to "connect" persons with each other. Facebook seeks no such connection.

For example, recently on Facebook, a friend posted: "I'll post more photos from the *** Pool Party last night, but here's my favorite so far. What a great *** family!" This is a typical type of personal post not intended to generate a response or to ask for any new information, feedback, or ideas. It is simply a statement: I did this, I am sharing this, isn't this wonderful!

I could note the tense and the use of "I" versus "we" or "us" or "them" or anything that would suggest anyone other than the poster even exists. That is the nature of Facebook: it is not, at its core, about feedback or advancing new ideas. It is a closed echo chamber of ideas shared by people who seem mostly interested in a one-way channel of information: they speak, but they do not necessarily listen. In the word of communication apps, this is a key difference that separates Facebook from e-mail: the former shares without thought of who is listening; the latter shares with intent as to who is listening. It is, in a way, much like a research paper. I am writing what I write without much thought as to who might read it someday. Of course, the difference is that I am not expecting a response to the book (though such research structures are rapidly growing).

The obvious difference between the pool party post and this book starts with intent: posting about a pool party seeks no intent, whereas the latter requires intent to not only inform but to spur further discussion. The conversational quality of the pool party post was never intended to be informative in the same way that we consider academic research, of course. But was it even informative in what we might consider a normal conversation? Consider a Facebook post the very same day as the pool party post by a person dealing with a serious illness involving her muscles. She went on for some paragraphs, posting the most intimate information in an effort, she offered, to inform others of the symptoms of the very rare disease she self-diagnosed based, at least in part, on her own family history. The post made me think of my own self-diagnoses of a malfunctioning thyroid and, some years later, issues associated with treatment of brain cancer. For the first, I relied on family history to convince—and it took some serious arguing—a physician to test and treat this ill graduate student. In the second, I relied on WebMD, a Web site created and maintained as an information source for patients, to self-diagnose diabetic shock due to the removal of high doses of steroids. In both cases, I felt no desire or need to share the details with anyone via Facebook or e-mail or with my family or my friends (much less complete strangers posing as "friends").

Facebook has rendered such activity as public information. The action of sharing the information, private though it may be, is not seen as public because it is posted to a "closed" group of those identified as "friends." Yet the poster likely has not considered whether those who read the post are sharing it with their other "friends," and so on. The actual private nature of information is not lost but rather ignored. It seems as if no information, no matter now private it might have seemed at one time, is seen as private now. Everything is shared with everyone.

But with such a transmission of information—one way, with little or no expectation of a response—the actual post becomes singularly important. We are, after all, all that truly matters. "I" and "me" are far more important in the Facebook universe than "we," "us," or "them," which seem to exist elsewhere. Even in the informational post detailing the user's health issues, the post focused on the personal issues encountered, the challenges faced, and triumphs (and warnings) earned.

Facebook offers us a way to see where we as individuals are taking the world of information sharing: from an exchange to one-way spewing. The presumptions, of course, are three:

1. The posts are read;
2. The readers care about what they read; and (oddly)
3. The information is not saved.

This last feature is perhaps one of the more fascinating and definitive differences between Facebook and other information storage areas, such as an academic journal. In these, the primary goal is to preserve, catalogue, and verify. In Facebook postings, information is not verified, not indexed, and, if stored, done so more by accident than intent. Yes, we might accept such a reality. But let us for a moment consider that even our use of e-mail is decreasing, largely, some believe, because of sites like Facebook. Now let's consider the time it takes to write a letter versus to post on Facebook. Finally, the time represented here reflected the thought we give to what we are writing. Dashing off a note is considered of little value. If so, what possible value would we give to a posting on Facebook?

Does it matter? After all, all we are fretting over are a bunch of letters. Consider letters as the sweat our bodies produce as we work out to remain healthy. Fail to train our thoughts by writing in a meaningful (and, at times, difficult) fashion, and we might as well assign ourselves to the lazy, slow, poor thinkers club. Facebook is too easy. Facebook is a child's toy that requires no effort and, in many ways, discourages real effort. For example, Pew posts their studies on a regular basis. Unfortunately, their charts are too small to read easily, thus encouraging users to skip their postings, no matter how informative they might be. Facebook is a narcotic, a drug for the mind that cares not so much for progress as for distraction.

I agree that we are becoming highly individualized. That's what technology has allowed us to do. I may have the exact same smart phone as someone, but they could use it completely differently. For example, I use Instagram and Twitter and my grandma uses her iPhone for solitaire and virtual poker games. Technology has allowed us to be individuals. You can use your phone however you please. You choose the apps you download specifically for yourself.
—Kaleigh

APPS AND GLOBALISM

Finally, what consequences can we draw from the potential impact of Angry Birds or Texas Poker on global culture? This is a relatively easy one: apps render the world cultureless. How? Via global, mindless sharing.

Culture relies first and foremost on one thing: difference. Without that difference, no culture can exist as a full culture. Consider that within the culture that stretches from Bar Harbor, Maine, to San Diego, California, we encounter many subcultures. Within Maine itself, there are several differences in language inflection (and words), food, music, habits, and all the other elements that comprise a culture. Each is different, but none stands as a separate, complete culture. I have a once-relative who might argue the point, but those in Maine are closer today to those in Quebec than they were fifty years ago and far closer to those who live in Boston than even twenty years ago.

Globally, when we consider cultures, those that are very much separate are growing closer and closer. They share a secondary language (English). They share commercial products (Apple, Coca-Cola, Nike). They share many other culture elements. True, many other elements stand out, perhaps some even more today than in the past. I have argued many times that we live in the age of the dying (nova) star, which explodes as it dies. Some cultural elements are on the edge of fading away; the list is long and need not be repeated here. Let's just agree that many people take up weapons to die for what they think is going away. And perhaps they are correct. As a culture is absorbed into another, some elements are no longer considered important, be it handmade store signs replaced by Coca-Cola and Pepsi signs or locally made shoes replaced by Nikes. Every time we share a cultural event, we are sharing, but we are also smoothing down the sharp edges that define one culture from another.

Apps speed this process of global culturalization, and their ability to remove the rough edges seems to take place with little or no notice. For example, Invesco is an app designed to allow users to not only store design ideas, but to do so with little or no sense of ownership. Here's the thing: take the name "Invesco" out and you can replace it with one of a few million others and they would all fit the sentence (if not quite rise to Invesco's standing as an investor's app). And yet they would all have the global standing of Invesco. The point here is that while we have individuals marching through the streets with pitchforks and AK47s, they are also using a global app to spread the information about what they are doing (very likely), gather data about what they are going to do (probably), and checking out their stock portfolios (maybe). And—who knows?—maybe playing Angry Birds!

What we have is a global culture that is more rapidly shared on a day-to-day basis by individuals less concerned about structures (including governments) and more focused on personal rights. This growing culture focuses on individual rather than group needs. We are no longer concerned about whether the group—expressed as a town or society—has the necessary tools to survive. We are no longer concerned about whether our existence hangs upon the success of our neighborhood or our state. We watch impassively as the stock market (in whatever country we are in) rises and falls. We focus instead on what is of interest to us: the latest style of clothing, the latest entertainment, the latest games. In some ways this reflects a supreme faith in the sustainability of our own world. In other ways it suggests a supreme disinterest in our part of the world beyond what we can see on our iPad. What we see is ourselves, what we are doing, what we see is important. After all, isn't me/myself/I what really counts? Who cares about *them* (and, secretly, even *you*)?

> I don't trust anything I don't fully understand. I get the general concept behind the Internet but I don't understand all the loopholes; this makes me hesitant to post certain things on Facebook or Twitter. Nothing is really private on the Internet, even direct messages/e-mail. I've seen court cases where some of the most crucial pieces of evidence are e-mails. Credit cards are the same; you don't need much to pretend to be someone else and rack up thousands of dollars in debt in that person's name. —Joshua

WHO'S DOING THIS?

Here are the verities that seem to be sweeping the planet, whether we like them or hate them. Yes, they are gross summaries; drop by some time and we'll have an ale at the LAB and argue over them in person (but not online).

  The younger we are, the more likely we are to be aware of what is happening elsewhere and the more likely we are to appreciate some of what is happening elsewhere;

  The older we are, the more likely we are to prefer people to calm down and just live in peace the way we are now;

  The more middle-aged we are, the more likely we would like things to be the way we think they were when we were children (and, by the way, we don't mind blowing up buildings to make a point about this);

  And, finally, roughly half of us love Coca-Cola products.

We are a global world dealing with a new, emerging global culture, adopting this global culture via advertising, and doing a remarkably good job when everything is taken into consideration. It could be worse. Some realities are present. Some good. Some not so good.

But in the end, a great number of us are willing to die not to change. We are willing to kill each other not to change. This is not a new thing. This desire to live as we have always lived is as old as our culture itself. What may be different is the amount of pressure exerted on us to change because of the nature of globalism pressed on us via the Internet and the use of very small, easy-to-access, and easy-to-use things called apps. But we'll talk about that in a bit (no pun intended).

Simply put, global cultures are merging into one culture. Yes, I am sure the majority of you fair readers are balking at this. After all, you still have foreign languages taught at your high schools, you still watch foreign movies, and from time to time, a touring group of Buddhist monks will drop by and create a sand drawing. We are different, you argue. We are not the same. We do not eat the same food. We have different gods. We like different music.

This is all true. But it is becoming less true at a rapid pace on a daily, hour-by-hour basis. What has been different about cultures that have existed for several millennia may be gone by the end of this century, possibly much sooner. Okay, you might be thinking, but how? Ah, there's the rub! In order for multiple cultures to disappear, languages must merge, religions must disappear, governments must change, and all the other elements that constitute unique cultures must melt together into a singular pull-down menu bar or an easily updated app-driven, hand-held (if not much smaller) device. So much of that is already happening that it is hard to claim much insight with much certainty. Consider what Trumka had to say to us regarding conducting business globally:

> People live, breathe, work, eat, sleep, shop, and raise their children in a global economy—for better or for worse—and it influences their lives in profound and complex ways. Globalization is about the extraordinarily cheap costs of moving data around the world, about the merging of financial markets and accounting systems, and about the creation of global labor markets by means of both high and low technology. Labor markets have been transformed in every part of the world. Today, because of the Internet, services as disparate as financial journalism and accounting work can be practiced anywhere people know how to communicate in English. At the same time, the market for unskilled construction labor in the US is now dramatically different than in 1990, largely because people traveled here from other countries, often fleeing countries with no economic opportunity. But some of the issues associated with globalization are willfully ignored by policy makers. (Trumka 2011, 42–46)

Trumka nicely sets out the ground rules. First, the conversation is in English. Second, these rules are based on agreed-upon globalism established by those who are less interested in the politics than they are in the economics. Finally, the terms of change are not negotiable: it is an irresistible force that works under and around the temporary and paper barriers of political institutions, largely ignores the rules followed for centuries by religious institutions, and makes up its standards much as a new game online, an app, makes its rules clear-cut and understandable (again, in English). We are at the edge of an era of very large change that has a force behind it that is more powerful than any political movement, that is more insistent than any religious tome, and that is cheap and easily adopted by consumers worldwide. But each of these apps carries with it a cultural time bomb. Each carries within it a guide for the user to a new world with new rules and new cultures. The only constant, reliably consistent factor within each is the economic engagement sought by the business sector with the elusive, difficult-to-target new millennial consumer. Such conversations between, say, Coca-Cola and its target global consumer revolve around an understanding of simple rules: entertain, engage, learn. In Coca-Cola's "Small World Machines" commercial, consumers are offered a way to communicate with people they live close to but with whom they rarely mingle (Coca-Cola 2013). Setting aside the strategies associated with the commercial (which is a globally common, but locally unheard of, three-minute-long spot), the result is an argument for more sharing. As one of those speaking in the background notes, "This is what we want: more and more exchange." But what is being shared is not just a Coke. Dancing, speaking, dress, art, and a wide variety of other actions that we would categorize as cultural are being shared, easily, seamlessly, and at no cost except the consumer's time and a can of Coke.

But is there no other cost?

Apps provide a distraction, even though some are created to educate, enlighten, and even make the user smarter. In the vast world of apps—between Apple and Google, we're looking at close to a million ("Apple/Google Use Numbers")—the desire or at least unintended result is to divert the user away from whatever is actually happening, of consequence, of immediate outcome. Global culture is made manifest by global sharing. We want to exchange our ideas, but such exchanges have the cost of pluralizing the very cultures we are intending to maintain. Consider world music. The very name reflects a sharing of ideas that would not exist without a sharing of musical ideas. The result is something less rock and roll, less tribal, less geographic, and far more blended. Examples are numerous (Sting, Paul Simon, Peter Gabriel, U2, and many others). Notably, this is led by the efforts of Western singers and musical operations, just as much of global commercialism is being run by Western corporations. Finally, advertising, perhaps much more than its brethren in public relations or its counterparts in journalism, has figured out the global key: use local culture to sell locally, use a consumer-created global commercial culture to drive the global message. Advertising executives know that the line separating the local from the global is not only fading, but it is of little importance. As a friend pointed out to me about twenty years ago when I was a graduate student at the University of North Carolina, Chapel Hill, his most recent travel home to India included a bus ride down a familiar road dotted with family-owned and -operated businesses. Not much had changed, he reported, except that all of the handmade store signs had been replaced by Coca-Cola or Pepsi signs. He regretted the change, but accepted the reality that the handmade signs were artifacts of a passing culture. The sterile, commercialized replacements were more convenient and easier to use and modify. The former signs were at one time advertising blended with local art and culture, but as advertising had changed, the signs had become branding artifacts, message conveyers of a different sort: less cultural, more consumer-focused information. The choice for the individuals involved was obvious and irresistible.

> I think that the Web has its pros and cons. Since information is more available, people can have access to whatever information they want, making things more transparent. We can have a better understanding of what is happening at all times in all parts of the world. However, how do we know what is a reliable source? People are always looking for a scandal and may blow something way out of proportion instead of focusing on the important issues. Sometimes the negativity is highlighted way too much, and it overshadows the good that some leaders are doing. —Nathan

CULTURAL EXCHANGE OR CULTURAL SHIFT?

Fishermen in the depths of the Amazon basin reported seeing hippopotamuses swimming nearby (Schultz 2014). The oddity was traced to a 1980s drug lord, Pablo Escobar, and his fascination with various exotic (defined as so only by their unusual presence in Colombia) animals from faraway places that he kept in his private zoo. When he was no longer a part of Colombia's drug war landscape, the zoo, including a handful of hippopotamuses, was turned loose into the Amazon jungle. What had been a wild beast located on only one continent is now on at least two.

This is an example of very direct, very immediate globalization.

So is distance education. This form of information exchange occurs in two forms: person to person and online. The former is older and traditional and involves the sending of students from one college, say in Texas, to another, say in the Czech Republic, for an academic year. The information exchange occurs in two directions. The student learns customs and education intended by the program. Teachers and fellow native students learn customs from the visiting student not specifically included in the study guide (music, style, politics, language, etc.). The exchange is powerful and tends to be seen as a net positive for the learner over the educators and cohorts (Butcher, Latchem, Mawoyo, and Levey 2011, 149–58; Kulapov, Anokhina, Kolesnikov, and Ponomarev 2012, 38–44; Meyer 2005, 1601–25; Pinto and Sales 2008, 53–74; Roushanzamir 2005, 24–29; Salas 2006, 33–37).

That is, the visiting student generally is changed more by the culture that is being visited. Consider spending a year in any foreign country in an atmosphere where you are daily placed in a place of learning, a place where others have already come to an understanding about elements of a culture that are unknown to you. Yes, you will learn your classroom subjects. You will do your ABCs. But you may have the opportunity to learn even more outside the classroom. I use the limiting term "may" because if you tend to "clump" together with fellow travelers from your native country (even if not from your native state or region within that country and even if those students are not studying the same area of academics as you), the amount of cultural exchange that might have occurred will be lessened. You will naturally create your own cliques, which lessen the need or opportunity to interact with those of a different culture. Part of the rationale of student exchange is blunted, lost, and a great deal of cultural exchange is also lost.

But what of online education, which is ramping up globally to meet a demand that is growing exponentially ("The Best and the Brightest Still Fill Our Universities" 2014; Hunter 2004; Kraljic 2010, 52–61)? Does this form of distance learning include even a modicum of cultural exchange? Hard question to answer with much more than "depends." Technology is a factor (is delivery via video or one-way messages?). Is the subject something that requires more interaction than simple content (perhaps English poetry analysis versus analytical geometry)? Is the distance learner expected to participate in something more than a passing note, a quick message board post, or something thin and containing little actual personality (and, therefore, cultural in nature)?

I am focusing on education in this area because it is both one of the more interesting areas that is undergoing rapid change and because it is an easy topic: most of us have some experience with our university's distance education program and the growing pressure being placed on it to provide leadership to meet a global demand. First, you see a lot of commercial selling of what looks like education. Second, as state governments in this country decide they no longer want to be part of higher education, you (especially if you are a parent) will get up close and personal with universities. And, by the way, complain all you want: your child's seat will be filled by a student from somewhere else. Demand exceeds supply. Finally, education carries with it several benefits: longevity, improved health, and social equality. None of these is an absolute but rather improvement: poverty engenders short lives, poor health, and terrible social inequality. This does not suggest that holding a PhD will guarantee that you are not racist, sexist, or elitist; I've met more than my fair share of people who fit into all these categories.

The drive to improve education and thus extend lives, improve health, and promote equality will result in changes on a global scale, changes that must include cultural transfer. And thus it carries with it some interesting consequences. The drive to learn globally will carry with it a drive to learn English. The drive to learn globally will carry with it a drive to become closer contextually. The drive to learn globally will carry with it a drive to adopt cultural standards, much as we accept turning right on a red light (once claimed to be California's only cultural contribution to modern society). Each of these seems as simple and small and, in many ways, as inconsequential as the right turn on red. But these changes will build on themselves, one added to another, until we—standing back from our cultures at some temporal distance—see a significant shift toward one place socially.

They may come in different colors. They may even seem to be different. But we will experience a world that wears the same shoes (we already do), puts on same shirts (we already do), listens to the same music (it is moving in that direction), appreciates the same art (and has for decades, if not centuries), watches the same sports (we already do, mostly, see FIFA World Cup), and increasingly expects the same political rights (the list is endless). The last of these is perhaps the greatest rubbing point, though it comes in more than just a political flavor. How will we describe this world we live in, where two fundamental cultural aspects—politics and religion—are seemingly inseparable? And with the adoption of the use of apps by religious groups (e.g., search "religious apps" on *Huffington Post*) and political campaigns (Davy 2010), every user can define his or her own world or reality. That is, if you are a deeply religious person who has a very real problem with equal rights for women, then you will be able to reinforce this belief, along with plenty of others, within your app world. The app becomes your echo chamber, a non-global device that isolates the user from the world in general but connects the user with other like-minded users, giving each a sense of belonging and a sense of being right.

But make no mistake here, the use of apps by religious and political groups pales in comparison to overall usage. We are not talking dozens of apps, but millions of apps being downloaded by users globally. Yes, many of these are used a few times and dumped. But they are tried. So what does this mean culturally? We have many possibilities: trial and error (I tried it and didn't like it); tried it and moved on (I found a better one); so many games and so little time (the instructions are overwhelming; they require actual reading!); and on and on. The bottom line is that downloads, as previously mentioned, are running in the three hundred billion range, while the users are just a billion or so. These aren't serious users. These users are serious about what they are doing. They couldn't care less about what is happening in Syria. They have zero interest in Bill Blah Blah coming before the Senate. Who are they? Look at the list above: the first two: young and old. When we talk about politics and religion, we are talking about the third group. Let's set them aside for now and focus on the overall use of apps.

> I think that the Web has definitely allowed for politics to become more personal. We have more negativity and opinions being shared over social media than we ever would without the Web. We have heard it over and over again: people who bully others over social media do it that way because they are too afraid to say it to the person's face. I believe that concept applies here; more people are willing to share an unpopular opinion because they can hide behind a computer screen. People with similar views tend to stick up for each other on the Web, so in that sense it does create a sense of bonding between people with like opinions. However, I think that overall when dealing with politics, the Web does somewhat does tear our sense of belonging apart. The fact that people have the ability to post whatever they want allows for people to post things that are not true or greatly exaggerated. This causes conflict between people. It has become more about proving people wrong instead of accepting the difference of opinion. —Steve

EN MASSE

Two possibilities present themselves when it comes to apps and global culture: apps may accelerate the blending, or they may heighten the cultural barriers that already exist. A third possibility is a combination, wherein apps speed up the adoption of a part of culture being adopted globally, in this case, the English language, while at the same time maintaining the walls that keep individual cultures and elements of these cultures apart. The argument for English becoming the global language is an old one and can be found in a sea of research. The language is already the adopted language in most countries where it is not the primary one. The keen part of this argument is the idea that apps might simply result in a preservation of cultures by providing individuals with the opportunity to maintain their own structure of beliefs, independent of others. This is even more likely as we look at the rise of individuality that is driving so much of the adoption of apps themselves. These stand-alone persons need no one, they want only those whom they want, and they have the ability to walk away from an online community whenever they wish with little concern regarding their personal safety. This ability to shift between groups gives the appearance that there exists a sense of community while at the same time allowing the singularly alone person to maintain his or her very much preferred singularity.

In their own way, apps are not so much creators of individuality. They are supporters of that wish on the part of those defining themselves to remain independent of judgment by others they have already "defriended." This is the self-created, self-maintained echo chamber that has nurtured the continued existence of groups that are totally convinced that they are correct in their beliefs because they listen only to those who support these beliefs. The same might be the case with culturalism. Even as more consumers adopt similar choices in commercial options (Nike vs. Adidas, Coca-Cola vs. Pepsi, Apple vs. Samsung, and on and on), we come to believe more that such choices matter, that such choices are deserving of discussion. This is where we cross the road of culture into commercialism: which is what? That is, what defines culture and what defines advertising, and how do they impact each other? Many books have attempted to address this, and many classes have focused on the issue. But at no time have we faced such an obviously more powerful challenge ahead. Are we to become a global culture defined by our commercialism, or are we to remain a commercial global market splintered into dozens of submarkets by cultural differences? Is some of what we are seeing in terms of revolts and uprisings a part of a movement against the Westernizing of cultures via the commercialization of their markets? We may not object to sharing a bottle of Coca-Cola with a neighbor across an ancient border or barrier, but what if that sharing not only leads to a more friendly, peaceful relationship, but also to a more similar culture that, by way of similarities, leads to fewer conflicts and wars?

The focus of all this has to do with peace and culture, and the two of them with advertising. Is it possible that if the world has one commercial "deck," we might also have less warfare? This is related to a question I love to pose to students: what if we were to see one world minimum wage? Setting aside the issue of currency and all that, what might be the outcomes to a global minimum wage? Check out the research already out there, and the feelings are mixed. Some see the issue through the business scope (Lee 2012, 261–75; Rani, Belser, Oelz, and Ranjbar 2013, 381–410; Rogers 2014, 1543–98; Williams 2003; Wolfson and Belman 2004, 296–311), while others feel that the correct view is more societal (Ashta 2011; Axford 2008, 1650–52; Bird, Vance, and Woolstencroft 2009, 405–25; Green and Harrison 2006; Valletta 2014, 101–40). None presents the argument in black and white. But few, if any, make an argument for the role of advertising in a direct fashion but as an indirect, culture-shifting influence.

Advertising is essentially intended to change, influence, or modify the beliefs, feelings, and attitudes of consumers toward a brand. Sure, we could spend pages discussing the definition, but at the end of the day (or, maybe, at the end of most days) the argument falls into the area of influence, brand, and attitudes. Few, if any days, end up dealing with the influence of culture on attitude shifts, the brand message, or the "stickiness" of the attitudes that consumers hold. I have no direct evidence, but after a general scan of advertising pedagogy, one gets the feeling that culture is, by and large, simply presumed to be Western and largely ignored, except for attributes associated with that one cultural backdrop. That is, the idea of global advertising starts with Western advertising and looks at other cultures as odd variants worthy of a chapter or two.

This may feel inappropriate. After all, culture has a massive impact on personal attitudes, which would logically lead to brand beliefs. Hard to imagine how culture wouldn't impact the uptake of advertising messages.

But this is not the question we face in this particular examination. The issue is: in what way is advertising—via apps—changing the world's cultures?

The evidence thus far seems to point to a few outcomes:

1. Global consumers are less interested in the nationality of the products they consume than they are in identifying likes and dislikes.
2. Global advertisers are less interested in cultural differences than they are in the successful communication of a message.
3. The advertising starts from a Western perspective, then adds what is necessary.

In the first of these, the consumer has disconnected product production from nationality. "Made in the USA" is certainly a still-used motto; product origins are meaningful elsewhere as well. No doubt the French are still concerned about wine names that don't reflect the regions where the grapes were grown. But do consumers care as much as they did twenty years ago? Hard to make much of an argument.

The effort of global advertisers in crafting a message is to reach the majority of potential brand adopters, not all of the potential brand adopters. Even Coca-Cola, which has fought hard to reach beyond a 50 percent share of global soda sales, recognizes its place in the world: not all humans will adopt Coca-Cola products.

What has changed and what holds the biggest challenge to those most interested in preserving culture is the use of apps to transmit brand messages. Here is one possible scenario that combines the growing individuality of consumers with the growing technology behind apps and computing in general: Suppose that a consumer using an app has created a shopping world using self-created words that are self-defined, with both a shared platform and a more private zone, with information posted on a regular basis, with most of the information in the form of videos (in fact, almost all video), with little or no historical tracking, and with little information or data beyond access and availability. (Price will play a role, but it will trump all other attributes—and, yes, shipping is free.)

Thus, as we see the continued rise in individuality enhanced by the role of apps within this shift from group to individual, the role of advertising will be largely a reminder of where the brand is available. Each of us considers ourselves unique and our relationships within our self-defined worlds equally unique. No thought will be given to the impact of the brand on our own personal culture because the brand will have replaced that culture with its (our) own artifacts: language, fashion, beliefs, finances, and so on.

What may be most interesting is that all of us will come to believe that we are uniquely different from everyone else when we are not. In fact, the act of advertising a product to seven-plus billion consumers is itself a singular act of global action that overwhelms all cultural barriers, all cultural distinctions. Yet, at the same time, the ability to operate independently from others, to manufacture false "friends," and to "defriend" these contacts gives us the false sense of individuality that we strive to find. It is an illusion of separateness. It matters not so much that tacos offered for sale in the next decade in Bangor, Maine, are so very different than they are in Paris, France; Beijing, China; or Melbourne, Australia. What is interesting is the point at which they will taste more alike than different. This is much the same as language: when will English be spoken like it is in New York versus York, West End, versus East End? We are on the path, and the ability to use apps to share videos, share ideas, and share the spoken word may not have much impact on adults of this generation, but it will on the current generation of four-year-olds who are on their way to a far more global culture without even being aware that they are on the path.

Perhaps this will make more sense if put into a form of online context. Going back to Suler's disinhibition, let's consider how an app user might consider the world within the context of the device itself. Here are what Suler calls the primary factors:

"You don't know me": The notion of "You Don't Know Me" renders the user invisible, thus able to do anything the user wishes.

"You can't see me": The Internet provides a shield to its users. That shield may render the user so remote from the network that the person who seems to be there is, in fact, not there at all.

"See you later": The asynchronous time-shifting nature of the Internet can also affect a person's inhibitions.

"It's all in my head": Lacking any kind of visual face-to-face cues, interactions will be filled in by participants. That is, you can't talk with a blank face (even if the person you are "talking" with is not a real person).

"It's just a game": What's the worst that can happen? After all, it's just a game. No one can get hurt, right? Welcome to Rationalization Central.

"Your rules don't apply here": Your status is an unknown. That means you can be a nobody being a somebody or vice versa. And all the visual clues that we use to measure this in the "real" world are not present. Good luck. ("Online Disinhibition Effect," 2007)

This is a global culture that will grow within the generation that is next, the appers or whatever they are called, who have never known a time when their world was not self-defined, self-maintained, and self-redefined.

So what happens to advertising in such a consumer-ruled environment? It may become the main source for information. It may become the starting points for consumer growth. For, if we combine the app generation with world access to products, we may end up with a far more similar global culture, perhaps one dominant with several subcultures. Whatever the ultimate characteristics of this next image in global culture, we know that the brand distance between consumers ironically will continue to decrease, even as individuals believe that they are becoming more uniquely different.

We are sharing a Coke with the world. The world will come to share even more.

REFERENCES

Anderson, Thomas C. 2000. "The Body and Communities in Cyberspace: A Marcellian Analysis." *Ethics and Information Technology* 2, no. 3: 153–58.

"Apple/Google Use Numbers." http://mobithinking.com/mobile-marketing-tools/latest-mobile-stats/e#lotsofapps.

"Application Software." *Wikipedia*. https://en.wikipedia.org/wiki/Application_software.

Ashta, Arvind. 2011. "A Minimum Wage Solution to Halving World Poverty by 2015: A Stakeholder Approach." Rochester, NY: Social Science Research Network.

Axford, Nick. 2008. "Social Justice and Public Policy: Seeking Fairness in Diverse Societies." *British Journal of Social Work* 38, no. 8: 1650–52.

"The Best and the Brightest Still Fill Our Universities." 2014. *Wall Street Journal*. January 3.

Bird, Frederick, Thomas Vance, and Peter Woolstencroft. 2009. "Fairness in International Trade and Investment: North American Perspectives." *Journal of Business Ethics* 84: 405–25.

Butcher, Neil, Colin Latchem, Monica Mawoyo, and Lisbeth Levey. 2011. "Distance Education for Empowerment and Development in Africa." *Distance Education* 32, no. 2: 149–58.

Coca-Cola. 2013. "Small World Machines." Commercial. Leo Burnett. http://www.youtube.com/watch?v=QGy-5hHQvVw.

Crow, G., and G. Allan. 1994. *Community Life: An Introduction to Local Social Relations*. New York: Harvester Wheatsheaf.

Davy, Steve. 2010. "How Mobile Apps Are Revolutionizing Elections, Transparency." *Mediashift*. February 25. http://www.pbs.org/mediashift/2010/02/how-mobile-apps-are-revolutionizing-elections-transparency056.

Fisch, Karl. 2012. "Did You Know 3.0." https://www.youtube.com/watch?v=YmwwrGV_aiE.

Goswami, Ranjit. 2011. "From E-business to Social Tool for the Poor—A Study on Internet Applications, Drivers and Impact." http://dx.doi.org/10.2139/ssrn.1868846.

Green, David Alan, and Kathryn Harrison. 2006. "Racing to the Middle: Minimum Wage Setting and Standards of Fairness." Rochester, NY: Social Science Research Network. http://www.politics.ubc.ca/fileadmin/user_upload/poli_sci/Faculty/harrison/Racing_to_the_Middle_2.pdf.

Hawe, Penelope. 1994. "Capturing the Meaning of 'Community' in Community Intervention Evaluation: Some Contributions from Community Psychology." *Health Promotion International* 9, no. 3: 199–210.

Hunter, William D. 2004. "Knowledge, Skills, Attitudes, and Experiences Necessary to Become Globally Competent." PhD diss. Lehigh University.

Ikäheimo, Heikki. 2007. "Recognizing Persons." *Journal of Consciousness Studies* 14, no. 5–6: 224–47.

Ikegami, Eiko. 2011. "Visualizing the Networked Self: Agency, Reflexivity, and the Social Life of Avatars." *Social Research* 78, no. 4: 1155–84.

Kafai, Yasmin B., Deborah A. Fields, and Melissa S. Cook. 2010. "Your Second Selves: Player-Designed Avatars." *Games and Culture* 5, no. 1: 23–42.

Kraljic, Peter. 2010. "What It Takes to Be Globally Competitive: Education, Innovation, Values." CEEMAN—Central and East European Management Development Association.

Kulapov, Michael, Marina Anokhina, Anatolii Kolesnikov, and Maxim Ponomarev. 2012. "Diagnostics of Corporate Culture of an Institute of Higher Education." *Interdisciplinary Studies Journal* 2, no. 2: 38–44.

Lee, D., and H. Newby. 1983. *The Problem of Sociology: An Introduction to the Discipline.* London: Unwin and Hyman.

Lee, Sangheon. 2012. "'Varieties of Minimum Wage System' through the Dubious Lens of Indicator-Based Rankings." *International Labour Review* 151, no. 3: 261–75.

Maghnati, Farshad, and Kwek Choon Ling. 2013. "Exploring the Relationship between Experiential Value and Usage Attitude towards Mobile Apps among the Smartphone Users." *International Journal of Business and Management* 8, no. 4: 1–9.

McKenna, Katelyn. 2009. "Through the Looking Glass: Expressing and Validating the True Self." In *The Oxford Handbook of Internet Psychology.* Edited by Adam N. Joinson, Katelyn Y. A. McKenna, Tom Postmes, and Ulf-Dietrich Reips. New York: Oxford University Press.

Mendenhall, Allen. 2011. "Emersonian Individualism." *Mises Daily.* December 16. https://mises.org/library/emersonian-individualism.

Meyer, Katrina A. 2005. "Common Metaphors and Their Impact on Distance Education: What They Tell Us and What They Hide." *Teachers College Record* 107, no. 8: 1601–25.

"Most Popular Apple App Store Categories in June 2014, by Share of Available Apps." 2014. *Statista.* http://www.statista.com/statistics/270291/popular-categories-in-the-app-store/.

"Online Disinhibition Effect." 2007. *Wikipedia.* http://en.wikipedia.org/wiki/Online_disinhibition_effect.

Peabody, Amanda. 2012. "Invasion of the Apps." *Global License.* June 8. http://www.licensemag.com/license-global/invasion-apps.

Pinto, María, and Dora Sales. 2008. "Knowledge Transfer and Information Skills for Student-Centered Learning in Spain." *Portal: Libraries and the Academy* 8, no. 1: 53–74.

Portio Research Mobile Marketing Tools. 2013. http://mobithinking.com/mobile-marketing-tools/latest-mobile-stats/e#appusers.

Rainie, Lee, and Barry Wellman. 2012. "Networked Individualism: What in the World Is That?" *Networked.* May 24. http://networked.pewinternet.org/2012/05/24/networked-individualism-what-in-the-world-is-that-2.

Rani, Uma, Patrick Belser, Martin Oelz, and Setareh Ranjbar. 2013. "Minimum Wage Coverage and Compliance in Developing Countries." *International Labour Review* 152, nos. 3–4: 381–410.

Rogers, Brishen. 2014. "Justice at Work: Minimum Wage Laws and Social Equality." *Texas Law Review* 92, no. 6: 1543–98.

Roster, Catherine A. 2014. "The Art of Letting Go: Creating Dispossession Paths toward an Unextended Self." *Consumption, Markets & Culture* 17, no. 4: 321.

Roushanzamir, Saeid. 2005. "Theories of Distance Education Meet Theories of Mediated (Mass) Communication." *Distance Learning* 2, no. 3: 24–29.

Ruby, Alan. 2013. "International Education Supply and Demand: Forecasting the Future." *NAFSA.* http://www.nafsa.org/_/File/_/ti_supply_demand.pdf.

Salas, Alexandra. 2006. "The Rosy Future of Distance Ed." *The Hispanic Outlook in Higher Education.* May 8.

Schultz, Colin. 2014. "Blame Drug Lord Pablo Escobar for Colombia's Hippopotamus Problem." *Smithsonian.* June 27.

Schultze, Ulrike. 2014. "Performing Embodied Identity in Virtual Worlds." *European Journal of Information Systems* 23, no. 1: 84–95.

Sharpe, Deanna L., Rui Yao, and Li Liao. 2012. "Correlates of Credit Card Adoption in Urban China." *Journal of Family and Economic Issues* 33, no. 2: 156–66.

Suler, John. 2004. "The Online Disinhibition Effect." *CyberPsychology & Behavior* 7, no. 3: 321–26.

Talamo, Alessandra, and Beatrice Ligorio. 2001. "Strategic Identities in Cyberspace." *Cyber-Psychology & Behavior* 4, no. 1: 109–22.

Trumka, Richard L. 2011. "A Global New Deal: Making Globalization Work for Labor." *Harvard International Review* 33, no. 2: 42–46.

United Nations Economic and Social Commission for Asia and the Pacific (UNESCAP). 2011. "Statistical Yearbook for Asia and the Pacific 2011." http://www.unescap.org/stat/data/syb2011/I-People/Population.asp.

Valletta, Giacomo. 2014. "Health, Fairness and Taxation." *Social Choice and Welfare* 43, no. 1: 101–40.

"Village." *Wikipedia.* http://en.wikipedia.org/wiki/Village.

Wang, Hsiu-Yu, Chechen Liao, and Ling-Hui Yang. 2013. "What Affects Mobile Application Use? The Roles of Consumption Values." *International Journal of Marketing Studies* 5, no. 2: 11–22.

Whitley, Edgar A. 1997. "In Cyberspace All They See Is Your Words: A Review of the Relationship between Body, Behavior and Identity Drawn from the Sociology of Knowledge." *Information Technology & People* 10, no. 2: 147–63.

Williams, Walter E. 2003. "Gephardt's Minimum Wage: Just Bad Policy Gone Global." *Investor's Business Daily.* November 13. http://news.investors.com/111303-393370-gephardts-minimum-wage-just-bad-policy-gone-global.htm.

Willmont, P. 1986. *Social Networks, Informal Care and Public Policy.* London: Policy Studies Institute.

Wolfson, Paul, and Dale Belman. 2004. "The Minimum Wage: Consequences for Prices and Quantities in Low-Wage Labor Markets." *Journal of Business & Economic Statistics* 22, no. 3: 296–311.

Chapter Five

Apps and the Small Screen TV

Yes, the advertising makes the Internet worse. This is because of all the personal information it stores. People tend to believe that with the correct privacy setting they are beating the system. I constantly update my privacy settings on my computer for various uses. The fact that the Internet remembers what I've looked into or just stumbled upon I see in advertisements directed to me on Facebook. Sometimes these advertisements can be offending or straight-up irrelevant to my life. This is frustrating and as you said can mess with my emotions. I can't stand that the Internet saves info just to advertise and manipulate their users. —Tim

I can vividly recall sitting on the couch with my dad and being told to change the channel on our whatever-width black-and-white television set. That was the remote control of the 1960s. You got up, walked across the room, and switched via a click dial from channel 3 to channel 11. After all, who needs a remote control for just two channels? I never fail to evoke stunned stares of disbelief when I share this with my students, grad and undergrad. None of them has known a time without cable television, and few know what led to that backbone form of information delivery upon which they are so reliant. Television was a single box, usually located in the living room. Owning more than one was a symbol of success and having one in your bedroom was certainly a major step up the social ladder.

But that first one was where the family huddled every night. It was a chance for the family to act like a family, and mine mostly acted that way (my brother, four years older than I, was far too cool to (1) be in my presence and (2) watch anything my parents watched, even if he liked Ed Sullivan, after all, who didn't?). It was what made the United States united, in a way. We all sat and watched television together. Together. That was during the 1950s and most of the 1960s. Families acting like families. The group was the dominant form of media consumption, and reaction to what was being broadcast was digested in a group fashion, with all of its moderation, mediation, and discussion.

The little breakthrough before the big one (cable) was ultrahigh frequency (UHF), wherein our wonderful "non-click-dial-it" feature on our cutting-edge color television could actually reach odd new channels like ABC or, in my case, channel 17, which connected us to an Atlanta-based "entertainment" operation still being concocted by one Ted Turner. Turner would eventually be a leader in cable television, a form of television communication that used telephone poles and other existing infrastructure to string wire capable of carrying—among other things—television signals. The change was seen at first as an extravagance; after all, television sets were intended to get the signal "free" through the air captured by wire "ears." Yes, the signal was poor. Yes, it often failed (due to storms, wind, or nothing in particular). But paying for access to more channels seemed, well, a waste. After all, who needs to watch Ed Sullivan with a clearer, yet still lousy, black-and-white image to which you already have access? Of course, this would change when signal clarity attracted even those not impressed with channel choices. Content would improve to take advantage of improved clarity; televisions would offer more clarity to enhance viewing. And there was the introduction of color, which made nothing more special than NBC's peacock.

For Turner Broadcasting, the leverage was a baseball team, along with other sports products. For other emerging channels, the attraction would be movies (HBO) and special programs. If you are older than fifty, you can recall when there was no cable and when watching television tended to be a group activity. I remember sitting with my sister watching *The Haunting of Hill House*, one of those black-and-white films that just seemed perfect for small screens. The net effect was gathering the two of us together (again, my brother was far too cool to join in). The movie was scary, but in some ways it was made even more entertaining because I had a companion to share the experience. It was not a solitary, isolated, me-and-the-screen thing. It was a chance to share a sweaty, scary, remembered event—if not the movie's content—sort of thing.

All this would change with the spread of cable television. More televisions appeared in houses, averaging nearly one per person in a large number of homes. Families might meet for dinner, but moments after the dishes were removed, the parts that made the family a unit headed to their own rooms, their own televisions, and their own channels and content. Individuality was enhanced and encouraged by cable television. Sharing ideas, questions, and worries with others was not.

Cable did not encourage television ownership. That was a done deal by 1970, well in advance of the cable revolution. In fact, cable moved in on a market that was saturated with just the right devices to carry a pay-to-watch product. All that was needed was the device necessary to watch the programming, which cable could argue would be more diverse and offered in a clearer format that was much more functional and reliable than rabbit-ear signals. And, of course, you as a cable consumer would be part of the population seen as more elite and thus "better" than those unfortunate ones still using ears. Besides, cable is better for the kids, right?

By 1990, cable was the given delivery method for urban households. The switch increased programming, expanded the sourcing of these programs, and spread production of the programs out from the former hubs of New York City and Los Angeles. But, more important for our discussion today, the format allowed for more individual choices. Consider Nielsen and rating services' abilities to track those watching particular programs. Prior to cable, with two to three channels (again, think UHF and ABC), a show ought to grab about 33 percent of the market. Nobody is going to go nuts if your show pulls a 40 in a three-channel land.

In cable land, the number of channels would increase, the options would increase, the choices would increase. Today—with hundreds of "channels" (we will come back in a bit to why I just put that word in quotes)—pulling 40 percent gets babies named after you at television networks, production companies, and advertising agencies. With your 40 percent share, you have broken programming's trend toward smaller and smaller shares. Only a few events can claim this kind of success, starting with the World Cup and the Super Bowl. Most programming on television today is happy with a 1 percent share.

But let's keep things in context. In the years since 1980 and the boom in channels, the population of viewers also boomed. Thus, a 1 share today is of more base value than a 40 share in 1965. And, of course, the nature of the viewer changed from white Americans to global, with an increasing variety in viewers and, of some interest, in programming. But this programming has split in two directions: one seemingly more concentrated and the other more diverse.

> I'm talking about the fact that almost all journalists across the whole developed world now work within a kind of professional cage which distorts their work and crushes their spirit. I'm talking about the fact that I finally was forced to admit that I work in a corrupted profession. (Davies 2011)

MEDIA AND OWNERSHIP: WHO RULES THE DAY?

At the same time that viewership and programming was increasing, the ownership of the media producing the content was being consolidated into the hands of fewer individuals. This was happening globally: Note Silvio Berlusconi in Italy, Axel Springer in Germany, and, of course, Rupert Murdoch's stranglehold over information flow in the United Kingdom. In the United States, the trend has been steady: fewer corporations own more of the traditional media platforms. In general, the majority of broadcast and cable networks, more than a hundred in total, is controlled by eight corporations: News Corporation (Fox and Murdoch again), Walt Disney (ABC, ESPN, and a handful of other Disney brands), National Amusements (CBS and Viacom), Comcast (NBC and all its brands), Time Warner, Discovery Communications, E. W. Scripps, and Cablevision.

But something else is happening. Or—perhaps more appropriately quoting Bob Dylan— "something happening and you do not know what it is." As more of the large information providers are being lumped under fewer tents and run by fewer individuals who have not the slightest idea what they are actually running, more platforms are popping up. I am always tempted to quote Princess Leia: "The more you tighten your grip, [fill in the blank with your choice of the mega–media corporations], the more star systems will slip through your fingers." In this case, what is slipping through is information collection points located at a particular URL. Gee, that sounds like a rough definition for a pretty simple concept, does it not?

I guess we will call them "platforms." Not sure what else to call them. They are not "channels" in the traditional sense. They are not movies. They are not programs. They are sites online (but, then, isn't everything we deal with today?) that provide access to content. Again, "content" being about the best term for what might have been called programs twenty years ago. Chris Anderson's long tail theory applies here (and again, applies pretty much everywhere that has anything to do with anything online). The point is obvious, but only when you redefine what actually counts as "content." In 2015-and-beyond speak, content is pretty much everything available via an Internet connection using any device. What we see are the big information providers on one side and an endless spread of much smaller "sites" that offer content to smaller numbers of viewers. The point here, though, is not that we simply read the chart and accept that big controls X and small controls the rest. Another overlay is necessary: credibility. And here is where it gets dicey again.

Before wandering into credibility land, let's consider for a moment the nature of the device considered here: generally a flat screen information projection that can carry information in a format and quality defined by the user. That is, it is on the user's end, defined by the user, and under the control of the user. The actual device is neutral; what passes through, in general, is completely under the control of the user, presuming the user has access to everything (and that is not a settled issue these days).

But is it what we would have called a television forty years ago? In 1975, I would sit down and watch one of a few shows. I had choices, but the choices were so limited that the sense of control was firmly in the hands of the program providers. They offered what they wanted to, when they wanted to, and in a format they defined. I had a choice, to be certain. But the choice was so limited that the idea of self-expression via the actual selection of what was being watched was irrelevant. I was, along with millions of others, watching the Beatles on Ed Sullivan. At no point was there any sense of control other than the very limited number of choices. Nor was there any sense that I was unique or an individual in the action of watching the show. I was not making an individual choice: I was making a choice to be part of a much larger percentage (if not in raw numbers) of viewers. But, at no point did I think that I was watching a fake, a put-on, a deception. These were, in fact, the Beatles, and it was, in fact, Ed Sullivan. The idea that it might not be never even came close to my universe. Total credibility. Three channels and total believability. The center of the action is what is on the screen. The center of what is real is on the screen.

Consider that if you have a choice from among three colors—yellow, blue, and red—your individuality is limited to the narrow diversity offered by the choices. You are one of three: red, blue, or yellow in a group of perhaps millions of other reds, blues, or yellows. But if your choices are from among hundreds, perhaps millions of content providers, then the sense of individuality is preserved in the user. You are just one of a few watching a particular video at that particular time. You are the one person making up a group of one.

And yet you are still watching the work of others. What if the content is no longer something created by some group of "special" people, but by "normal" people—like you? That's no longer a what-if issue. At dinner last night, my better half showed me a video put together by a group of eleven- and twelve-year-olds that had all the attributes of a movie trailer. Clever, attention grabbing, fun. Put together by preteens at a summer camp. Using what? Their iPads and free software. This is not a "gee, that's nice" moment. This is a "what does this mean to future content?" moment.

I haven't had cable for three or four years now. I do, however, have Netflix and Hulu accounts and watch some TV shows there. I think that watching TV shows on apps gives you more control, depending on what app you use. For instance when I log into Netflix I have the option to choose whatever I want to watch and can watch it without commercial interruptions but when I get on Hulu there are commercials and I have to wait for those to play out. But after I'm done watching whatever show I wanted to watch I get off of the apps and go do other things. With cable though I'd sit around and aimlessly flip through channels in hopes of finding something that I wanted to watch (or to pass the time while commercials played). —Jasmine

PROGRAM CREATORS: GREAT IDEAS WITH NO BARRIERS

The original thinking about television was that it would provide movies and programs on a small screen. This did not always work so well, especially when it came to presenting especially widescreen movies on not-so-wide television screens: something was always lost. The examples often used are the dance scenes in movies like *Seven Brides for Seven Brothers*. The television screen's restricted width required part of the original scene to be eliminated: cut off. Television's disrespect to the video content of older movies is carried forward today in the way reruns are manipulated to allow more commercials. As television audiences per channel drop, advertisers demand more placements per dollar, with channel owners taking existing programs and editing them to squeeze out five to ten more minutes of commercials per hour. This means a movie that is an hour and forty-five minutes long runs for three hours with commercial breaks. It also means that scenes are deleted from programming like *Law and Order*, with the hope that what is left still makes sense.

At the same time, the percentage of the population attending movie theaters continues to plummet. This has resulted in tighter movie budgets for some, short runs for some, fewer theaters in some communities, and virtually no promotion of new releases compared with past campaigns. It is as if movies in theaters are déclassé. No one bothers to go sit with total strangers in a dark room to watch a movie that they can watch at home with a beer and their friends on a seventy-inch screen. The costs at theaters are higher, the chances of adolescents acting out their childhood much higher, and the likelihood of the viewer's space being invaded astronomically higher—no, let's watch it at home.

But what makes home viewership even more interesting is that what may be watched is just as likely to be something created by someone at home. That is, the increased friendliness of the technology necessary to create a movielike production has lowered the barrier between home movies and Cecil B. DeMille. That technology has moved past point-and-click into even easier production. The previous barriers that separated the technically trained and therefore machine-ready cameraperson are now resolved via a software solution that fills in what is not known in 90 percent of given situations. That is, while the users are unlikely to create a cutting-edge, Sundance Award–winning film, they will be ready and able to create something light years better than what their parents created on vacation thirty years ago. The cutting, the splicing, the sound mixing, and all the other basics of an okay movie are placed in the hands of an otherwise novice. Imagine babe-in-the-woods meets Alfred Hitchcock. That may be a stretch, but the barrier between creating something for your own entertainment and creating something you would gladly show to your parents is much lower than it was even ten years ago. The software has rendered the challenge a matter of willingness to spend time putting the pieces together.

Of course, the ownership of the content itself is an issue only if the result is shared publicly, if only because it is likely that the background music, artwork, and other elements will be, well, how shall we put it? Not exactly public property. Legally, any use of copyrighted material is out of bounds. Practically, that's just not the case. I could spend the rest of this book citing chapter and verse regarding the use (and abuse) of copyright to protect intellectual property. I could examine the back and forth between the rights of the copyright holders versus the use of materials within the confines of fair use. I could revisit a paper I and two others published a number of years ago regarding the misinterpretation of the Copyright Act of 1976 as amended. Bottom line: the Internet has moved on in two important ways: (1) It is global; (2) It is individual. The first of these suggests that there is little of what might be considered an agreed-upon definition of intellectual property rights, in many cases because culture gets in the way. In the second, online users simply do not get it: if they can access something, then they should be able to use and share it. After all, it's not like they are charging anything for the finished work. And they created the thing. And what's the harm in borrowing a bit of Metallica, much less U2 and Dick Clark?

Part of the issue here is that they—though they know it not—are right. To a point. The continual stretching of the Copyright Act, largely to protect the Mouse, has rendered it, well, silly. Remember, as I am sure we all do, that the wording in the U.S. Constitution includes the words "for a limited time." The way some seek to continually extend author/owner/copyright holder rights with the Copyright Act negates the "limited" spirit of the Constitution, at least in the minds of many. After all, life plus a thousand years (which one feels like the law is headed) is not that far from author's life plus infinity. Is that what's hanging in the balance here? Well, and this is important, the tradition within all societies (with the exception of one or two, which we need not discuss) has been to take A and B and make C. That means A, created by Fred, is mixed with B, created by Frieda, to create C, a new idea, a new thing, what might be called progress, if it works. Lots and lots of "A + B = C" stuff happens on a daily basis. Most of it is a bust. Most of it does not work. But the only way progress happens is if we, as a society, accept that the process of change is anything but perfect. The individual creating the video by borrowing a bit from Fred and some from Frieda is trying to create something new via a bundle of technology that has lowered the creation barrier. "Point and click" has almost become "think and it happens."

But something is missing. Something the technology cannot supply: ideas.

It seems that cable is so heavily dominated by commercials these days that to sit down and watch a thirty-minute TV show, you are gonna watch ten minutes in commercials. It is so much easier, less annoying, and more efficient to watch TV shows on Netflix or Hulu. Also, they engineer TV shows to be addicting and when you can watch back-to-back episodes it allows you to find out what happens. Yes, is absolutely puts more control in your hands and is more enjoyable to stream television or watch prerecorded shows that you can skip all the advertisements. (Funny that I'm an advertising major.) —Zachary

GOOD IDEAS

I got a call the other day from a "coordinator." I love coordinators. They coordinate things. In this case, the objects being coordinated were very smart high school kids. The coordinator in question wanted to know if I, as a speaker who talks to high school kids as part of Kansas State University's Presidential Lecture series—I must note my department's director has decided I am no longer suitable for this program; why, I have no idea—would be willing to talk to her very smart kids about a topic that was not precisely a subject I usually tackle. Sure, I said, I can modify to fit what is needed. She seemed skeptical, I think, because she had not quite defined what she was looking for in my presentation. She knew she wanted someone to talk to her kids about new media and where it was taking the world globally but was not at all sure about what the actual gist of the lecture would be. After all, this was unplowed ground for her.

I could sympathize. After all, having a textbook is much more comforting than relying on scans of recent journal articles (one is more convenient and neatly put together by a publisher, the other not so much). Feeling comfortable with a topic begins with being familiar with the content. New ideas are all well and good, but are they accurate? Are they reliable? Are they going to get me in trouble? Again, progress is a nice idea, but most of us really do not like the idea. Progress involves change, and change involves the danger of errors, and errors are just a bad idea.

But it is the idea of change that drives the progress that we desperately need. What easy-to-produce technology has provided is everything but good ideas. It is a semester-to-semester reality: students love to take pictures and hate writing words to go with them. Technology does the first part. Brains have to do the second part. It's a given that hijacking an advertising phrase like "Got Milk?" and substituting the lactose part with almost anything else is so simple, so easy that almost any lazy, got-no-effort college student will rationalize that the theft is clever and worthy.

The sad part is that while we are seeing technology do such a great job of creating an easier pathway from A to B for those seeking C, we too often are missing out on the heavy lifting of actually coming up with a good idea. We are confusing the process with the end result. I had a professor at University of North Carolina, Chapel Hill, who restricted his advertising students to index cards. No computers, no large sheets of paper. Index cards. Students had to put the advertising idea on an index card. Frustrating? You bet. But it forced the students to think efficiently and uniquely. No massive missive and no simple rip-off. The success had to be carried on its own. No use of video to hide the fact that the video was barren of actual imagination or new ideas. No use of video to be entertaining without actually projecting a message (though admittedly similar to three-quarters of the television commercials today).

This idea of requiring students to actually think as part of the creative process is bound to show up on the teacher's evaluation as "mean and cruel." It is also bound to generate thank-you notes years later from those who learned out in the wide world that progress-bound ideas are not images alone. I know because I have received a few.

Bottom line: coming up with great ideas is rarely a solo act.

Consider this story, the veracity of which is less important than the story itself: When the owner of Absolut vodka looked to save the brand many years ago when it was hardly selling anything in the United States and the marketing team recommended abandoning it, one of ideas presented was an ad still seen today. How was that arrived at? The art director reported standing in his shower at home, imagining a halo above the bottle with the words "Absolutely Perfect" under it. He raced to the office and showed it to his copywriter teammate, who made a small change: "Absolut Perfection." Rewriting is always required to make things perfect.

Sometimes it takes Mrs. Einstein for Mr. Einstein to come up with the theory of relativity. Sometimes it takes a curmudgeonly keeper of planetary motion data to provide a theorist the gist necessary to devise the four rules that explain how the solar system works. But we are working away from teams, are we not? We are individuals who need no one but ourselves. I must confess, I rarely write with others and prefer to work alone. But I know that I must seek the works of others to fill in the gaps in my thinking. Reading the works of everyone from Jenkins to Hofstede to Wodehouse to Jerome to the Bard is more than entertaining. It is illuminating. But I am not sure that merely reading the works of others is the same as sharing new ideas with others. It is much like trying to convince students that their time at the university is not to learn everything but to understand that they do not know everything and will spend the rest of their lives learning.

The individual on Facebook is unaware of this flaw, perhaps. Whatever the thinking, the act of an individual as a sole creator, sole maker of a new idea, is more than a bad idea, it is anathema to progress. Yet our technology encourages the sole creator to create without engaging with others. We have removed the barriers to creation without creating the incentives or pathways to actually create the kinds of progressive ideas that move societies forward.

> I never have watched much television, even when I was a kid my parents only let my siblings and I get thirty minutes of TV a day (unless it was family movie night, of course). This has really carried over into my college years. I pay for cable with my roommates only to have a common gathering place for when our friends come over, but most of the time we just plug in the HDMI and stream Netflix anyway. I watch about an hour of Netflix/TV a week. I prefer to watch Netflix because I can watch what I want, when I want to watch it, and don't have to be bothered with all the commercials. Having control of what I view is important to me; that is another main reason for why I prefer to stream my TV rather than watch cable. —Rachelle

CREDIBILITY: WHO TO BELIEVE

We have a world of pundits, some actually expert, some just experts in their own minds. They present themselves as having the answers to the questions confronting us on a daily basis, even though some questions seem to come up every day or at least every week. Oddly enough, the patterns are very similar, so much so that we can see that the events of today are not so different from those that started World War I, got us into a made-up Spanish-American War, and buried the mantra that was said over and over again prior and during the Vietnam War (it had to do with dominoes). We rely, seemingly, on these experts to make sense out of what is a plethora of data, a mountain of news and information—all gathered and disseminated by those who claim to be wiser than we are and certainly better trained and educated than we are to deal with the challenges that face us. But are they and are the issues that face us actual issues or are they manufactured? Users of apps have withdrawn from the day-to-day issues into a world of non-issue-driven strife and stress. After all, pigs stealing eggs is hardly a matter that generates a lot of stress, right? But the experts persist, challenging the world to believe they have the answers to problems that they suggest face us. In education, these are the experts in pedagogy, accreditation, assessment: areas that are pressed forward with such zeal that one wonders how we ourselves were ever educated in a non-zealous world not so keen on these areas of education. Yet suggest that these areas of "research" are of questionable value, and you will face scolding from those who have invested their lives in selling bottles of cures from the backs of their wagons. After all, we all want a better world of education, right? So, let's start by talking it to death!

But are these self-proclaimed experts, pedagogical and otherwise? After all, they put their shorts/pants/dresses on like most humans do. They have no superhuman powers. They attended okay universities (if they attended really good ones, they probably aren't being quoted but are working for a lot more money generating data that is not shared with very many people). They seem like regular types with regular types of vocabularies. So why should I believe them over someone else? Or, perhaps, why should I believe them over *me*?

The experts who appear on small screens are suspect regarding their "expertness," but also equal in rank and status to those who read or watch them. One of the equalizers that has rendered the role of these experts is their ability to create their own apps. That is, they present themselves much as the experts who appeared in 1995 as the Web site creators, the experts who appeared in 2000 as the Web site rules experts (who could make your site legal), and the countless other opportunistic bottom feeders who have used timing as their best tool in selling themselves to a needy audience. I can recall, shortly after moving to Kansas, attending a conference where I offered a free analysis of community Web sites. One such site for a county in southeast Kansas was particularly troublesome for the owners; its administrators complained bitterly that their site rarely showed up in online searches. I took a quick look at the metastatement—a bit of code within the HTML of the site—and found that the site referred to a regional electric company, not to the county. Whoever had set up the site had used an existing formatted code, poured in content, but had neglected to update some of the site identifiers. They had not forgotten to charge the county in question $10,000.

The positioning of such experts online must be considered one of the factors that drive users of apps. Nothing quite like being your own software. It carries with it its own weight of credibility. The rule is simple. You believe yourself completely and others based on varying, largely superficial sets of rules. Your app is the basis of credibility within your own world. Rather than living by the rules of Second Life, you create your own set of measures, valid or otherwise. As Nakamura puts it in *Cybertypes*,

> The Net is, like other media, a reflection of the cultural imagination. It is a hybrid medium that is collectively authored, synchronized, interactive, and subject to constant revision. Because it borrows liberally from other media like television, film, and advertising, it is particularly sensitive to shifting figurations of race, thus a good place to look to see how race is enacted and performed. (Nakamura 2002, 55)

Nakamura's perspective is insightful but misses a key element: individualism trumps all. We all, every one of us, base our belief on ourselves. Even those of us who have little trust in ourselves have even less in others. Those who have signed away their trust in themselves to others, well, that is a religious function that, frankly, all polls are indicating is happening less and less. In fact, the rise in atheists worldwide—those who admit it openly and those who skirt the issue for fear of being treated badly by believers—may be linked to a rise in the use of apps. The two track along with each other. It seems that the two have one constant in common: the persistence of the individual. The singular nature of the person, this rise in the appearance of each personality and the resulting willingness to express this uniqueness, especially among those who are the highest users of apps—the young and the old—lead to a world of self-defined, self-determined credibility. This world is hardly scientific. It does not value science. It values its own reflection, a measure of itself within a world that it defines with varying characters of likeness. The degree of credibility required is measured within its own scale created within its own rules, themselves defined within their own set standards. If this sounds like a religion, perhaps it is. But given the continued slide in the identification of the public with organized religion, it must be a religion of the self, a religion so personal in nature that no one else shares its beliefs. It is not egotism in the traditional sense: these apps users have self-doubt. They do not believe they are always right. They just do not seek answers in traditional places. Each user has their own user handbook of credible answers that can fix a nonworking situation based on criteria established, tested, and adopted by the user. Of course, these answers are usually wrong, but "wrong" is such a fluid word, right? That is, one person's wrong might be another person's "not so wrong" and another person's "maybe right." This is what we get in an echo chamber: the certainty that no matter what we think, it is always right, no matter how much of the universe might judge it as wrong. The inherent problem with this, of course, is that progress becomes a victim of roadkill. Nothing defeats new ideas quite as effectively as bad ideas that suggest one of two outcomes that cover 100 percent of all possible outcomes: (1) we tried that before; it did not work; (2) we have never tried that; it cannot work. As an aside, this is generally what happens at academic faculty meetings. Sigh.

The issue of credibility among app users is more than a matter of who owns the echo chamber. We (that is, the universe) must step up and suggest that standards of right and wrong do exist. This is easier to argue than to see implemented.

In the app world, users have their own caves to retreat into, far, far away from the land of reality, where they see no real need to be deemed correct by those they feel are not correct. This presents a dilemma, especially in education. We are, so it is said, charged with teaching those without knowledge how they might learn. It does little good to teach specific knowledge outside the basics. Yes, Biology 101 and 102, *Hamlet*, *Much Ado about Nothing*, and Introduction to Sociology are all valuable courses. But the best university product is a student who can use an app to learn. That is, why can't we use apps to reach our youngest and oldest users (keeping in mind that those between twenty-five and fifty-five are too angry to be taught much) how they might actually learn to learn? Consider that with little effort I can find two dozen critics of Shakespeare, each with insightful, useful views of the works by the genius who worked among us four hundred years ago. Are just some of them right? No. Does it matter that they disagree? Yes and no. The work of such critics is not the world of finding out how much copper is in a rock. It is something completely different but equally valuable.

The app user can be reached and shown how they can find the critics—from Jonson to Auden to Bloom—and use them to develop a greater understanding and perspective. This is more than just reading a criticism and then reading another. It is understanding that each criticism is right in its own respect. That there are no "right" answers—even when it comes to the theories in physics. The simple answers to complex issues, as former U.S. Senator Daniel Patrick Moynihan was fond of pointing out, are always wrong. In app land, too many users seek a world of simple answers solving complex issues. After all, it is so much nicer when A resolves B. We like that. It feels simple, easy. No muss, no fuss.

But it just is not the way the universe is, whether you are in app land or not. Simply using an app, even one built just for you, does not promise truth any more than opening a book will. Opinion? Yes. Truth? Well, that is another kettle of fish.

Yet in the face of rising individuality, we are all facing the rising certainty among some that they have Truth living with them exclusively. The credibility factor for them is settled. Yes, they are using their apps to back up their beliefs, but even more important, they are using their apps to create a world that reinforces their beliefs as Truth. Oddly, this truth issue matters little among the young and old, perhaps because they are creating a virtual world that is largely benign and largely happy. But those troubling twenty-five to fifty-five-year-olds wandering around, blowing things up, building fences, throwing people out, among other acts of certainty are doing so based on a world that they have created within their app land. Facts? They have plenty (or so they argue). What they actually have are opinions presented as facts ("after all, I got it from Fred's site"). Apps reinforce this issue of certainty. They are confident that the U.S. president was born in Kenya. They are confident that many other opinions are facts within their self-replicated opinions-as-facts echo chambers. Is there a hazard here? Only if actions are taken based on false information.

If your app, for example, suggests that the appearance of a new meteor means that the world will end and it is time to check out, you might want to verify the data. But how? As mentioned above, in today's world of thousands of Web sites supporting the end-of-the-world argument, some even within the established app you are using, how can you not leave the buffet of Web sites supporting what you believe without a degree of certainty? After all, how can a thousand people be wrong?

Let's do the math: one thousand users out of the total number users on the Web. Result? A very small percentage. The app does not guarantee that you are correct, but it may impart the sense that you are. After all, one thousand good, close "friends" agree with you on your very own app site. What more could verify your "rightness"?

I know—some or maybe a lot of you think that I am getting upset over nothing. Okay, maybe I am. But let me suggest the following model. I have written much regarding the flaws of the peer review system and the desperate need to address these flaws before the nature of the network simply turns away from the peer system completely (Gould 2011, 1–18). Peer review is homophobic, xenophobic, misogynistic, and a few other things. It allows friends to help friends to help friends and generally games the system unfairly. And no, I do not accept that this is okay, because even with all the error within the existing peer review system, it is better than what we would have without it. That is a foolish excuse for foolish behavior.

However, simply walking away from any kind of review process puts us all in app land with no sense of what may be accurate and what may be just the opinion of the poster. With a nod to Mr. Emerson, this is bad; this is worse than it seems. How do we determine what is accurate, valid, reliable information versus the opinion of one? Easy question to pose; difficult to answer.

We have tinkered at the edges of peer review for more than sixty years, since the major shift toward anonymous review in the 1950s. We have even considered allowing authors to step around peer review and post works to university e-reserves, usually maintained by college library staffs. We have attempted to correct the problems cited earlier with little or no success. In some ways, peer review itself has fallen victim to the rise in individuality. Professor Smith publishes a work that makes him feel as if he is the leading expert in marshmallows. In his own mind, any further work in this area ought to be cleared by him. Various journals often feel the same way, raising Dr. Smith to the status of supreme leader in his field. He may even be generally admired and liked as a gregarious, fun, seemingly fair sort of guy. The kind of scientist you would be honored to work with. Ah, but perhaps Dr. Smith, by his very easy-to-work-with personality, has a way of shifting all research to fit within his view of life, the university, and everything. This is fine, if you care little for progress. Progress requires change. Progress accepts the possibility of being wrong as part of the equation, part of the experience. No one can guarantee accuracy except those who allow for no new ideas. If your obsession is consistency and a perfect match with what is already allowed, then you can be certain progress will never be attained. This can be applied not just to academic research but to almost all aspects of life. We are most comfortable where we are. We are most uncomfortable hanging around the edge of change. For some of us, especially those in middle management, consistency and tradition outweigh all else, no matter the possibility of the new ideas moving the organization forward. The act of an individual within an organization to keep the organization in stasis is often rewarded—unfortunately—as an act of good management. The same can be said about academic research. The historic barriers to new ideas are well known, from Einstein's theory of relativity to Kepler's laws of planetary motion to dozens of other now-accepted proposals all representing what had initially been opposed by those protecting their own territory, defending their own turf.

But what about the other end of the equation, you might ask. How can we verify a new idea as a valid idea? After all, creationism popped up a few years ago, backed by those seeking to work out an alternative to traditional beliefs in Eden. Placed in perspective, this was not even the most contrary of ideas posted. After all, some form of logic can be followed and ultimately rejected in this case. But the arguments of some individuals, starting with those capable of enhancing their position via upscale video technology, seem to be able to use the platform to convince the masses. Romancing a few hundred to do everything from committing suicide as a means of jumping aboard a passing comet to blowing oneself up in a crowded market to please your god are the acts of individuals, a few individuals. Yes, they are still working within an organization, but when the organization is so loosely defined and lacking centralized control, we can and should define this as individualism.

The fact remains that we see individualism around us daily, in everything from published books to online postings. Individuals are stressing their beliefs, and in this individual-driven and -defined world, there are fewer methods to critically and accurately assess the credibility of such arguments. Think of this like Chris Anderson's long tail theory, this one with a few dominating ideas: Christianity, Islam, Hinduism, and others. Add in a few ideas about forms of government. Shove all of these to an increasing thinner and thinner left side of the graph, with an extending and more diversified tail stretching out to the right. In a world that previously defined its group activities as those carried out by one thousand or more, a group defined as five or six people seems individualistic. In fact, if this period in time offers anything, it is that small, independent groups will seek ways to influence larger and larger populations. Oddly enough, it is the very individuals who fear the influence of individualism who are acting as individuals, seeking influence within the world of larger groups.

Credibility becomes a sideline issue. It is almost as if credibility is mixed up with sustainability. If your idea is right, if your political movement is correct, if your religious stands are valid, they will verify your credibility by their survival. You and your ideas are right because you persist, not because of any testing or independent evaluation of the ideas.

Yes, we are focusing here on the activators, those between twenty-five and fifty-five who in general seem to care enough about their society that they want to influence its future. Those younger and older, for very different reasons, are elsewhere, distracted by their own interests. But they too have a level of credibility that they require. It simply deals with issues of style versus belief. It seems more changeable and open to new ideas and new inventions. The middle-aged activators are, perhaps, looking for validation. But then so are the other groups. We all need a sense of validation, that what we are doing is right, where we are going is the right destination.

As individuals, we look for keys to notate the credibility factor attached to a bit of information. Does it seem correct? What do we know about the source? Has it been right in the past? Yes, we ask and answer these questions as individuals. But asking these questions at all is of some importance. Accepting information as fact without seeking validation is beyond even the act of political fervor that might elect an otherwise incompetent candidate. How do we gain a sense of validation in the two worlds we are examining— twenty-five to fifty-five-year-olds and everyone else? More and more we use apps. And within this construct we open up a new possibility. What information is so carefully controlled, so carefully biased, so carefully politicized that information seekers are not only unaware that they are being misled, but become part of the validation of what is invalid?

> I don't watch TV anymore at all. I used to watch all the time before I moved to Manhattan, but now that I don't have cable I have stopped watching altogether. I've noticed that even when I come back home for breaks, I still don't watch TV even though I have access to it. Most anything I watch will be on YouTube. I only watch one show and I can find most every episode with little effort on YouTube in decent quality. I think it gives me more control because a problem I had with TV in the past was not being able to find anything to watch, but now I can just search it on YouTube and find the content that I want. —Matthew

"NETWORK" CONTROL: WRESTLING A WIDE-OPEN INTERNET INTO A CLOSED MESH OF APPS

I work in a school of journalism that claims to be interested in mass communications, which, I imagine, it is from time to time. Just recently, though, it showed its true colors with a symposium involving a part of journalism. Very nostalgic. Very sweet. Not particularly relevant to much of anything that is happening in the wide world today or really to anything that has occurred since about 1990. That's okay, I guess. What such events make me wonder is whether participants are aware of the battle royale that is under way globally over control/management/suppression of the Internet ("Compromise on Internet Control" 2006, 7–8; "Sen. Franken Presses FCC to Issue Net Neutrality Rules to Keep Internet Free & Open" 2014; "U.S. Control of the Internet," Prabir and Bailey 2014, 1). The outcome of this battle will determine far more about how information is transferred and shared than seminars on past events, of course. But so will the role of apps within this warfare. They are the wild card, the under-the-radar communication channels that will reshape the information shared, often to the point that the modified data bears little in common with what was initially created.

This ability to redefine, reconstitute, reshape the world worries some, obviously (Brower 1999, 36; Davis 2000, 4–6; Krause 2009a, 2009b). In fact, the fear of what may come is of so much concern for some governments that information sharing is controlled (or attempted to be controlled) among app users. The ability to efficiently research target consumers is of such prime importance that some corporations are seeking ways to modify the ways in which app users can use the Internet. If it seems that these two groups have much in common, it may be a matter of similarity in methods than in actual results. One—governments—would like online users not to use apps to get ideas like freedom of thinking, sharing, democracy, individualism. The other—corporations—just wants to make sure that these app users remain loyal consumers, and by "loyal," they mean singularly sold on one set of brands. Yes, we can see much in common here: both want a brand/country to dominate the thinking of the consumer/citizen. Both are attempting to control the largely uncontrollable. They might as well attempt to nail a jellyfish to a tree, as a former professor of mine, Robert Louis Stevenson (not the poet), once noted. Apps are, well, largely like the Internet they run on: they simply route around efforts to control it. Yes, it might run slower, but the information will get through. In the case of Time Warner and others seeking to slice up the Internet, deciding who gets the fast part is at the core of the debate. For China, Russia, Iran, North Korea, and other countries troubled by users accessing whatever they wish, any speed is bad, slow or fast. Apps can be built to defeat specific barriers.

Let me repeat that. An app can be constructed in such a way that it can get around a specific barrier built by, say, the Ministry of Freedom in LaLaLand. This means that information now flows. All information. Information about spying by the United States. Information about bomb sites in Russia. Information about movie stars (as if anyone intellectually older than age thirteen really cares). Apps render efforts to stop conversations kaput.

The effort reminds me of samizdat, a tradition during the Soviet era in Russia of using photocopiers as printers. Ten, twenty, or more copies of a book were made and passed along to another person who then made more copies of the copies. This was done until the copies of copies of copies became unreadable. The habit forced Soviet regimes to register photocopiers, much the way some academic departments do today, to determine how they were being used. Of course, even photocopiers can be manipulated to allow use without registering activity.

With apps, the solution may simply be in the numbers. It may be easy to stop five people from circulating thousands of photocopied books. But how do you stop millions of users from accessing a site from a variety of ISPs using a wide variety of apps? Some of these apps may be registered, known, and clearly predictable. Some, even though they are known, may be difficult to stop. But what of those not even known to exist? And what of those that are shut down and reappear slightly different, just enough to escape regulation? Controlling information is very much like trying to put toothpaste back into the tube: messy and rarely successful (Bullinga 2002, 27–33; Cukier 2005, 7; DuBord 2005, 12–17; Gábris and Kovár 2013, 6–21).

Cultures are not built to change. Just the opposite. Cultures are built to sustain, to provide a psychological shelter for individuals wondering where to fit, how to act, what to do, and when. As a tool within an app, culture becomes disposable. That's a hard idea to accept. If we create a hierarchy of what is important to the world as a whole, clearly culture rises near the top. However, if we apply that same process to individuals using an app, suddenly culture is just another game, something to manipulate, play, figure out, solve, and toss away for a new version. Western Culture 5.0. And don't worry, we can assure that you will be kept on the cutting edge with updates (Western Culture 5.1, 5.2, etc.). The actual content becomes something to examine, consider, and then file or eliminate. Keep in mind that billions of apps are downloaded each year, but only millions of them are kept by users, and even fewer are actually used.

At the end of the day, apps are our new communication platform. Like it or not, they will provide us every form of communication we wish and offer the ease of eliminating objectionable facts, individuals, conversations, situations, or anything that does not fit into our otherwise perfect self-manufactured app world. The idea that they can be controlled is an open question. Can we (the overarching rulers of everything) prevent Fred from sending out a new version of Obama the President 2.0? Unlikely. Can we suppress the number of units he might have sold if we did not object? Of course.

But that's where the fine line of distinction will settle: not whether apps can be prevented from sharing (as some governments would dreamily prefer), but rather how fast that sharing will occur. In the days of television, the channels offered were the very controllable units that could shut off access. But the structure of television has changed to perhaps more accurately reflect its name: images at a distance. Moving content into an uncontrollable, unrestricted, unreviewed world—whether a movie world or academic world— makes it something wholly new, wholly different from whatever it was prior. Yes, it may look the same, but it is not. The model of television—the structure of how content was created, promoted, and viewed—might as well be tossed out the window. Whole sections of the pathways—as we have noted— have not been replaced; they are simply gone. The app has not only taken over TV land, it has renamed it, refined it, and, for all intent, erased its past. It matters little, in 2015, the who, what, when, where, and how *African*

Queen was created. What matters is not how it will be disseminated, but by whom, under what conditions, as well as how it will be viewed. The old mass communication model of sender-message-receiver has been replaced by something more like receiver-pathway-message, with the central element looking more and more like an app.

> I think that users would prefer to watch on their own time since with so many different channels, being able to watch something live means to miss out on another one of your shows. The impact this puts on the viewer, or for me at least, is that I feel more in control and do not feel like I am missing out on some of my favorite shows. It also makes TV timeless by bringing back old shows and letting you be able to access it from another source, Netflix in this case, it is basically media convergence at its finest. —Andrew

WHERE DO WE GO NOW?

Good question. Unlike Thomas Friedman, I can offer few certainties (and he offers few to begin with). The power of the app to redefine how we communicate (and if we communicate) with each other cannot be underestimated. It will be underestimated. But it should not. What is happening in various places around the globe involving those hyperactive middle-agers who want to change the world backward or forward is more than enhanced by apps, it is empowered by what can be transmitted using the app: video. Everything we know in communications regarding the power of the message (and that's not a lot) is that the video/audio is more powerful, more memorable, and carries a greater impact than any other form of communication short of face-to-face communication (and, for some, even more than that). The barriers to this form of communication have largely been ones of devices: mostly screens, in the forms of television and movies. Take these down and this powerful communication structure has no barriers and with this, no filters. Anyone can send anything to anyone at anytime, and as many times as they want. I know—some of you are worried about pornography. Others about copyright. And others about little details like anarchy, whether in the form of civic protest or armed militia. Thus far we have no means to control the free information sharing offered via apps. Doubt this? Consider that ongoing efforts to prevent online copyright violations of everything from writing to film to products should indicate that the issue itself is persistent. That is, we would not be chasing the issue of copyright online as virulently as we do if it were not such a problem.

Of course, we rarely talk much about the "problem"—violations of fill-in-the-blank rights—but instead focus on the solutions that we think we have or will have. We—the group—believe we can control the individual. Of course, it should be clear by now that I for one do not think this is possible. The individual, no matter where they are around the world, will use whatever apps available to access whatever information they wish, even if some of that information is "protected," hidden, buried away. The small screen we used to call television and the big screen we used to call movies are at the end of the search for information conducted at light speed, moving in and out of barriers, around locked doors, over burning moats. No information will be kept "safe" except that not intended to be shared electronically. Consider the bits of data I presented in this chapter, attributed to no author. It is not that a particular person did not create the work. It is that at some point they cared not, it seems, about being known as an author of the work. And fewer works are created every day with the intent of authorship. If the information is perceived to have value, it is shared. If it is shared with anyone online, it eventually will be shared with everyone. And what form of information is the most valuable, the most likely to be shared by those interested in passing around data? Audio/video, film, movies. You know, live stuff.

REFERENCES

Brower, J. Michael. 1999. "U.S. Government Must Maintain Control of Internet." *Computerworld* 33, no. 10: 36.
Bullinga, Marcel. 2002. "The Internet of the Future: To Control or Be Controlled." *The Futurist* 36, no. 3: 27–33.
"Compromise on Internet Control." 2006. *Newsletter on Intellectual Freedom* 55, no. 1: 7–8.
Cukier, Kenneth Neil. 2005. "Who Will Control the Internet?" *Foreign Affairs* 84, no. 6: 7.
Davis, Charles K. 2000. "Private Corporate Nets and the Public Internet." *National Forum* 80, no. 3: 4–6.
Davies, Nick. 2011. *Flat Earth News.* London: Vintage.
DuBord, Steven J. 2005. "The UN's Desire to Control the Internet." *The New American.* December 5.
Gábris, Tomás, and Ladislav Kovár. 2013. "Restraining the Information Dissemination on the Internet." *Communication Today* 2. http://www.communicationtoday.sk/restraining-the-information-dissemination-on-the-internet.
Gould, Thomas H. P. 2011. "Fear and Loathing in the Fog: The Perceived (and Persistent) Vagaries of Tenure Standards among Mass Communication Professors." *Publishing Research Quarterly* 27, no. 1: 1–18.
Krause, Reinhardt. 2009a. "Control of Internet Is at Issue." *Investor's Business Daily.* September 21. http://news.investors.com/technology/092109-506654-control-of-internet-is-at-issue.htm.
———. 2009b. "U.S. Loosens Control over the Internet's Global Traffic Cop." *Investor's Business Daily,* September 30, 20019. http://news.investors.com/technology/093009-507547-us-loosens-control-over-the-internets-global-traffic-cop.htm.
Nakamura, Lisa. 2002. *Cybertypes: Race, Ethnicity, and Identity on the Internet.* New York: Routledge.
Purkayastha, Prabir, and Rishab Bailey. 2014. "U.S. Control of the Internet." *Monthly Review* 66 (July-August), no. 3, http://monthlyreview.org/2014/07/u-s-control-of-the-internet.
"Sen. Franken Presses FCC to Issue Net Neutrality Rules to Keep Internet Free & Open." 2014. Press release. https://www.franken.senate.gov/?p=press_release&id=2665.

Chapter Six

Individualism and the Rise of the Global Consumer

I believe there is a different impact viewing something in one sitting versus over the course of twenty days (as per the example). The ultimate goal for the director and actors is for the viewer(s) to enjoy their work and get engrossed in the story line (keep them coming back for more). I personally prefer being able to watch an entire season in one marathon session rather than having to wait week after week for the next episode. For "normal" television, I find it too easy to forget to tune in, remember the time/day, miss an episode, et cetera, and then ultimately lose interest. For me, having the ability to watch one show right after the next actually fuels my excitement for what's to come. Such is the case with movies; the capability to replay a funny part over and over makes the experience that much more enjoyable. Instant gratification, voilà! —Crystal

Free shipping. Few elements of an advertisement capture the attention of modern consumers—including my mate—as effectively as the expected value in not paying for the delivery of a purchased item. It has become expected. In fact, some purchases are not made without free shipping. It's almost as if distance has become null and void. At one time, we paid attention to the old insult, "made in China." It's as if it matters little to the consumer where the product is made, who makes it, how much the laborer is paid, what raw materials are used. Yes, we fret that 3.25 billion people in the world average $2 or less a day in wages. But someone has to do the work, right? And who are we to set the wages? After all, it's not like the laborer went to Harvard. Yes, we pay some attention to the "greenness" of what we are purchasing. But in a world that generates more than $75 trillion in sales, a billion or two here and there by way of being kind to the Earth or fair to coffee growers and in deference to the economic impacts of transmigration societies hardly adds up to much. Yes, billions in dollars, euros, or whatever the currency is used seems like a lot. It is not.

The hyperbolic nature of a global domestic product (GDP) racing toward $100 trillion leaves the average national production in the shadows. Yet the average consumer can be left believing that on a global scale, a billion dollars is meaningful. After all, the world has only twelve hundred or so billionaires. Yes, more than ten million are millionaires, but only a relatively small handful are billionaires. And, of course, we might reassert that more than 3.25 billion—almost half the population of the planet—make less than $2 a day ("World Economy" 2003). But that is a discussion for another day (and chapter and verse).

This chasm, which is growing wider as the rich become richer and the rest of us stand in place, is the cause of much of the strife that has beleaguered our planet for a few centuries. Much of the "difficulties" seem to have arisen from the idea of individuals thinking of themselves as individuals, which, of course, led them to think of themselves as equals in every way, especially economically. That sense of equality resulted in marches, sit-ins, and barricades of every imagination. It has resulted in some of the elites acting nice and giving some of their money to the less fortunate. In extreme cases, some have given all of their money to the poor. But not much has changed except that the gap is getting wider between the richest and the poorest.

But it is not the gap that we speak of now. It is how fast information flows in this land and to whom it flows the fastest. After all, it is one thing to know a thing; it is an entirely different thing to know that thing even a microsecond before another knows that thing. That is how fortunes are created today. Of course, nowhere in these sentences were the words "creativity" or "genius" used. No one suggested that being the fastest was the same as being the smartest. In fact, while some might suggest that being "certain" is far more important than being "first," the engine that pushes society forward seems to be more focused on those who are by definition "innovative," which is both new *and* different. It is better to be accurate than to be first to publish (we know this is not accepted by our present critics, but it feels good to suggest it is). Thus, the laboratories with billion-dollar grants are expected to be better than those with only million-dollar grants. But those researchers with far more powerful Internet connections, backbones capable of carrying far larger files at far faster speeds, are the ones more likely to win the race to "the answer."

The engine that forces apart the haves and have-nots is hardly new: the age-old elements of capitalism composed of trading and economics. What may be new is the way in which the age-old tools are being used in a very different style focusing more on individual action. Time past provides us with a picture of trading conducted by groups largely defined in some way, which over time broke down from nations into trading groups, and from these groups into the individuals we see advertised today. The path now has allowed for forms of trading never seen before, with previously unmatched losses suffered equally by investors out of their depth in decisions far beyond their ken. They might have been angry about the poor advice they received, but they were lured by promises of massive returns out of balance with reason. Hard to feel much sorrow about what we would—were we more hard-hearted—simply refer to as greed. Add the speed of these returns to the massive returns, and one might appreciate the rewards generated by the clever, the nimble. After all, all we were experiencing was an extension of what was already a market that valued not only access to information, but also the timing of that access. That is, we not only reward those who know what to buy or sell, but those who know when to make the transaction based on access to the information necessary to make the right decision. As is often said, timing is everything.

In many ways, the changes in the ways that consumers act like consumers provide for us a descriptive example for how to model the rise of individualism within the global economic marketplace. We have evolved as consumers from visitors to a market to markets visiting us. But what does that mean? It's hardly news that catalogs account for much of modern consumer sales. What has changed beyond mailboxes stuffed with catalogs (and not letters from friends and family)? And is there a cultural or national (and which of these two is dominant?) identity attached to the way in which consumers now interface with their selected markets? And, at the end of the day, does time still play the same role that it did twenty years ago or fifty years ago or has it become so exquisitely narrow in its differences that it matters little for the average humanoid? Have we turned some decision making to large apps (but still apps) that can make "decisions" based on the most precise differences in timing? Too many questions. Let's see if we can ferret out a few possible answers.

> In my opinion, the Internet has been so far the best thing that has happened to the world in terms of global communication. It has indeed made the world a smaller place. True, people from older times like my parents lived without the Internet and were still able to survive; even till this day quite a number of people still do. But you'll agree with me that the Internet makes living and learning a lot easier and most of all convenient in this new age. As an international student here in K-State, I feel like if it wasn't for the efficiency of the Internet, I probably wouldn't be here talking about how easy and convenient it was for me to research the school, apply, and communicate with the admission department. It is only normal for such a great invention to have its little adverse effects like insecurity and intrusion of privacy, which pertains to those who are a little careless with their private information on the Internet, especially with mistrusted Web sites set up by fraudulent organizations. I do a lot of shopping online from various Web sites that require my banking details [but] only after I do a little research on them by looking up the Web site on Google,

which gives me access to different blogs set up by Internet users reviewing the Web site and the products or services it poses to render before inputting my bank details. By doing this I get a broader knowledge about the Web site and what to expect. I know for a fact that every single activity on the Internet is being monitored for security reasons, and at the same time a platform for fraudulent activities, which I'll say is almost inevitable in such a major invention. One just has to always have his or her guard up when surfing the Internet. The Internet renders way more advantages to the world than disadvantages, which makes the Internet route worth the risk. —Tosan

Online catalogues are not really catalogs. They are apps disguised as catalogs. I suppose it just would not work so well to call apps what they are to those who use them: sols; that is, solutions. These highly adaptive, narrowly defined, carefully crafted software products are called "apps" by those who make them. That's all well and good. But in this particular case, the consumer's view might be more important in providing us a better idea of how the devices are being used (beyond killing pigs).

Let's compare consumer products for a moment: say, for example, a refrigerator, an automobile, and a handheld mobile communication device. Notably, all can be modified to accommodate the demands of the user. But the last of these, the handheld, computer-based, portable memory manager, synced calculator grows to become more like the user than the other two. Stepping past the use of passwords, the handheld has hundreds of user-defined options that, taken together, make it a unique machine, a device that comes to reflect the personality of the user. This is not to suggest that the refrigerator will not come to provide you with specific enhancements for only you or that the car you have just purchased cannot be made very personal with add-ons and elements not "standard." The computer just has more of all these, so much so to the point that it can nearly disappear in its size and magnify in its impact beyond any prediction.

Part of that capacity, in fact a majority of that capacity these days, is likely to be an app, something found and adopted by the user. In some cases (Second Life, several years ago, comes to mind), the app can be modified by the user to accommodate individual demands and needs. It may start as a game and turn into a business tool.

Thus, both the device and the application running on it are unique to the user. What could be a more individualistic act than this? Yes, a large number of us use iPhones, and many of us play Angry Birds, but few of us actually set up our devices the same way. This is much different than computers were thirty years ago, when the machines defined user behavior with only a few options available.

Our behavior online has, in many ways, resulted in a profile that can be tracked and predicted by the seller. We do not feel comfortable talking about being "tracked" or being "predictable," but there you have it. Every time we say "yes" to a site's inquiry regarding our status, we are handing out a bit of our privacy to a machine. But, hey, it's just a machine. It's cool.

And it probably is, given that the machine has already figured out how to do something very clever: modify communication (advertising) to match the audience's expectation.

Let's consider what this might mean.

Clearly, I want my pitch to include what my target has already indicated a predilection for; say, for example, a particular brand of lemonade. Thus, my message within an app will include that, but what else?

> I believe that, yes, it is a very real possibility that someone can be watching what you do on the Internet and that all my personal information could be saved. Because I believe this is a possibility, I take caution in what I put online and do my research before sharing personal information. I think we can definitely live without the Internet but we would lose out on easily accessible information. Having and utilizing the Internet is worth it but just caution yourself and do your research before trusting your personal information with any site. —Cheyenne

CULTURE CAN BE SO CLEVER

Now culture steps to the forefront. A clever advertising app that can take a message such as "your family's favorite lemonade" and translate that into, say, two hundred cultural, linguistic "events" has a fair chance of generating consumer response in more markets than one of the traditional quadrants of Foote, Cone, and Belding (high involvement, low involvement, high feeling, low feeling). That is, the ability of each individual/consumer to define and craft the message via an app that, at least in its roughest stage, will be cultural at first, will result in a greater brand adoption. Take that message to the consumer level via an app that translates that advertising message into the language (cultural communication pathway) that the consumer speaks, and, well, you have something much more powerful. Add to it the specific details of each consumer's life, and you have a communication message apparently crafted by an app but really created by the consumer to "translate" the advertising message into something far more relevant and meaningful. Using the Ad Speak app, the consumer completes the sales circle by making the argument not only contextual, relevant, and persuasive, but oddly enough, complete.

Thus, the "catalog" that we are familiar with today—those seemingly uniform, non-unique mailbox fillers with pictures and offers—will soon be created by the consumer. Part of this is made possible by an individualized printing operation that allows the advertiser/ad agency to create a package designed with only those pages of information that are relevant to the target, as defined by the target, not a marketing team "guessing" what the target wants. What the Internet has done to the speed of message transfer, it has, in nimble and skilled hands, done to the ability to target each consumer, one by one. The interface has not been perfected but is certainly well on its way in that direction. It proves to be not only efficient for manufacturers, but also consumers. It also may create channels of information. And there's the rub.

As we know about humans, they are generally bipeds with two unfortunate synergistic attributes that work well together: complacency and habitualness. We are not very demanding, and we create habits that we expect to meet with a degree of consistency. This frankly explains how billions of a certain mediocre hamburger can be sold: it's not for their culinary magic. The consumer receives the same boring, lackluster burger each time it's ordered. As the Bostonian said: "foolish consistency is the hobgoblin of little minds," and we love that certainty.

Within a system of apps delivering a new message for a new product, it is highly unlikely that the target consumer will respond without some degree of certainty that what is to be consumed, purchased, or used will not stray far from what is already known. Thus, our efficient consumer service system will become an efficient server of the same stuff. Where does progress fit into such a highly efficient, seemingly closed off communication network as that offered via an app that offers consumers a pathway with few, if any, digressions? It does not.

Such catalogs will, no doubt, be very efficient vehicles. But new products will be restricted to carefully considered line extensions. In such a consumer-defined communication network, it would be hard to imagine, for example, a product like Mountain Dew breaking into a high-sugar, highly caffeinated drink category unless it already existed there. That is, if consumers are ultimately in control of what information they receive, it is likely that information will be very narrowly focused on what they already use and are familiar with.

The advertising media planner reading this will argue that this is already happening. Readers are selecting the information by magazines, programs, stations. Yes, but not down to the message level. No doubt that same media planning director would now be proposing that the consumer only pays attention to what they have already adopted as their brand. And this is true, but the chance of grabbing a stray, picking off a point or two from a competitor, is so much more likely in a world where the target consumer at least sees your commercial or print ad than in a world where the only messages are those dealing with what they already have adopted. The argument here is not that somehow we have a solution to this. The argument here is that this is very likely and will persist with little or no cure. As the consumer increases the control wielded over information flow via apps (which is much more individualized than any Web site can ever become), the possibility of ignoring (blocking) unwanted channels of information increases. Why should it not? Consumers have the ultimate power over what is watched, or so they would like to believe. We can at least agree that the consumer would be choosing to watch what is watched, setting aside for now whether there was any real choice in accessing that particular app (marketing/political/economic blocks). What is included in that version of products shown to the consumer would be defined by the consumer, if only because showing hundreds of possible options is not as satisfactory a shopping experience as seeing only those items preselected.

Where does global fit into this, you might be thinking? And well you should. Setting aside the cultural issues for a moment, consider just the problem of how consumers look at information gathering based on their network limitations. Not everyone sits on a fat tree network, invented by Charles E. Leiserson of MIT. Some of us may still be using a dial-up over foul—or slow, at the least—copper. The speed and reliability of our connections are so globally diverse that it is hard to even start a conversation in 2016 or 2017 about information gathering without first admitting it is uneven and by nature largely unfair.

So much of what we end up talking about is some time in the future. This future is an unspecified time. This is a time when Thomas Friedman might take a stab at being more precise than I will. Let's just say "within your lifetime" (I may not have that much longer; that's a separate story), if you do not recall watching the previously mentioned Beatles on the *Ed Sullivan Show*. We can agree that everything seems to happen faster these days than we think it will. Part of this is because we have people being paid to sit around thinking about stuff like this (Google comes to mind). Part of this is the certainty that demand will require we provide a supply. Pizza was created because someone wanted something like a pizza; convertible cars were made because someone wanted a car with a removable top. Consumers call the shots. Always will.

But the consumer-defined, consumer-driven, consumer-dominated world of advertising and marketing information like that surrounding a new product will be controlled by consumers themselves more than it ever has been in the past. This starts with access. How consumers decide what information will be shared. Let's set aside the over-the-top, earth-shattering items like the latest iPhone, which everyone wants to know about, and focus on the more mundane: laundry detergent. How is Procter & Gamble going to introduce a new product without first connecting it to consumers via what the consumer already knows? In an app-driven, app-defined world, the consumer will know about a new version of Tide only if the line extension makes it past the barrier the consumer has created: the app itself. The app becomes an extension of the consumer's brain, already set to avoid change, avoid risks, avoid anything perceived as "too new" (at least in a majority of cultures) or too

boring (in fewer others). This is not to suggest that the consumer walls him-
or herself into a small room with no choices; it suggests that those choices
will not be too far afield, too risky, too strange. And, of course, this willingness to be risky will vary with age, from young to old, and, of course, by
culture as it still exists.

But the massive sieve that controls all information, all branding data, all
consumer outreach will be nominally controlled by the consumer or at least
by what the consumer *does*. That is, it will be the consumer's behavior that
sets the parameters of data barriers. The consumer's use of the app and the
app's opportunity to interact with that involvement will create the ultimate
behavioral overlay, an interpretive network or grid that acts as a sort of fence,
setting the boundaries of where the consumer's wants and desires can go,
and, of course, where these wants and desires cannot wander. It's not hard to
imagine a self-defined search engine, personalized by the past behavior of
the user to such detail that the app knows what to include and what not to
include. The quality of this prediction is largely a function of the app's
interpretation of the user's behavior in other areas. Now we're getting into a
more vague landscape.

I tend to rely on software and common sense to keep me safe online. I use
Google Chrome to browse, because it's a bit safer than other alternatives such
as IE. When I download files, I usually check to make sure that they are safe
first. I also only give out as much personal info as I need for various sites. My
name and e-mail address are everywhere, I'm sure, but other than that, only a
few sites such as Amazon, PayPal, and Bank of America have my private info.
I trust these sites because they have good security.

I trust their security in spite of what seems like a lot of hacking attacks
lately, because most hacking attacks are DDOS, or distributed denial of service, attacks. These do exactly what it sounds like: they deny service. They
can't access information; they can only shut a site down due to traffic over-
load. So, in the end, it is definitely worth having a small bit of personal info
online in order to gain access to such a huge wealth of information and resources. Finally, even if it wasn't worth it, there are plenty of tools such as Tor
or regular proxy servers that allow a user to redirect their traffic and their info
so that they are better hidden. You can browse anonymously if you really want
to.

Browsing anonymously sure does have its various levels of security, but
for the most part you can browse completely anonymously as long as you
don't actively enter personal information on sites that you visit. As far as
keeping my personal data goes, I trust mainstream bank and commerce sites,
with PayPal being a good example. I don't think that we all have our own
standards, but there are some companies trusted by most people. Finally, as far
as your "stroll through the living room" analogy goes, that's not quite how a
DDOS attack works. It's more along the lines of your front yard being filled
with a hundred people so that you can't get to the door in the first place, but
they can't get in. It may be annoying, but your data is safe. —Daniel

CONSUMERS SERVED BY APP-DEFINED BRANDS, NOT BY AGENCY-DEFINED MARKETS

The reality already exists: Procter & Gamble can deliver the vast majority of the center of any grocery store's inventory direct to the consumer for far less, including the free shipping alluded to earlier. And why not? As we have seen in other areas of commerce, the layers between the manufacturer, farmer/ rancher, and consumer are disappearing. The ability to ship directly from the factory/farm to the consumer is becoming more and more commonplace, so much so that the once-common barrier of distribution has been replaced with virtual shelving and automatic carts. The shopping experience has changed in another, very significant way relevant to everything we are dealing with in this book: it is solitary. What is left for these roaming nomads are faceless, bodiless blog notations, some curiously 180 degrees from what others are posting. It makes one wonder: are they "paid posters" and do their moms know what they do for a living?

That issue of believability is not a minor issue. Consumers are coming to rely more and more on what others say on Web sites and blogs, and they have become more clever about sniffing out public relations "plants," whose job is to not respond to complaints but to post positive "consumer comments." Misleading? Sure. But it is, again, hardly the first time consumers have been misled regarding a product or service. Snake oil was not invented by individuals who had performed decades of scientific research and who were genuinely committed to the welfare of the potential user. They were back-of-the-wagon ne'er-do-wells whose existence and profession continues today.

Online consumers continue the traditional habit of relying on data available only through information-collecting magazines like *Consumer Reports* or polling centers such as Gallup or Pew. Is the accuracy as certain? No, as just mentioned, comments can be added purposefully to mislead consumers. It remains the duty of the potential buyer to hunt out valid evaluators (negative posts can be just as invalid as positive ones, after all; competition is competition). So, what might be a more obvious landscape for apps designed to hunt down valid evaluations? That is, given that apps are designed to meet consumer demand—including the desire to kill egg-stealing pigs—might an app builder come up with a tool for consumers to measure information sites?

Consider My Products, an app marketed by Mize, which "helps consumers manage products they want and own, and connects them to support from brands as well as family, friends and social networks." Containing no advertising, the app (and many others like it) allows the consumers to build their own histories of information. "Our app puts a genie inside the consumer's smartphone they can call on for help, anytime, anywhere. Consumers can discover and learn about products, get advice, as well as access support from trusted friends and brands" (Burke 2013). This eliminates the need for consumers to rely on traditional sources for information—such as advertising, which is questionable by its very nature—as the sole or even major basis of a brand adoption. The shortcut from "what" to "when" in the purchasing cycle is pushed forward via information supplied by those largely unknown to the potential brand adopter. This is no small change. In the past such changes were based on at least some information exchange among friends, relatives, known wise ones who were the keepers of what we wanted to know.

Some time ago I started thinking about bees. Well, not so much about bees as beehives. We have a new home on a large piece of land, large enough to think about adding some hives in the back. Yes, they are a nice conversation starter. But that can be handled at a distance. To tackle this issue, we went about in our usual way: Google. Then we asked around the local tavern we spend some time in and actually encountered two gents who keep hives. The information they provided largely matched up with what we had found online. But there were points of difference. So whose word do we go with: the local experts or the online sources?

If the national/international brand/information source was positioned in direct competition with a local one, which would do a better job of swaying the consumer? I guess we have to start with some definitions. What does "national," "international," and "local" mean? What constitutes a brand or information source? We each have our own thoughts on these terms, so I need not waste time and space on my own take. Let's say that we all possess a difference of some significance that we have each measured for ourselves. The decision at the end of the day resides within each consumer (that would be each of us) based on our own experiences, our own beliefs, and our own set of advisers in whom we place some degree of trust. Perhaps the last of these standards is the most important. It certainly fluctuates the most. The degree of trust we lean on can arise from what others say about these "experts," the track record we each experience (the experts seem to get it right more often than not), or a sense of trust that arises from intuition rather than logic: the experts are reinforcing what we already believe.

It is this element that the commercial world spends so much time trying to influence, if only because advertisers know that the last of these three is connected to and greatly impacts the previous two. The irony, of course, is that the app user defines the degree and importance of this impact. In a world of online branding—if such activity actually occurs—the consumer rules the information flow in a fashion wholly new and difficult to predict and seemingly impossible to control. Predicting how consumers would react to messages within commercials was never a precise science, no matter how much those in marketing wished it were. Information uptake was measured based on group activities, relying on demographics or psychographics that provided rough guesses.

What we have now is a reaction scheme that occurs at the level of a single person. What is even more difficult is that this one person may or may not agreeably fall within a given demographic, as they roughly did in the past. Our measuring skills have gotten better, but what we are measuring is still hard to define.

Part of the problem is that the engagement of the consumer in defining the brand is shaped in part by the app itself. Facebook has a real presence in all conversations within its blog world. The way in which a brand would be discussed in a Facebook group is likely to be different than that same topic on a different platform. Part of the difference might be the structural issues (restrictions of words, aka Twitter). Part of the difference might be the nature of the anticipated users (Facebook versus Myspace). Whatever the difference, the app is driving the nature of the message far more than television ever played a role in the shaping of the commercial beyond the size of the image. The ability of the user to set the when, where, how, and, to a great degree, the why of watching a commercial message will have an impact on that message itself. Simply taking a sixty-second commercial and putting it on a Web site like YouTube or tagging it into a blog post will not satisfy the consumer. Perhaps most interesting, over time the actual presence of the app—that is, the actual physical place of the app—is less and less obvious. Television was always obvious. Hard not to notice that the information you're receiving is coming to you via a television "set." Information coming to you via an app is still connected to that app, and users still feel that the app is the delivering element, but the presence is far less than a television.

As a computer science major, I find a lot of loopholes in the Internet and in different computer programs. Nothing in the Internet world is 100 percent perfect because all of the components of the Internet are made by humans who are not perfect. So I feel like there is always a way for someone to get around Internet security, whether it is to see what a user is doing online, lift their credit card, or find out personal information. However, I feel that I still could not live without the Internet when I use it for so many important things, such as school and work on a daily basis. —Eric

CULTURAL IDENTITY DEFINES THE CONSUMER APP MARKET INTERFACE

We spent time at a wedding in Barbados a few years back. Wonderful place. In addition to being a place of wonders, it came complete with lines of demarcation. Some in our party remained on the grounds of the holiday resort, filled with all that would be necessary to enjoy a week away from home: food, drink, music, and a beach complete with an ocean. Others ventured forth, driving rental cars past the gates of the resort into the "actual" places (tourist culture) of Barbados. Some went further: they rode the Yellow Bus. I would attempt to describe the experience, but why ruin it for all of you heading to that idyllic isle? Bottom line: it was a group that experienced the ride as individuals, each getting out of the trip their own impressions.

The Yellow Bus of Barbados stands in many ways as an example of what the consumer experiences using an app within a market online. A crowd exists within the site, yet the visitor does not need to interact with others to attain a unique interaction within the site that involved no outside (other) interference or assistance. The ability to be at once within a crowd and yet not part of that crowd is what makes the online app consumer market world so very different from other iterations, including Web versions. We have no required sharing of information. The experience can be simply the user gathering what everyone else is doing without doing anything themselves. This might be likened to a "lurker" within a blog site, but the power for the app to gather information is so much more refined.

The curious part of the visit to Barbados was the lack of a sense of legal presence. In fact, my wife and I never really felt we were in a "country" as much as were on an island that happened to be a country. The culture was so thick that any presence of a legal system seemed buried layers deep. Again, Barbados offers us a way of looking at online apps: these electronic games, shopping devices, information gatherers care very little about nations. They are saturated within the culture they are born into. National boundaries are not only ignored, they do not exist: again, they are much like Barbados, an island with no defined borders with nearby nations. What one experiences within Barbados is its culture, not its rules, its court system, its legal policies or political parties.

Apps are culturally driven, culturally created, culturally defined. We can see the differences between versions of Japanese and American anime, even if they share the same heroes. We can equally see the differences between the way an app operates in Syria versus in India. We can also see that the differences matter little to the actual user; that makes sense. They are not the researchers, after all. They are citizens, consumers, parents, active or nonactive members of a group. The app is the tool defined by what is sought, not by what it can find.

The searcher becomes the channel of information; the searcher defines its depth, its direction. Yes, such was always the case with direction. But the degree of depth was not as much a control left to the consumer: it was, instead, left to the control of the advertising agency. Now the information is posted, much like a highway billboard sitting and waiting for a consumer to drive by and see and gather the data.

This described individuality that drives the modern Internet consumer is not bounded by cultural lines of tradition. Consumers seemingly make decisions within groups, but they are, in fact, making decisions on their own. This may give us some idea of why so many more consumers are self-defining even while acting as though they are within a self-defined "group" such as Facebook. They choose what they believe and then believe it.

This has always been the case. Someone influenced the individual as they grew from child to adolescent to tween to adult. ("Tween" refers to those between their teens and when they come of age at thirty-three, according to one Bilbo Baggins.) But the influencers were a bit closer to home in the form of family, neighbors, community. The modern influencer can exist anywhere, be anyone, exist in any culture, provide answers based on any past, any belief.

Here we enjoy a challenge for an advertiser. In the past, knowing who the influencers were, where they lived, and what influenced them was a pathway to success. Textbooks in most college classes even today discuss targeting influencers, identifying the opinion leaders, and knowing how to reach them. Failing to do this was a certain script for failure.

Today, the opinion leader may still be present. The question at hand is more where, who, why. Culture may play a role. Product usage may play a role. The opinion leader's status may play a bigger yet thinner role (Elvis is not your mom, after all). In fact, no matter how we choose to measure the impact of the Internet and all its devices, that impact is thinner, more changeable, less durable. The idea of maintaining an icon like Tony the Tiger for a century or more may be a thing of the past. As products and their brands go global, some will carry their status as leaders (Coke: Open Happiness) more effectively than a cereal suggesting that it is "Great!"

> I know there are people out there who can track and hack into literally anything. Even the United States national security has been hacked into. My policy on keeping myself safe is to just simply not put things out on the Internet or even my iCloud/Apple account that I wouldn't want to be shared on the off-chance someone did hack into my personal computer/phone/account of some sort. I change my account passwords frequently and check all of my financial statements regularly to avoid any type of hacking. I feel that the Internet is as safe as you make it. If you put things out there, you should accept the risks of someone hacking into your stuff. . . . If you cannot handle those risks then it may be best to stay away from surfing. —Kaleigh

IS TIMING AS IMPORTANT AS IT ONCE WAS?

At what point/place/activity does faster not count as an advantage in the app world? Being the first kid on the block with the SpaceSeven Rocket toy must still count for something, at least on the block. Does it count even more somewhere else? Does wearing the latest fashion count for anything outside of your small, fashion-focused world? Does being able to load, solve, or identify the solution make you special anywhere other than in the game that defines the solution? Does it even begin to matter if everything posed above is solved by an isolated, limited, irrelevant-to-the-world-in-general sort of element, be that a game of Angry Birds or an issue of *Wired* or a box of Kleenex? In this century we are not exploring the world as we did in the nineteenth century, nor are we filling the world as we did in the twentieth century. We are *playing* in this century. Playing with whatever we think we can play with, starting with toys and ending with human lives.

We use technology to enhance the play, speed it up, increase the "fun" factor. That "fun" can come in the traditional entertainment mode, or it can arise as a "feel-good" sort of emotion that convinces us that we are doing a good thing for the world and for us. Advertising is all about ensuring that we understand the speed factor (which, as we all know, is deeply related to our own limits on life). Getting one hundred things done must be ten times better than getting ten things done, even if the "things" being "done" are—well—useless, meaningless, and frankly a waste of time.

The secret role of advertising has been to ensure that the consumers believe that the product being purchased is the best one, the right one, the only one for them. Whether it is or isn't is irrelevant. The consumer in this equation is an elite. Such special consumers are not keenly focused on un-biased science to prove "the best," even when such a decision has health ramifications. Consider that we regulate medical advertising to protect those able to purchase such products based on the advertising (which presumes a degree of education). Do we need to protect medical professionals from medical advertising? That's a healthy argument we can have over an ale and a biscuit at a local pub.

Consumers—these elites we refer to above—want information, and given their certainty of a soon-to-be death, they would like the information as soon as possible. Whether this information is verified is a secondary matter. Fast is first. Truth is somewhere in the top ten, along with size, price, availability, and so on. Now we're dealing with a cultural issue here, best summarized by Hofstede's uncertainty avoidance index: risk. The more consumers are likely to be fearful of decisions made, the more likely they are to avoid making risky decisions. This varies by culture.

But we have already decided that consumers everywhere value the speed of access to information first. How are we to reconcile this?

Let's start by considering that we are not dealing in absolutes. The habit many of us, including some academic researchers, have in presuming that we are all Western in our thinking is silly but easy. We are not. But we all start from a base. That is, our cultures all have points from which we change. And, yes, all cultures are changing. This is a certainty that many studies in culture also overlook or ignore. Cultures are growing together. But of particular importance in this consideration is that the average consumer in any culture is shifting. Consider what Hofstede notes on his Web site regarding why consumers should participate in his culture compass survey:

> [It] was developed by The Hofstede Centre in collaboration with itim International, a culture consultancy. The purpose of the survey is to make you aware of potential cultural pitfalls and to increase your effectiveness in dealing with those being born and raised in your country of interest. Since you as a person [in] all likelihood differ from the average person of your home country, this survey will measure your personal preferences in terms of Hofstede's model in order to give advice as accurately as possible. Your personal preferences will be compared to the average value pattern of your country of interest. (Hofstede Centre n.d.)

This proposes the obvious: you and your culture are not the same.

And of all the factors involved, whether it be individualism, risk, or the other factors that Hofstede has identified, one not directly dealt with is speed. Add to this advertising's main purpose, which is to connect the consumer with the wanted device, service, or whatever when the decision to purchase has been made. The sooner, the better. In fact, some commercials are pretty blatant about stating that automobile insurance research takes only fifteen minutes, as if taking longer than that on something that costs several hundred dollars and protects things that cost several thousand dollars is a waste of time. We live in a do-it-now culture where taking time to actually think through an otherwise important, complex decision—whether auto insurance, marriage, or presidential elections—is important, but just to be made, like, immediately.

Apps help us do this by focusing the gathering of information to one subject: let's consider building a new house so that the choices can be narrowed to a particular architect whose design includes just what we are seeking. Of course, this leads to the information seeker getting information snarkled (*snarkled*: misled without knowing you have been misled).

> I do not think that I could live the life that I live now without the Internet. I rely heavily on the Internet for a lot of things such as online classes, communication with people, and finding information quickly. Of course if it came down to it I could live without it, but it would take some adjusting. Even at K-State I rely heavily on the Internet in order to find out information about my classes, upcoming events, and enrolling in school. Without the Internet, these activities that would normally take me a couple minutes would take a lot more time out of my day. For the most part I do trust the Internet. In my opinion the Internet is safe if you are careful about which sites you visit and what information you give out. If you put out all of your personal information onto the Internet and it gets hacked, it is really your own fault for giving out that information. The

only time that I have been concerned is when buying something online and having to put in information such as my address and credit card number. A part of me is always worried that somehow someone will get ahold of the credit card number and use it! —Mackenzie

TIMING IS IMPORTANT, BUT SO IS CREDITABILITY . . . MAYBE

The economic barriers that served to maintain a degree of difference among cultures (and brands) are evaporating. Driven by global advertising messages, global consumers will buy globally, without preference for locality, except as it adds to the purchase decision. That is, a consumer in Texas will be as likely to purchase a sweater made in South Africa as in Dallas, without consideration of the design, fabric, or colors. Cultural icons will no longer be tied to geographics, but to online groups that defy demographic, psychographic, or any other traditional marketing "boxes." Advertising will be targeted to the individual and that individual's behavior.

Project ourselves forward fifty years, and it is likely that we will have each created our own marketing channel, or at least we will believe we have. Each channel will be built on what we have learned from market information devices (that we currently call "apps"). We will channel our desires through the device, which will learn and adapt its "thinking" to anticipate our desires. Now here's the interesting challenge: will our new device be built to change as we do now, or will it be likely to "defend" an existing set of consumer beliefs and preferences? Good question. The average global consumer in fifty years will be very individualized, yet very similar culturally with others (so much so that the idea of culture may be only that of subcultures). How could such a disparity come to be? Easy: apps. Apps reflect our desire for information, largely advertising, in a form we choose to access (versus having it shoved at us) and in an environment of our choosing. Apps will have raised advertising to the highest form of information by rendering it available to the seekers when and where they want it.

Of course, apps do not guarantee accuracy. But then, what does?

REFERENCES

Burke, Bruce. 2013. "My Products." *m-ize*. http://m-ize.com/my-products-from-m-ize-helps-consumers-shop-smarter-socially.

Hofstede Centre. n.d. http://geert-hofstede.com/cultural-survey.html.

"World Economy." 2003. *Wikipedia*. http://en.wikipedia.org/wiki/World_economy.

Chapter Seven

Online Advertising and Risk, Elitism, and Gender

Whenever I am online I always think about if people can see what I am doing and it is kind of scary to think about. You look at all of these hackers these days, such as the Lizard squad who hacked Xbox and PS4, [and] it is hard to feel comfortable putting personal information out there. However, it is almost like the Internet is a necessity in this day [and] age. For example, look at us all now, typing on the Internet. Although I am guilty of using the Internet on a regular basis, I do not know if it is worth it putting personal information on it, such as addresses and credit card information, because you can never ensure that it won't fall into the wrong hands. I am very cautious though going about what I open on the Web and what Web sites are worthy of my personal information. —Ryan

In many ways, advertising has acted as a creator and maintainer of groups. You were cool if you used brand X, certainly cooler than those who used brand Y. Notably, the message was couched as being part of a group that used brand X and their general coolness compared to the group that used brand Y. Advertising acted as a glue that pulled people together and kept them together. The role of advertising has not changed much, but perhaps the interpretation of its role has. That is, advertising may have become both a general method to reach a general audience (the masses) and also a method crafted to reach an individual with an individualized message actually created by the information target. And, if you are curious (and, of course you are, otherwise why would you be reading this book?), the trend seems to be heading in the direction of the latter. Individuals are crafting messages for themselves, or at least they think they are. Revisiting the Coke "commercial event" involving machines in Lahore, Pakistan, and New Delhi, India, made clear that the actual "commercial" was both the shared video of the idea, the

137

creation and use of the devices, and the actual event itself (Coca-Cola 2013). That is, we watch a commercial while those in the commercial create a personal commercial for themselves. The brand is not overtly expressed but always present as the positive result of sharing and friendship. The understated brand message embedded subtly in the event may be the big brand method of the future.

This ability to create and be created—an act and an action that are both active and passive—provides the brand a way of reaching and communicating with those who are moved by the message while they watching passively and at the same time motivating those who are actively present to create the message. The passive commercial is "narrated" by the active innovators who are anything but passive. They are engaged in the event, in the act that they see as unique and personal, edgy, and new. The brand becomes a gateway to solutions to a bigger challenge, something unsolvable by nations. Culture becomes the baseline, not so much the nations, which—at least in this Coca-Cola commercial—are seen as ineffective at best, if not harmful to the togetherness sought by those present. The subtle need for the individual is to sense a power over the outcome suggested by the advertising. Inclusion of the consumer in the "conclusion" suggested by the commercial empowers the individual to believe in her- or himself. Ensuring that each individual feels that he or she has a significant role in the discussion/evolution/dialogue is more than simply carrying forward a conversation with a target consumer; it is everything that will mean anything in modern advertising. Making absolutely certain that the conclusion arrived at in the commercial is presented— as in Coca-Cola's "Small World Machines" commercial—is both the film crew working for the agency and those participating in the creation of the spot itself. They are not presented as actors, but as "real" people, "normal" people, people very much just like everyone else (but also unique).

Is this the future of advertising (at least for big brands)? A far more complex conversation with the target, an engagement with the participants in the creation of the message, an enchantment with those watching the message as it seems to be created in front of their eyes?

Likely.

The ability to engage the target in creating an advertisement is too alluring to miss. The chance to capture the honest reaction of the target consumer in what amounts to an honest appraisal of the brand is too valuable to pass up. Here we have advertising at its height: the consumer is the actual creator and consumer, one and the same. Of course, the same issues are involved: is the message so narrowly crafted that only one person understands it? Is the brand so narrowly defined by the consumer that the message cannot be shared with other consumers and have any efficacy?

For the consumer, the issues are the same, just ramped up a bit (as all things are when the Internet is involved): is the new product too risky/boring?

Are advertising messages more keenly created with dialed-in accuracy to match the right message to the right personality, to the right elite, to the right gender?

Will new advertising messages require new media planning, which changes the roles of those who were once called media buyers into something more than just advertising planners, but rather someone who tracks consumer activities, seeking a pattern that reveals the "sweet spot" that has been desperately sought for decades: what is the target doing right now that matches the intended commercial message? This coincidental matching of a consumer's headache with a commercial message for aspirin is the golden key, the X factor that advertising creative directors and media planners have chased for decades: trying to blend a lot of talent with a little luck. Online, it is a ramped-up world requiring more of all-of-the above talent, plus even more luck. No one knows for sure who is on the other side of the computer screen, but then no one never knew for sure who was watching the television, either. What is different, of course, is the ability of watchers to become players, and players to become creators. Ideas spun off each other in the earlier days, and they still are. But more ideas are generated and launched into actual "programs," whether Angry Birds, FarmVille, or who knows what.

Yet, in a way, the message is changed from something connected, however remotely to other different content, to a stand-alone series of programs: we have dozens of versions of Angry Birds. We never had more than two or three spinoffs from sitcoms and dramas. Yes, we have *NCIS, NCIS-LA*, and *NCIS-NO*, and no doubt a new *NCIS* at some point. The recipe is pretty simple. In fact, most stories are similar, whether online or on the air: we have a hero, a fatherly sage, a perky youngster, a romantic figure, and a smart one who seemingly knows everything. That works for *NCIS* or Dungeons and Dragons or most works by Shakespeare.

So what makes the online world so attractive for viewers, and how can an advertising agency actually track this with something other than a generic advertisement that suggests the viewer purchase product A? Does the app define the user or simply the user at the time the app is used? That is, can someone who plays Age of War also play FarmVille? Of course they *can*, but, more to the point, *do* they? Or are the apps so different that users define themselves as members of another category? You are an online card-game player, or you are an online story game player. Of course, this is the challenge that plagued agencies in the now-fading television age. Who watched what was always the biggest question. Online watching adds a few more elements: when and where. With the exception of sports, as we have discussed, online content is largely asynchronous. Watchers watch when they want to watch it. Setting aside the debate over sports, which is still largely unresolved (and getting more so), online watchers are users of content when they want to use it, where they want to watch it, and how they want to watch it (uninterrupted or in bits).

The solution to date for providers like YouTube is to offer viewers an advertising opt-out bar that they can manually close. Irritating? You betcha. Is the advertising related to what is being searched for/watched? Theoretically. Doubtless thousands, perhaps hundreds of thousands of surveys are being conducted (uselessly) in an attempt to find out how users feel about opt-bars, when even those conducting the surveys (a lousy social science research tool, IMHO) know that the bars are irritating for 99 percent of the viewers. These bars are simply the easiest, not the most precise, way to reach potential targets. Yes, they sometimes offer some accuracy, as defined by the agency/client, but rarely is the definition anything more than a broadly defined term: after all, we do want hits, right? That is, even today, when offered a tool that offers incredible precision of matching the right message to the right consumer, the copy/image still will be somewhat generic to ensure some responses. The logic is that a message that draws a thousand hits that generate five leads that provide one close is more comfortable for the agency than a message that draws five hits that provides one close. Logical, no. Predictable, of course!

Let's look at a handful of online platforms intended to reach the consumer, starting with Amazon.com.

> I believe the Internet can be as invasive as you allow it to be. In other words, if you throw around your credit card and personal information on shared public domains and blogging Web sites or whatever, there's a better chance cyber theft might take place. On the other hand, if you are tentative with giving out personal information, use firewalls when in public venues, and don't purposely go to malicious Web sites, the Internet is not all that dangerous. Yes, if someone who is capable of hacking wanted to, they may be able to access your information, but you could compare that to robbery. Someone could break into your house and steal your stuff. Is it likely? Probably not. Is it possible? Of course it is. We are only as vulnerable as we allow ourselves to be on the Internet. I for one am very protective of my information on my computer and hardly ever give out personal information even on social media. I believe I do have control over my precious data through the use of antivirus programs, firewalls, multiple passwords and data encryption, and by not being ignorant of the dangers the Internet holds. So, yes, I absolutely believe it is worth it to surf the Web and discover the endless opportunities it holds and will continue to do so. However, I will not be doing that blindly and will always have my guard up to its pitfalls. —Connor

EVERYTHING SOLD TO EVERYONE, EVERYWHERE, AND—OH YEAH—FREE SHIPPING!

I could fill a lot of pages with recent data about how much Amazon.com has sold lately. I could relate the history of this massive economic wonder. But in the first case, the numbers would be ancient by the time this book is published, and if you are at all interested in the latter, well, the whole story is available on Wikipedia. No, let's consider a different tale, one that considers not so much how Amazon.com was created or who created it but why. Why would something that requires such an incredible amount of trust and willingness to take chances be rewarded with millions of transactions daily? The tale to be told goes back a bit.

Over the centuries, we've witnessed a variety of financial meltdowns in the Western world. One common denominator has been a degree of trust placed in certain individuals or groups to do some particular thing, whether that be mining copper in South America, growing cotton in Georgia, or farming in a variety of places around the globe. All of these activities were accompanied by financial loans that guaranteed success or that at least presumed success when perhaps that was a bad idea. And, as might be argued, as time rolled along, more of these presumptions were guaranteed by individuals than groups. That is, whereas we had groups and corporations in London backing copper mines in South America in the nineteenth century, we saw individuals putting together deals more and more as the twentieth century passed. Some of the most famous failures occurred in the last years of the century.

So, how could a company in the new century convince an individual to put money "out there" with the hope of actually receiving the paid-for property, be it a book, a frying pan, or a ball of twine? Good question. But a question answered quite successfully by Amazon.com. For its success was not born of the advertising (there was little), the marketing (again, very little), or even the public relations (for which there was a modicum). Something else happened, and it was not at Amazon.com but in the brains of millions of potential consumers/users.

Students who have taken any of my courses that deal with advertising and who—purely by accident—encounter this text would be shocked to learn that I do not believe the success of Amazon.com was due to its brand. At least, not its early success. Brands are created by consumers based upon expectations and satisfaction that the expectations were to be met. That is a very brief definition of branding, an idea that has generated books. Bottom line: consumers do not like to be disappointed. McDonald's sells billions of hamburgers, and most will agree that these are not the greatest hamburgers ever made. But consumers know what they are getting. Expectations are met.

So what does Amazon.com provide?

Well, it wasn't trust, at least not early on. Trust requires some degree of a track record, some history that transactions occurred and product was delivered as promised. This may be the biggest barrier to the success for another major online market vendor, eBay, which has had some cases of products being paid for but not sent to the buyers. Such cases were few, but it doesn't take many to spoil the stew.

The success of Amazon.com may be, at least in part, due to the readiness of certain global consumers—yes, largely in the West—to take the risk. This is no small thing. Yes, it required a degree of trust based on little or no information. Yes, it involved relatively cheap transactions of books, for the most part. Yes, the minimal trust extended by Amazon asked for little beyond the understanding that what was not acceptable could be returned, no questions asked, and—as would become more important—no shipping would be required. And unlike eBay, Amazon.com is a very large operation that involves so much more than, well, seemingly edgy, slightly strange things.

But the individuals performing this act of risk were doing so in numbers not seen historically. We are traditionally cautious regarding some actions. So what makes Amazon.com a "safer" risk than prior similar challenges? Perhaps it was the timing, not so much of Amazon, but of more in numbers, and more in willingness to take more and more risk "iUsers."

Amazon.com did not create new risk takers. It did not create a new brand of people willing to enter credit card numbers into unknown sites for uncertain results. The relationship between Amazon.com and the online user was defined by the user, both in terms of timing and frequency. The actual purchase was an afterthought. What we have here is no less than a fifteenth-century risk taker whose willingness to take a risk shifted from the parting of the head from its shoulders to the parting of currency from the wallet. Early users of Amazon.com were hardly hanging around East End alleys, but they were—at least in terms of online behavior—taking a major chance of being robbed.

The thrill of getting a book must have included the actual method in which the book was received. Of course, today books are more and more the product of the download: printed books are giving way to ebooks. We could spend pages and perhaps chapters discussing the shift from paper to bytes as I have in other books and research, but what is striking here is not the shift from print to electronics, but rather the willingness of consumers in very large numbers to conduct what amounts to an act of elitism with those they do not know, over property they have not seen, with outcomes not guaranteed. Posed to Supreme Court Justice Kennesaw Mountain Landis some decades ago, he might have repeated his declaration that the courts could and would not protect fools.

And are these consumers of online goods actually fools? After all, they have no recourse; in some cases, the seller turns out not to be in Atlanta, Georgia, but in some far away, largely (more) unregulated country. Indeed, in some cases, recouping losses domestically can be drawn out and difficult. So how is Amazon.com so successful?

Because, in a global world, numbers mean almost everything.

Elitism, defined in terms of a total global perspective, places millions of online commerce users into a class that they might not belong to in any other way. That is, you may be a uniquely elite online shopper but in all other aspects of your life remain in the terribly safe, dull thrall of suburban life. You take care that your hoses are stored and nothing is left outside, but you freely and seemingly comfortably shop online. That individuals do this, uniquely enough, is precisely why computers were built: use by one person. Groups find it hard to work on one device. Special group work sites have been created for individuals to work with other individuals.

Thus, when we consider global commerce, we think in terms of billions of users and trillions in rewards. Even the success of Amazon.com in such a landscape is minuscule. Here is an area that is moving past Anderson's long tail theory: even those who can claim to be the largest suppliers of a product are just blips in the global commerce occurring now. Anderson's thinking that there would be a few dominating players may be overwhelmed by the acts of individual consumers who choose individual sources based not on their Walmart-weight quality, but their subject specificity as defined by— who else?—the users themselves. We in the advertising world have worked within an environment where we controlled pretty much everything. No more. Consumers will use Amazon.com and the hundreds, perhaps thousands, and eventually millions of sites that will deliver what is desired: the right product for that unique consumer at the right time, the right place, and the right price. Advertising's role is important, make no mistake. But the precision and control it had in the 1980s is gone. The consumer elites are at the steering wheel. The direction that consumers take will be based in no small way on the opinions of other users not perhaps on the advertising. Not to suggest that advertising won't have a role in narrowing the selection field, but the ultimate decision will no longer be based on some form of physical interaction created in the 1960s. When it comes to the choice of who delivers a product, the decision of the consumer might be based in part on the experiences of others (chat rooms, blogs, etc.), but that secondhand information itself may be based on information provided by online users or sellers.

Bottom line: the clarity of information is being overwhelmed by the quantity of information. In the case of Amazon.com, a great deal of effort is put forward to enable users to provide information to other users. The accuracy of that information is, well, not part of the discussion. In fact, given that many information providers (we used to call them publishers and corporations) have hired public relations professionals to post on sites without revealing their associations, we have or should have very real doubts about message boards. But users seem not to be as fearful as we are, perhaps in part because the goal for information gatherers is to locate the negative posts on boards versus the positive posts. The logic is simple: negatives can be trusted more than positives.

But can they? After all, what keeps a representative from company B from posting some trash about a product sold by company A on product A's blog or Web site? Some critics of "modern" public relations wonder if this is at least a day's lecture in a universe course: how to fudge your competitor's product in their territory. Muddying the waters works both ways: both positive and negative. Lies are not always pointed in one direction, though I doubt many online information seekers keep that in mind. How hard would it be to trash a new, otherwise superior product? Not hard at all. The strategy may not be something you'd be proud of, but it works just fine to diminish or even increase a competitor's user information collection zone (this used to be called "consumer letters"), filling it with lies about new products or services. Has this happened? Who knows? We seem so much more obsessed with big events (North Korea blocking the release of a film) than whether the average post regarding a product on Amazon.com is valid. The lack of any real involvement to clarify valid posts from scum posts is more an issue of the far simpler "hands-off" mantra of the corporate site provider, even though the initial use was by the network provider, not the content provider. That is, it is one issue to suggest that a cable provider has no responsibility for content than to suggest that Amazon.com or other such sites have no responsibility for content in their user-generated areas.

The fascinating part about the "discussion" that occurs regarding whether a post is valid is that Amazon.com (and the thousands of similar, smaller commercial sites) has remained neutral on the issue, almost as if they can act as information providers in much the same ways that AT&T acted as copper providers with little or no interest regarding what passed through the wires.

> In answering your question, I do trust the Internet, but I always have to have my guard up. I think the amount of trust we put into the Internet is pretty interesting especially considering how easy it is to access information and how easy it is for others to access your own personal information. With the recent hacking of Sony, I think people are starting to realize just how unsafe the Internet can be and it serves as a good example that maybe there should be better security and online regulations that can save people from losing their identity. But at the same time we do need the Internet and we rely on it every day, so it is all about finding a happy medium and having the will to see past the risk in order to get to the information (the reward). I believe it is all about figuring out the risk and deciding whether the information that the Internet possesses is worth it, but at the same time at what cost is it worth it? This is a

problem people face every day when deciding whether they want to check their bank statement online or buy something online even though they are faced with the fear that their credit card information and bank information could be stolen. In today's society, the Internet is very high risk, high reward, and my hope is that we realize this and turn it into a low risk, high reward tradeoff. —Andrew

CHANGING THE PURCHASE EXPERIENCE

You have selected what you think is the best item for you and now approach the checkout counter. How well the person behind the counter handles the exchange of cash or credit for the item is part of your shopping experience. If they are grouchy, angry, spiteful—well, you get it. That person puts a negative exclamation point on what otherwise might have been a great shopping experience. If the experience had already been a rough one, well, so much for ever returning to that store.

But does online shopping remove this possible negative outcome?

Well, the personal touch is gone, which of course means that the ability to saunter up to the bar and be recognized is gone. The consumer is #13836492384701 as far as the computer is concerned and holds all of the personal traits that #13836492384701 would have. But the computer is never angry, never grouchy, never short with a customer. If you are selling something bereft of emotion, maybe concrete or rocks, a pleasant checkout is hardly necessary. But if you are purchasing flowers to plant or fencing to install, wouldn't a chance to create a personal relationship with the consumer be of some value to both the seller and the buyer?

Amazon.com eliminates that, though it tries mightily to seem personal, with its personalized lists of books to read and suggested items "also purchased" to help consumers consider other options. But is that really anything other than an attempt to extend the sale?

Becoming cynical about the sincerity of commercial sites is too easy. All attempts to present a personalized front come across as just that, a personalized front to an otherwise computer-driven, mechanical, impersonal, switch-bound, neutral, colorless, emotionless device. Of course, one might argue that this device is far more accurate than a human, but is it? It can be and has been argued that computer programs that drive mechanized devices are no more accurate than the humans who created them. Thus, the ability of Amazon.com to guarantee 100 percent accuracy of every transaction is more of an advertising ploy than a legal promise. No one is perfect.

But, consumers expect everything (except themselves) to be perfect. So what Amazon.com must deliver is the illusion that everything that can be found can be found on its Web site at the lowest possible price (including pricing for used versions), along with the option for free shipping for the patient consumer. This somehow is a substitute for the personal transaction one receives at the local bookstore.

And although now many of us can deny ever having a "personal" relationship with the bookstore cashier, few of us fifty years ago didn't know our pharmacist. I must admit that I have a brother who has several certificates on his office wall proclaiming his abilities in pharmacology. It was he who related to me the general ignorance of physicians in the area of drug science, given, as he noted, that most are required to take only one course in pharmacology in medical school. Pharmacists are the ones to trust when it comes to making sure that drug A and drug B do not result in convulsion C and death D. "Docs," he said with spirit, "know nothing."

Yet consumers are willing to deal with pharmacists online, which is a step more removed from those at big box stores. Yes, these online pharmacies are cheaper, but we are not talking about an air filter for your car engine. We are considering products that can (and have) led to death when taken incorrectly. This risk taking in some areas may defy Hofstede's dimensions of culture: need may overcome fear, cheaper prices may justify taking uncalled-for leaps. Nothing defines risk so well as the willingness of a person to do something dangerous based solely on need versus logic, weighing of options, and consideration of all outcomes.

In all of this, the elimination of the person-to-person relationship for the sake of convenience and price seems a poor choice, no matter how much time or currency is saved. We are trading our own selves for little. Yes, we will likely always have Kramer's Bookstore just off Dupont Circle in Washington, D.C., but that store is for the elite. Just as universities are more and more becoming a place of learning only for those who can afford them, a bookstore with actual books in it will become a place for those who can actually afford to purchase one at an elevated price. I imagine some will allow the rest of us to look and not buy, but not that many.

At the end of that day, Amazon.com is a circus maximus for the non-elite: those served at a distance, those who do not deserve personal attention. This all sounds far too personal and cruel. But the culture of an online-based global economy is not based on equality but efficiency. We are not cooing over the petite madeline of Proust but the wafers at 99 cents for five pounds. In a very real sense, Amazon.com represents in concrete terms the division between haves and have-nots: we can, at best, make the life of the lower middle class more efficient, less colorful.

Finally, here's a nugget to consider: what if the ability to easily publish has rendered our works less challenging, less worthy, less valuable to the world of progress? Publishing's barriers didn't always guarantee that great books were allowed through the gates of review, but they presumably kept more of the poor works on the author's shelves and not in the bookstores. What if everything is published? What if the act of publishing is no longer part of the standard of good versus not-so-good? How will we be able to tell if what we are about to purchase is Proust's standard or something not so good? As Emerson pointed out two centuries ago, it will forever be the silly writers who will be the most popular, but we have taken that population of poor authors to a universal limit that does none of us any good.

> It really is hard to say if I, or anyone in my situation, could live without the Internet. Logistically speaking, yes, of course we could survive, but many of us have grown up with the Internet as our biggest source of information and entertainment. Because we have grown up with it, we tend to have some sort of innate trust in its inability to betray us and share or exploit our personal information. I have had a new way of balancing privacy and my need to surf since my grandma has found her way onto social media. It quite literally is the concept of only spouting out information you would want your grandmother to see. Also, the possibility of future employers having the capability to view what I have published to the Internet has made me err on the side of professionalism. I think the value of the Internet varies from person to person. Someone who is starting their own business and looking for a platform to get themselves out there is going to find more worth in the Internet than, say, Bill Snyder. After weighing the pros of the Internet and how I apply it and its resources in my life versus the likelihood of the cons, it becomes easy to say it is very much worth the risk. —Carolina

HAVE AN IDEA? MAKE IT AVAILABLE NOW!

Publishing has over the centuries progressed from cave walls to papyrus to lambskin to paper to bits. As it evolved, the ability to create works has moved from the group (society, community, government) to the individual. The shift is irresistible. Individuals wish to express themselves without the constraints of opinions once offered by others (peer review). What we have is wholesale publishing in an environment that allows authors to create printed volumes on demand and online volumes in infinite, inexhaustible amounts. What is not included is quality as a measure of purchase, and, given the success of some authors, nothing could be more obvious. But the real issue is how the information, created in the billions of volumes, is used by others. Here's what is hanging in the balance: progress. Without quality controls, how do we ensure that we are moving in something remotely like forward motion? That is, merely creating lots of "stuff" is no substitute for creating smaller amounts of "good stuff."

Google provides a landing zone for a lot of information, including what might be categorized as advertising or public relations (i.e., information promoting the sale or image of a product, service, person, or corporation). The problem—at least for some—is that neither advertising nor public relations offers any verification of what is being posted. In advertising, verification has not been an issue until recently. The Federal Trade Commission's (and its international equivalents') dealings with national and local advertising's evils were always seen as limited. In public relations, the assumption has been for decades that the "flack" was always pushing the best side, despite what the truth represented.

Google and other major information sites provide the data but fail to offer the seeker any way to determine whether, for instance, what is being posted on a blog within the site is filled with honest posters or paid shysters. The difference is significant. Most potential buyers are looking not so much for positives but negatives, working on the naive but understandable notion that negatives are more likely to be more "honest" than positives. After all, a positive post could be a paid representative for company A posting on company A's Web site or blog. What is not always clear is that nothing prevents company A's paid representative from posting something negative (found or otherwise) on company B's blog without revealing the connection to company A. This is just one form of using a new media device to attack a competitor. No doubt offending company A would argue that it is merely providing valuable information that company B is failing to include. But then, the nagging question remains why, if not self-evident, the connection between company A and its posting representative remains unrevealed.

Another possible danger hangs out "there" for information seekers and corporations: phishing. As Wikipedia describes it (and yes, I like Wikipedia for some citations):

> Phishing is typically carried out by email spoofing or instant messaging, and it often directs users to enter details at a fake website whose look and feel are almost identical to the legitimate one. Phishing is an example of social engineering techniques used to deceive users and exploits the poor usability of current web security technologies. Attempts to deal with the growing number of reported phishing incidents include legislation, user training, public awareness, and technical security measures. . . . Phishing is a continual threat that keeps growing to this day. The risk grows even larger in social media such as Facebook, Twitter, Myspace etc. Hackers commonly use these sites to attack persons using these media sites in their workplace, homes, or public in order to take personal and security information that can affect the user and the company (if in a workplace environment). Phishing is used to portray trust in the user since the user may not be able to tell that the site being visited or program being used is not real, and when this occurs is when the hacker has the chance to access the personal information such as passwords, usernames, security codes, and credit card numbers among other things. ("Phishing" 2004)

The interesting element in this is the reliance on trust. So much harm caused in modern human interactions evolves from a violation of trust, as interpreted by those who feel wounded. In peer review, violations of trust go back centuries and are examples of the depth of rationalization to which some can rise in order to cover their foul behavior. In academic interactions, the use of power and rank forever have been tools of those lacking ability to further stall and frustrate those more able. In research, it has been used as a way to steal, delay, cancel, deny, and in so many other ways destroy the solid work of some, at the false betterment of others (Gould 2013, 174).

But where does Google fit into all of this? After all, in a way, all it provides is a better highway, a faster elevator, a smoother access. It does not have a role in directing or pushing people one way or another. It is the highway. The accidents that occur on it are not its fault.

Or are they?

Consider if I build a road (we might as well stay with this scenario) of the quality of an interstate highway, complete with on and off ramps, four lanes separated by concrete barriers, and set the speed limit to ten miles per hour. I would expect few, if any, accidents. I would also expect few, if any, drivers (users). I would also expect few, if any, police (regulators) watching what is happening on my highway. Finally, I would expect, little, if any, traffic (productivity and hence progress). Somehow this is not what we think is happening with Google.

What if the Google highway has no limits regarding speed. Anyone can drive as fast as they wish (gathering as much data as they wish)? Okay, the anarchy would be a bit of a nuisance, but that nuisance would be visited upon everyone in something of an egalitarian sort of way. No rules, no barriers, no standards. Yes, progress would be popping up from time to time, but few would notice, and fewer would be available to make the judgment.

Finally, let us consider a Google thoroughfare that provides a variety of lanes available to different types of users based on Google standards. Yes, I am raising the issue of elitism again; however, in a world driven by economics, what would not define and shape the future world of an information controller than currency and status? Either would gain a user access to information in the fastest, most valuable fashion. In a universe of individuals, elitism is a standard accepted and valued. Consider a post to a blog by a student in an online class I taught during the winter 2015 intersession here at Kansas State University:

> I personally don't watch much TV at all. When I use Netflix it is usually just to watch a movie, every once in a while I might go and watch a series that I liked or new ones that people have suggested, but I don't keep up with it. The one major difference I can say would be the commercials; people enjoy the fact that they can skip the ever-growing ads and commercials on Netflix and You-Tube. . . . I don't pay for cable at all and I enjoy saving that bit of money. Watching TV via Internet does put a lot more control in the consumers' hands and makes for a more individualized approach from advertisers and Web sites because not everyone is watching the same thing at the same time anymore.

This thing that Internet-based TV watching is changing [is] the amount of
young people that watch or pay attention to their local news. —Erin

Here we have traditional television being delivered via a network platform
that seemingly changes the actual programming so much that the user does
not consider the program something originally built for a technology that is
clearly fading into the background of this new generation. Yes, a mouthful,
but worthy of some consideration. We are stepping away from using the
source of the information as part of the way we value and measure the
veracity of the information.

If you are younger than thirty, that may not seem like much of an issue. If
you are older than fifty, the lack of a source as a measure of veracity is a big
deal. Information supplied to you via the *New York Times* was of more value
to you than the *Detroit Free Press*, which was of more value than the *Savannah Morning News*. The comparisons are easy and transparent, at least to
those born before 1960. Those born after 1990 couldn't care less.

The comparison becomes even more extreme when we examine advertising pre- and post-Google. Advertising's veracity lies upon a few standards.
Does the message actually contain information that requires some evaluation
as to its truthfulness? Lacking that, the rest of any advertising evaluation is a
short trip. Any history of advertising analyzed for the use of information
versus the spending for time or space would suggest that we have gone from
lots of information (however doubtful in its veracity) to less and less as the
previous century passed. Today, most advertising is entertaining, informing,
persuasive, but not presumptively irritating or insulting. What Google allows
is a complete reversal of the traditional advertising model from the advertiser
confronting the potential consumer with a message to the potential consumer
seeking out information possibly related to a potential purchase.

Two injured elements lie upon the field of Google (global) commerce: the
big box stores today and, soon, "the brand." Now, I admit that many will
agree with the first as fait accompli (I like to toss in a little French now and
then). But the second? Now, that's a step off the board at the deep end. For
more than half a century, advertising has been built on the singular concept
that "the brand" is not just number one, but it is everything in the mind of the
consumer. Protecting that brand, nurturing the consumer's feelings toward
the product or service that bears that brand is not just advertising's number-one job, it also represents the certainty of losing a client by seeing the brand's
share fall.

So, what do I mean when I suggest that Google will strip a brand of its
consumer loyalty (note that I am not putting this as "stripping a consumer of
brand loyalty")? If the consumers know everything about the product, what
can a commercial possibly transmit to them? Emotion? Yes, but much as
successful commercials of the past used emotion to succeed, they presumed

the target consumer knew next to nothing about the product and could be convinced by a deeply affective story. Consumers are armed with tools that allow them to know information about products and services to a degree that no advertising agency has ever had to face. Smart consumers are just part of what advertisers are dealing with here; this is setting that consumer at the center of the decision-making process and hoping that something good happens. Such wishful thinking is not the "sold" rationale for a multimillion advertising campaign.

So agencies are adding new media, looking at new methods of analysis, and promoting new methods of reaching the target consumer with a message. But, at the end of the day, the consumer is far more powerfully armed with just Google (let's not even consider the dozens of minor, more exquisitely targeted search engines) than are all the agency's copywriters and art directors. The battle is lost.

Using Google to learn about "what I should buy" has rendered advertising moot. User-generated content, whether valid or not, is the current trusted tool of the shopper. Using what others say about this shirt, those screwdrivers, that bar, this car is much more common and seems more effective than the countless advertisements that extend a one-hour-and-forty-five-minute movie to three hours. Oddly enough, consumers do not like commercials. Perhaps the dislike arises because 98 percent of the commercials are not targeting them to begin with.

What Google has done is turn the information management power away from the client and its advertising agency and given it to the target consumer. But the real damage here is not the profits of Procter & Gamble (which are at an all-time high, as is its stock). The damage is to all the brands held by P&G. They are all now competing with everything on something other than a brand-reputation basis. Is it price driven? Possibly. Is the reputation of Bounce what it always has been? Possibly. But the erosion of the impervious brand is already under way. Alternatives are being offered. The very real possibility exists that the danger may be generated by the consumer's access to information, not just to some information, but to all information. That is, the consumer cannot be swayed by information.

So what is left? What are we losing with Google-like advertising information systems? Perhaps the ability to influence consumers to make the right or wrong decision. But, really, was that ever ethical? If it was, why would so much of advertising education be spent on ethics of the trade itself?

I KNOW YOU ARE OUT THERE — I CAN SEE THE APP

Many of us who teach advertising and were once in advertising professionally consider the shift toward apps a very dangerous pattern. We are still struggling to deal with social media in general and a great number of us do not believe that the Web is as powerful as it actually is, much less that the Internet rules the universe and all that. We are solidly convinced that our math can predict who buys what. We, for whatever reason, trust numbers more than we do emotions arising with cultures, and we cling to the myth that our consumers act in groups rather than individualized buyers and brand creators. But all the evidence tells us that consumers are creating their own worlds, and a major way this is happening is via apps.

Oddly enough, the ability to use applications has more to do with the willingness of an individual to spend time creating a small program that pretty much does one thing and one thing only. This takes us back to the very early days of computer entertainment in the form of two moving panels on opposite sides of the screen with a ball that bounced back and forth between them. Pong pitted two players against each other. A number of apps do that today, while others allow individuals to join teams that go out into the wilderness to seek both individual and a form of (possibly real) group victory.

But in general, apps are tools for individuals, whether the task involves a quest or balancing a checking account; the individual takes on the task at hand and earns a solo victory. The need for any allies is limited, minor, and entirely voluntary. Thus, even when an ally is added, that act is one of an individual acting as an individual with the assurance that at any time the alliance can be broken (sounds like "defriending," yes?).

We have no other way to characterize it: apps encourage individuation.

We are at the very edge of this new form of information transfer. Frankly, we have only hints about the directions it might take us (plug "future of information transfer" into your browser's search function). What we do know for sure is that the direction will not be unified, but instead diverse, possibly with millions of directions. Apps are certainly capable of providing what we would describe as "fun" and "entertaining." They can share what is useful and helpful. They can even give us information that might save our lives (think: WebMD on a handheld). But they can also offer a hate group an echo chamber of information vile and evil in nature, which allows it to justify any act, including the massacre of dozens of schoolchildren. These tiny tools are a perfect example of faulty human thinking that either presumes that something is right because it always has been judged as right (tradition) or cannot right because it is not like anything heretofore experienced (risk). In neither case is the value of progress included in the calculations. We are not interested in the success of change but the certainty of solidity. Thus change, when it does occur, is highlighted as a huge event, a massive risk taken and overcome.

Apps are small victories offered to the individual to succeed, whether in straightening out vital financial reports or eliminating certain rascally pigs.

And perhaps the two actions are drawn a bit closer to holding equal value to the user, though that frankly deserves some research not conducted to date.

Perhaps the most interesting part of the entire app world is the arrangement of finances. Here is where things get very interesting. Nowhere is the application of Chris Anderson's long tail theory more appropriate and useful in a descriptive way. Prior to the app world, millionaires were made—at least for those who were not inheriting wealth—through the creation of a better invention that probably sold for much more than a dollar. The creation of such an invention involved many and generally required something akin to a factory.

Now I can become a millionaire through the creation of a simple game that I can sell for 99 cents online with no packaging, no advertising, no shipping, and no handling (whatever that is). An app that sells for less than a dollar, if even mildly popular, can make the inventor wildly rich. We are in a world of millions of users, perhaps over a billion (depending on who is doing the counting). Let's agree that a billion is a reasonable number. A million in sales is around one-tenth of a percent. Yes, we are in the big numbers world, and it doesn't take much to generate a very rich individual making a simple online app in her or his garage on the weekends.

And did I mention there is no (traditional) advertising?

I did not mention it because none was used. Sorry, just not necessary.

BETTER HOMES, BETTER GAMES, BETTER MEALS, BETTER WALKS—JUST BETTER

Honestly, I hate that the Internet has made life easier. The only reason I say that is because if the Internet was never used as a simple tool to find information, it would be less appealing and less addictive. But of course it is as simple as can be to use, and as a result I couldn't live without it, just like everyone else on this planet. I do think that the Internet is pretty invasive if you don't manage your personal information wisely. I was always taught to monitor what I put on the Internet and all other forms of social media. It's worrisome to think that the second that personal information is on the Internet, there is no return or permanent delete. It's scary stuff, if personal information gets into the wrong hands! But then, it is impossible to define whose hands are "wrong" or "right." That's why the Web is such a scary place. I will just continue to remain on the safe side of things by keeping as much personal information to myself as I can. —Ashlynn

The results were so predictable. Just as we as individuals are separating ourselves from others (with the few incidents when we act as groups highlighted as a big thing), sites and apps online are becoming more individualized. This presents an opportunity and challenge for advertising agencies. Let's just toss out the idea of the mass buy, the easy eight-page ad in the *New*

York Times as the sure thing, the solution to all consumer challenges, and better than anything else we can imagine. Let's also accept that not only does the message require quality creation, so does the selection of where this message will appear.

The options are becoming massive and varied. But they are mostly, at least initially, free. Some remain that way, relying on a revenue structure that leverages users with advertisers in a crude, Google-like pay-to-show advertising scheme. Others are more subtle, attracting advertisers without making the involvement so obvious.

Houzz.com is one of the former, targeting a mere twenty-five million homeowners and fewer than a million businesses. The concept is basic: promote a site with images and ideas for homeowners to consider for remodeling (mainly), though some attention is given to new construction. The sharing is done mainly by professionals, though there are some private individuals with their own ideas. The sharing of millions of images within a somewhat narrow subject area (home design) is hardly a new idea for any Web site, much less a site launched in 2013. However, the sense of exclusivity (elitism) just oozes from its pages. These are not traditional homes. These are exclusive, expensive, uniquely designed homes with great ideas. If you are building a home, a source for images is a boon. Comments about the ideas are even better. Add to that a sense of professionalism missing from the far more popular Pinterest and you have what amounts to an elitist Web site for a few million users.

It is not clear that this is what founders Adi Tatarko and Alon Cohen intended on their site:

> A place to browse and save beautiful home photos. A place to find the right design and construction professionals. A place to connect with others who have been there too. Houzz started as a side project but has become a community of more than 25 million homeowners, home design enthusiasts and home improvement professionals—across the country and around the world. ("About Houzz" 2015)

For starters, this site—also available as an app (of course)—is pitched as global, which results in shared ideas (culture) from all areas to all areas. It is also clearly individualized. Nothing about Houzz.com suggests that it is intended for groups. Ideas arise from what feels like singular input to what are clearly singular downloads. That is, the ideas posted are uploaded by a group or corporation but presented more as "Molly's idea." The downloads—like everything else online, it could be argued—are done by an individual. Houzz.com is a great place to share ideas globally, but the result cannot be mistaken or ignored. Sites such as this blend cultures, blur distinctions, destroy uniqueness. We are living more and more like each other, no matter where we are globally, and sites like Houzz.com make it more and more possible.

Does it also diminish the "power distance" as defined by Hofstede? Clearly not. It has just the opposite impact. Elitism is stressed, highlighted. Numbers using the site are presumed to be those who both appreciate its upper-class appeal and the architectural design. This is no site for the neighborhood. It is a great site for some advertisers. Of course, it requires agencies to reconsider the use of traditional media, and that continues to be a hard pill to swallow, whether you are in Kansas City, New York City, or London Town.

THE WORLD IS MY PLAYGROUND (RIGHT NOW), MY KITCHEN, AND MY BACKYARD

ESPN is a world leader. They may or may not be *the* leader. After all, we have lots and lots of sources for sports information. And sometimes a sport that attracts the lowlife pub crowd turns out to be popular elsewhere among those who consider their knowledge regarding the theoretical in-and-outs as signs of their elitism. Some places, the uniform matters. Sometimes, the goals versus midfield steals matter.

Ah, we have a challenge, yes?

As we consider the globe as our marketplace, Houzz.com provides a narrowly defined population. On the other hand, ESPN.com measures viewers in the hundreds of millions. However, whereas Houzz.com faces few competitors, ESPN.com has much more fierce competition, Univision being one that beat it out in broadcasting the 2014 World Cup.

For advertisers, the ESPN site is a challenge. It lacks a uniform audience, such as Houzz.com. It lacks a sense of the specificity that makes talking to a narrow group so much easier. After all, a narrow group might as well be one person. The wider and larger a group gets, the more diverse, more difficult to sharpen the message, and the more likely that the message will be the sort of general nothingness that we see too much of today.

Even more troubling is that sports are generally culturally diverse, even within the fans of the same team. As alluded to earlier, fans of a soccer/futbol team in Spain are likely to draw a culturally different crowd in that native country than in Russia, India, the United States, and Britain. But they are all watching the same game and likely watching it live. That's another distinction between ESPN and all sports sites: the live nature of the message. With exceptions such as the British Open, events are played and watched live, without delay. No saving and watching later, as is the case with almost all other types of programs. Of course, this habit may change. After all, what's to be lost from watching some sporting events the next day, besides betting, online gaming (fantasy teams), and a few other elements that make waiting highly unfavorable? Okay, sports may resist the delayed online viewing that is so successful with almost all other content.

We can also presume that the choices are far more regional and far more narrow geographically (though fantasy games are eroding this). People in Chicago generally pull for Da Bears, people in Detroit not so much. It's a geographic thing.

Two cooking magazines, *Cook's Illustrated* (with no advertisements) and *Cooking Light* (with lots), are great examples of rapidly growing, highly popular printed publications that are as present online as they are in print. Like ESPN.com, they are diverse; unlike ESPN.com, they present few regional offerings that appeal to readers in a specific part of the country. But, at the same time, they are almost exclusively intended for U.S. readers. This isn't obvious, but it is certainly present:

> Recipes in the magazine often utilize unorthodox, but easy, inexpensive, and commonplace ingredients and instructions. For instance, a recipe for Chinese barbecued pork substitutes ketchup for the traditional red bean curd, which can be difficult to find in the United States; a method for improving inexpensive beef roasts suggests turning off the oven during the final hour of cooking to improve the beef's texture; and a recipe for low-fat cookies includes pureed dates, an unorthodox ingredient that the author preferred over more traditional low-fat alternatives. ("*Cook's Illustrated*" 2005)

Cooking Light has experienced roughly the same rise in subscription rates but has a boatload of advertising. The natural desire to compare the two is rendered moot, if only because the two are both small and well targeted with only one exception: advertising. So why are we even talking about both here?

Good question.

The more subtle differences between these two publications are shared by thousands of others within the still-healthy magazine marketplace. Magazines have carved out what seem to be very similar readerships. Consider Eddie Bauer, Patagonia, and REI. One might easily think that these three have much in common when dealing with walks in the woods. One would be demonstrably wrong. Online readers can utilize one to shop, one to scope out a location, and one to research equipment. The purpose of magazines—and with magazines, I include catalogs with varying amounts of reader content like Eddie Bauer, Patagonia, and REI—is to both inform and persuade. It takes only a quick read of the latest issue of almost any magazine such as *Wired* to encounter suggestions about best purchases.

The argument, and a persuasive one at that, can be made that the Web has actually made print journal magazines include content that is more catalog-like and commercial magazines to include content that is informative and newsy. The two food groups are growing together. Now please understand that I am not suggesting that Duluth Trading Company's catalog is a magazine or that *National Geographic* is a catalog (though the latter of these two is more so than one might think). What I am suggesting is that the blending of editorial content and commercial speech is driven by the demands of online readers who want more than a sales pitch and who are open to more than just a story about a great dress but would also like to know where they can buy it.

AND IT ALL ENDS UP ON AN APP

The most fascinating part of the discussion regarding advertising and apps is that most universities that teach advertising still teach media planning as if the calendar still read 1980. I can say this because even at my school, we are just getting around to radically changing media planning, calling it something very different and trying to address the media-driven force: apps. Will it be easy? Absolutely not. We will make changes and edits to the course over the coming decade, I certainly hope.

As apps stretch to create their massive impact on media consumption by readers/consumers, advertising agencies (and eventually schools that teach the craft) will face the reality that the degrees of separation that made placement of commercials so easy are still there, just not as obvious as before. I am certain that some of you wonder exactly what the nature of the new media will be. All I am certain of is that it will be very different than it is even now, and it will be a great deal closer than it is now. Magazines and catalogs, seemingly polar opposites, will become more consumer-defined, one-stop content providers.

And won't that be fun. Maybe.

REFERENCES

"About Houzz." 2015. *Houzz*. http://www.houzz.com/aboutUs.
Coca-Cola. 2013. "Small World Machines." Commercial. Leo Burnett. http://www.youtube.com/watch?v=QGy-5hHQvVw.
"*Cook's Illustrated*." 2005. *Wikipedia*. http://en.wikipedia.org/wiki/Cook's_Illustrated.
Gould, Thomas H. P. 2013. *Do We Still Need Peer Review? An Argument for Change*. Lanham, MD: Scarecrow Press.
"Phishing." 2004. *Wikipedia*. http://en.wikipedia.org/wiki/Phishing.

Chapter Eight

Children Consumed by Convergence via Apps

I think you're right; we are heading towards individualization and I believe that you can see this trend even in different areas other than apps. For example, phones now can be purchased in a different variety of colors, and no longer do we have to settle for the generic stock design. Going along with apps, I think it also allows for a sense of expression. An app, and even where you place it in your phone, can say a lot about someone, and it also allows for the user to control where they place it, whether it be for easy access and efficiency, or placing some apps in groups within the phone to free up space on the screen and clear clutter. I actually like this trend that we are heading towards because in the not-so-distant future, I want to be able to customize and personalize as much as I can to make for an optimal experience with whatever product or brand it may be. —Andrew

In 1900 London (and elsewhere), children were considered nothing less than small adults, dressed accordingly and treated with the expectation of being able to read Greek and Latin and knowing a great deal more about society than our Western children do today. That's a broad statement. Perhaps too broad, but close enough to describe the children who lived at the core of mid- to upper-class societies in the "civilized" world.

Consider the novels of those days that dealt with children in the prior century. Consider the great expectations upon such children to act as adults, to love as adults, and to share their feelings as adults. The bonds were not just tight, they were unbreakable, which of course added to the class stratification that my friends over in sociology love to chat about over tea and stouts.

So, all that has happened in the past century (this is where I get myself in trouble with everyone, starting with my editors) is that our children are not so clever (in fact, perhaps just dumber), they are not dressed so well, they are taken care of and act as if they always will be, from cradle to grave, and they are as well read as my cat was before her sad (but quick) travel to feline heaven. We have created a new class of not terribly smart but terribly techno-literate brats, and what we have is a society (largely Western) with little chance of mass success, but with a great chance of mass glee. Things could be worse. Of course, there is the terrible irritating thing called progress. I'll come back to that.

Grandchildren are a wonderful creation. They are the perfection of individuation as expressed by the words "me" and "mine." They learn early in their lives, mostly by observation, that everything they need is the same as what they want. After all, who needs to live without a Transformers Generations Leader Class Armada Megatron figure when one can be ordered online and delivered (free shipping!) to your home almost immediately? Okay, you have to wait. No, the small person thinks, forget that "wait" idea. Let's hit the nearest toy store! Bottom line: life hangs in the balance, and this toy is on sale, is available, and solves the whole issue of survival.

What else have they learned? Perhaps that it is a certainty that the want/need in question is immediate. No waiting as mentioned above is acceptable. No Santa watch: What a stupid idea to wait! Let us have Christmas/Hanukkah/Ashura/Magha Puja/Diwali/ Navaratri/Yule right now, even if it is a few days (weeks?) early. After all, what makes one day so special over another that we have to wait? By the way, the same argument is used in colleges to delay finals.

The issue of time is a forceful one. The inability to wait for gratification can be directly connected to a term called *maturity*. But the value of even that idea; that is, being more mature than the person next to you, is questionable to millennials. After all, what's the benefit of waiting for any event or object to manifest itself? Having it now is just as useful, perhaps more so, than waiting to have it some years, months, or days later. The argument can be offered strongly that waiting is a weakness on the part of those too fearful to risk failure.

Somehow, I doubt the possibility of failure is what's on the mind of a ten-year-old.

What I can say with some degree of certainty is that the subject of what children think about is at the core of a multitude of academic research, little of which is in agreement. Some of this disagreement is part of the effort to be different and thus "special" in academics. After, let's keep in mind that what we are studying falls into the field of social science, and we all know what the abundance of research in this area has added to the human condition. So it can be forgiven if some professors spent their time impressing students, wooing cohorts, grabbing grants, and adding not much to what we might understand about otherwise interesting bipeds.

Some of the academic research results and their disagreement are genuine. That is, I suppose, the great thing about being a researcher in social science: no one knows for sure if you are an egotistical bastard or a real addition to the field. The bottom line, though, is that the subject being discussed—children—is a fascinating opportunity, especially today in this world of direct-to-brain technology. If we set aside for a moment the likelihood that many of these gloriously wonderful cherubs are likely to become insufferable little monsters armed with all the technology necessary to maintain such an existence, they can provide some idea of how information, especially advertising, is processed. We are not suggesting the usual shot-in-the-dark experiments or who-knows-what-will-come surveys. Rather I'm suggesting that simple observation may give us some idea of what is actually happening. And is that not what we are struggling to uncover? Perhaps it's just me, but when it comes to research in the social sciences, I think we too often skip over the very necessary sense of what is defining the subject to get to some sort of countable—and thus publishable—result. Easy, I suppose. Unfortunately, filled with too many possible errors inherent in social science but sadly overlooked or ignored in the research of this field. Humans do not—I and many others hold—render a simple number between one and five (the Likert scale).

However, if we are to consider the impact of children on advertising and vice versa, and all of this through the lens of miniature applications, we must spend some time looking at numbers.

> It is very sad to see, but we are all becoming more individualized. It is sad to see because it seems nowadays when there is a bunch of people in a room, they just have their face planted to their phone screen. However, it was not always like this. Technology, such as smartphones, I feel has taken over generation after generation. I think this does matter because it is creating an antisocial feel because everyone is so used to texting and never talking to people face to face. I often think of this matter and it is frustrating to see everyone always so caught up on their phone, because it is hard to have a conversation with someone without them pulling out their phone, or if a student is using a cell phone during class, and even people using them while driving. They are just a constant distraction for people day in and day out. (Granted, they have many great uses, don't get me wrong.) —Ryan

IN THE BEGINNING: TONY AND THE GANG OF "FUN" SELLERS

I have always been a believer that if one is told something is "fun," then it probably is not. After all, "fun" as an idea varies from person to person, so right off the bat, a third person's belief that I would find a second person's creation as "fun" is a bit of a leap, yes? And, by the way, if you are told that something is really a lot of "fun," then it is very likely to be really no "fun" at all. No, "fun" must be self-evident, just as a joke cannot be explained and remain funny. "Fun" must be so from the instant it takes the stage and remain so until its exit to be considered truly entertaining. After all, if I consider the possible barriers between my considering what you think is "fun" and what I consider so, the cultural chasm may be its biggest and most challenging. We are, in the end, individuals within individualistic cultures. However, more on that later.

What we face now is what we think of as comics generating laughs and comical characters selling cereal. Is there a difference? More important, is there a difference in the head of a three-year-old or an eight-year-old or a twelve-year-old? And do these groups think about what they see in these two manufactured, separate groups differently or is that simply something that we as more wise adults create in our minds?

Much social science research has been conducted about television and specifically the advertising in the 1960s, focused in large part on the impact of television commercials on children. A large portion, rightly or wrongly, presumes a degree of consumer ignorance that the researchers happily bestow on adults. The assumption that we can accept and work with is that a larger portion of little people are accepting what they see on television as truer than what their larger, seemingly more mature cohorts (many of whom are parents) do. Frankly, we have no real research backing this up.

Much of what children see and latch onto are characters that are animated, initially in the form of little more than an onscreen pencil drawing (Tom Terrific) of white against black. As we got more sophisticated and Walt Disney and Warner Brothers stepped into the fray, we were introduced to new, full-color, talking animals, people, and even inanimate objects. The 1950s and 1960s were the decades of huge leaps forward in entertainment, specifically that which was aimed at children. As children exhibited more need for immediate stimulus via television, more specifically, television commercials, their attention spans shrank, or so the research seems to suggest (Christakis, Zimmerman, DiGiuseppe, and McCarty 2004, 708–13). And as others suggest, this shrinkage was global in nature (Tai and Chang 2005).

As noted by a child psychologist,

> Albert Bandura found that children acted out the violence they viewed on television. Educational programs such as *Romper Room* and *Captain Kangaroo* taught children letters and numbers, but they were the exception. By and large, broadcasters were airing programs not to positively influence children but to captivate them with colors and music. Once captured, advertisers were free to offer their wares for unsuspecting eyes. (Clark 2004, 66)

Of course, it can be easily argued that this "offer . . . for unsuspecting eyes" has continued on into what passes for adulthood for many. However, the subject and focus of our discussion in this chapter are children and how advertising changed in the 1950s and 1960s.

The impact of this change was judged to be so significant that regulatory groups were not only created but spurred to act. Advocacy groups were gathering around the idea that television commercials had an effect not yet measured in any real way, not yet parsed from the impact of modern society and the waves of new information pouring out of television sets. It seemed (and, frankly, still does) that commercials were created to convince the target consumer that product A was better, more pleasing, constructed in a superior way, and, in general, the right answer. Whether that target was a forty-year-old white male or a six-year-old Latino girl, the argument remains the same. As long as the claim is accurate, where's the problem?

Well, it tends to be a matter of who is in a position to make an informed decision (about cereal?). That is, the forty-year-old white male may seem to be in the best position to decide what is the best cereal for his body rather than the six-year-old Latino girl, especially when the character making the pitch for one brand is a Spanish-speaking mouse resembling a famous Mexican rebel. But, again, this is cereal we are fretting over. How much damage can be caused by a bowl of cereal, sugar packed or otherwise?

Unfortunately, quite a lot. Sugary foods lead to obesity, and this country and the world in general are going in two directions: Fatsville Hells and Starvation Heavens. Sugary cereals do not help us get better. Raising children who see sugar and fats as solutions to depression and the boatload of other issues they will face as part of life as intelligent humanoids only leads to more special groups, special programs, special drugs, and early deaths. The short and sweet happiness in a bowl of sugary cereal is certainly a choice to be made in a world of individualism. However, when that individualism relies upon the group to provide what eventually will be the necessary medical care, it's not long before that group starts to feel that it should have a say in what the consumer consumes at six years old, parents or no parents.

Research on all of this is extensive, of course. I could spend chapters on just what's been done in recent years. Instead, let's consider a few of what I think are stellar works.

Tim Hollis, creator of such childhood giants as *Bozo the Clown* and *Romper Room*, had much to say about how the Sugar Crisp Bears became perhaps the first cereal characters to be used in expensive, time-consuming, stop-action animation in his books dealing with advertising and its small human targets. As noted by critic Carmen Luke, Hollis

> traces the evolution of advertising campaigns and characters, such as how the Sugar Crisp Bears went from three to one and how Tony the Tiger, Cap'n Crunch, the Trix Rabbit, and Lucky the Leprechaun developed over time. Those interested in animation history will be drawn to sections of Hollis's

book on how the Walt Disney and Hanna-Barbera Studios contributed to character advertising and how major animation industry personalities, such as Mel Blanc, the voice of Toucan Sam, lent their talents to cereal commercials. Finally, children's broadcasting scholars will appreciate discussion of how parental groups in the 1960s, such as Action for Children's Television, put pressure on the cereal industry for both its products and its advertising and promoted changes. (Luke 1990)

The result was more than the persuasive techniques of previous advertising professionals of the 1950s, such as Howard Gossage and the dozens of others like him who believed that what mattered in advertising was making the target believe what was being said, if only via repetition and irritation. What the Creative Revolution of the 1960s suggested was that capturing the consumer's attention—especially that of youngsters—was far more important. But why would this suddenly be necessary when it wasn't such an issue in the earlier part of the century?

Many blame the shift toward more consumer control of the advertising process on the medium of television itself. What is it about television that renders a consumer any more malleable than a newspaper or magazine? More to the point, the consumer reads these products alone, as an individual. So, if anything, isn't it more likely that the consumer would act as a group when watching television?

Possibly, if that consumer was the forty-year-old white male we have been referencing. But would that be the case if the issue involved that six-year-old Latino girl? Probably not. As Jackson noted recently,

The sixties were the age of youth, as 70 million children from the post-war baby boom became teenagers and young adults. The movement away from the conservative fifties continued and eventually resulted in revolutionary ways of thinking and real change in the cultural fabric of American life. No longer content to be images of the generation ahead of them, young people wanted change. The changes affected education, values, lifestyles, laws, and entertainment. Many of the revolutionary ideas which began in the sixties are continuing to evolve today. (Jackson 2014, 97–98)

Children quickly and often without much oversight adopted what they saw as truth, whether in politics or in consumerism. The realism that would strike that same generation in the 1970s and 1980s would create a far more cynical crowd, but that is not really what we are interested in here (our sociology and political science friends can handle this). What we are interested in is what this generation created, and what the generation created by that generation created next, who have come to be called the millennials. As is often said by those wiser than I, effects can skip generations. What the 1960s generation experienced may now be at least part of what drives the post-2000 generation of little ones. What is important, at least by these two "me generations," is a real focus on what makes the individual happy, what makes the individual feel fulfilled, what makes the individual feel satisfied. And, yes, that starts very early.

Innovations can have impacts far greater than what is perceived immediately. Color in newspapers added a great deal to viewer enjoyment, but that cannot be compared to the degree of enjoyment when color was added to television. In fact, that seems to be one element in common with all innovation: the newer, the greater the impact. Thus, when animation was made a part of online information processing, the six-year-old Latino girl no longer felt a need to watch television along with others. No, this exchange of information would be hers and hers alone (at least until her parents intervened).

The animation that changed everything in the 1960s had much the same impact (but in a smaller way) as the impact that apps provide today. Individuals were struck by an innovation meant for them. The use of that earlier innovation by advertising was something agencies of the era found so much easier and simple compared to their struggles to integrate themselves into the world of online apps and online individuals.

> The golden era of animation for advertising was during the 1960s and early 1970s. The problem with using a character animation in a commercial involved deciding what type of character would appeal to the viewer, especially if the viewer was a child. Tony the Tiger and the Quik Rabbit were hits, but they were special. Nevertheless, animation has led to the creation of other types of graphic arts. While character animation is seldom used by advertisers, a new form—computer animation—may be successful. This is the type of animation used in the latest Levi's commercials. It appears that the original art form will be replaced by the new form. (Chalmers 2005, 6–11)

Advertisers, especially those without university pedigrees but with great industry legend, faced a new challenge in the new century. Consumers were discounting the advertising they were viewing on "television"—a device they were also turning away from. The ultimate choice of direction was moving away from advertising agency control to consumer control. Trouble was, of course, that the consumer was becoming more global both in status and behavior.

> While I agree that we, as a society, are becoming more individualized as a whole, I do not think it is necessarily a bad thing. I for one don't want to be seen as another number in a poll and look to distinguish myself from everyone else, and I know others probably feel somewhat like I do. No one wants to be just another statistic. So with these new individualized apps, phones, tablets we are utilizing, we are showcasing our individuality. Personal apps within our customizable phones have empowered us to feel like we are individuals and are unalike anyone else in this world. Yes, it seems to be leading towards a more unsocial way of life, especially within younger adults (as you can tell by

everyone staring at their phone in any public venue), but I think that trend will soon pass as we start to realize that we can be the individuals we want but still socialize with others. Individualization is not a bad thing, we just have to balance it out by not completely shunning basic human interaction. —Connor

WHAT ABOUT PROTECTING THE LITTLE ONES FROM BAD PARTS OF THE "NEW FORM"?

Let's consider the bulwark of past decades, in fact, the century in total. The Federal Trade Commission (FTC), as part of its responsibility, is charged with protecting consumers. The FTC was established in 1914 as one of the earliest independent regulatory agencies. Part of its mission is to regulate false or deceptive advertising; however, Congress chose not to define "deceptive," leaving this up to the FTC and federal courts (Karns 1987). Since the mid-1980s, the FTC's position on what constitutes "deception" has followed then-FTC Chairman James C. Miller III's definition: "Material representation that is likely to mislead consumers acting reasonably in the circumstances to their detriment" (Karns 1987, 399–430).

Although the FTC was formed during the previous century, much of its work in consumer affairs started after World War II, especially after 1960. With a staff of twenty-eight lawyers and eleven ancillary employees, the Division of Advertising Practices (DAP) in the FTC's Bureau of Consumer Protection cannot hope to survey even a fraction of the tens of thousands of advertisements that run each year. Furthermore, with caseloads slowing decisions from months to years, the division is not in a position to survey the entire spectrum of advertising or advertising techniques. The division chooses, therefore, to focus on specific areas. Since 1960, when the agency became increasingly more active in consumer protection (Harris and Milkis 1989), some products have received consistent attention, such as health products, real estate, food, and vitamins. At the same time, some practices have also received attention, such as fictitious pricing, false demonstrations, scare tactics, and misrepresentation. This is not to suggest that the agency was not prosecuting such practices prior to 1960, but rather that the Bureau of Consumer Protection and the creation of the Division of Advertising Practices in 1969 institutionalized the practice and expanded the focus from primarily advertising techniques to specific categories (Harris and Milkis 1989).

The FTC's activities in regulating advertising have undergone demonstrable change since 1960. In the 1960s, the agency was blasted by Ralph Nader as "a self parody of bureaucracy, fat with cronyism, . . . manipulated by the agents of commercial predators, impervious to governmental and citizen monitoring" (Cox, Fellmeth, and Schultz 1969). However, given the pro-consumer policies in the 1970s, the prior decade might be considered a period of innovation (Jones 1988, 1–9). Certainly, as my long-ago dissertation suggested, the activities of the FTC in the 1960s were sufficient rationale to spur the National Advertising Division (NAD) of the Better Business Bureau. Of particular significance was the FTC's decision to abandon the "mail bag" as the source for oversight. "Consumers could not complain unless they knew their rights were being violated" and where to file a complaint (Jones 1988, 1–9). That is, the consumers were basically lawyers. By 1966, the FTC had instigated a consumer awareness campaign to "both publicize its activities and to find out directly from consumers which aspects of the market were giving them the most difficulty" (Jones 1988, 1–9). But still, it has and will always be a world of legal language exchanged among legally trained individuals and with little or no involvement by six-year-olds.

By 1978, the FTC had transformed itself from "the little old lady of Pennsylvania Avenue into an energized suffragette" (Baer 1988, 11–20). Most of this transformation—still filled with lawyers—was accomplished because of a wave of legislation, from the Magnuson-Moss Warranty/FTC Improvement Act of 1975 to new, stricter credit disclosure rules and the Hart-Scott-Rodino Antitrust Improvement Act of 1976. The major weapon during this period was rulemaking, a relatively new enforcement tool that allowed the Bureau of Consumer Protection to cast a wide net rather than to take matters on a case-by-case basis (Baer 1988, 11–20).

The decade of the 1980s saw the resources of the FTC shrink. Industry interest in the late 1970s acted to rein in what these interests considered a far-too-active FTC. The interest of business in slowing the regulatory activism was heard by Congress and started a period of budget cutbacks and "legislative vetoes" of commission actions (Harris and Milkis 1989). Between 1979 and 1989, the work years at the FTC dropped from 1,746 to 900, almost half. The number of cases involving deceptive advertising remained fairly stable, between fifty and eighty a year. This trend has remained consistent, with the agency expected to do more with less, as are all federal agencies.

A less-talked-about but much more child-focused "agency" is the Children's Advertising Regulatory Unit (CARU), also part of the Council of Better Business Bureaus. I could go into a lot of detail here, cite chapter and verse, discuss who established it and what it has been doing of late. Instead, I'll simply summarize: when it comes to regulating the advertising targeting children, CARU has established itself as the expert. Those who seek the opinion of the lawyers running CARU include the FTC and the Federal Communications Commission (FCC). CARU handles cases dealing with national advertising, such as setting rules for commercials regarding the use of "flying" toys that do not actually fly on their own. Bottom line: the most egregious actions by advertisers aimed at children on a national basis are identified and pursued by CARU (Bryant 2004; Campbell 1997, 1999; Fried 2006; Simon 2006; Steiner 1988; Thomas and Newman 2009; Villafranco and Lustigman 2007; Villafranco and Riley 2013).

In the long run, the FTC, FDA, FCC, CARU, and all the other regulatory groups that seek to rein in advertising abuses face a simple eventuality that no one has solved: globalism. The worst and most notable advertising might be noted and corrected here in the United States. I say the "worst" because federal agencies are all on starvation budgets intended to ensure they cannot truly do their jobs though they appear to do so. Facing millions of hours of advertising, the FTC cannot track down all advertising abuses with a handful of attorneys.

Interestingly, many advertisements are now being carried and watched on devices that cannot be regulated by one country or even a group of countries. All it takes is one country to allow the posting of the kinds of advertisements other countries would like to prevent—especially those aimed at children— and all the regulatory units in all the countries around the globe will face a challenge they cannot meet short of shutting down the Internet completely. Consider China's effort to keep its citizens on a network controlled and approved by the government. The losing battle is so obvious. Globalization is occurring much faster than global legal statutes are being fashioned. And the fastest, most uncontrollable, most irrational, most consumer-driven part of the global economy relates to children, mainly those with access to disposable income who are in places like Europe, the United States, and China. Certainly other countries have such areas, like India, parts of South Africa, and Brazil. But children rule the day in places like Beijing, Los Angeles, and Paris. Part of their impetus is advertising, especially that which ignores the "rules" set out by regulatory agencies. In fact, the only entities with any real control over this multitrillion-dollar market whirlwind are parents willing to step in and simply say "no." Given the desperate drive of the advertisers targeting children, including those in this country, the "interference of parents can add up to serious losses" ("Scrimp on the Kids?" 2001, 1).

No doubt many of those reading this will simply say, "No! Children are not doing anything that radical or that unusual!" However, I have found that many of the students in my classes are in deep denial about what their younger sisters and brothers are capable of these days, activities that outstrip even what they are doing at college. Some admit that they have been surprised by what their cousins, nephews, and nieces as young as three are doing online with laptops, things that were impossible ten years ago (or even five years ago).

Consider what *Direct Marketing* reported in "Generation Y—Not Just 'Kids'" back in 2000:

> Of the $6.5 trillion spent annually by consumers in the U.S., some $4,600 billion is spent by members of Generation Y. These children (now ages 1–20) are the offspring of the Baby Boomers, and marketers can expect their effect to be similar to the impact their parents had during the 1960s. The sheer size of

the market (some 80 million strong) makes it worth the attention of marketers. Add to that the influence that the 12- to 17-year-old segment has over another enormous market—their parents—and you have a group of teenagers with an unprecedented amount of economic clout. Despite these factors, however, many marketers have ignored Generation Y (also known as Millennials or Echo Boomers) because they think they are "just kids" without the cash to spend. (Gronbach 2000, 36)

It's almost humorous. We are so blinded by our cultural oneness that we often cannot see past our passports. The world grows closer and closer, more and more interested in what others are doing, more and more interested in acting alone without the bother of others. In many ways this is no more true than in the way we "talk" to our children. So many parents trust that advertising is being regulated online as it was on television. But even great researchers are stuck on an issue that they simply miss or ignore when it comes to advertising, especially that which is aimed at children (Bernhardt, Wilking, Gottlieb, Emond, and Sargent 2014, 422; Berning, Huang, and Rabinowitz 2014, 507–25; Castonguay, McKinley, and Kunkel 2013, 420–32; Dietz 2013, 1652–58; Elliott, Den Hoed, and Conlon 2013, E364–68; Jackson 2014, 97–98; Kunkel, Castonguay, Wright, and McKinley 2014, 263; Lee and Nguyen 2013, 225; Mikailova 2014, 327; Opree, Buijzen, van Reijmersdal, and Valkenburg 2014, 717; Patil, Winpenny, Elliott, Rohr, and Nolte 2014, 561; Reid 2014, 721; Scarborough, Payne, Agu, Kaur, Mizdrak, Rayner, Halford, and Boyland 2013, 815–20; Smithers, Lynch, and Merlin 2014, 386–92; Verhellen, Oates, De Pelsmacker, and Dens 2014, 235–55). The reality is that much of our research, as strong and as statistically valid as it may be, is myopic. Those who are responsible for conducting research into the effects of advertising believe that what they do reveals and describes. It likely does but only for a small portion of the world's population: that in the United States. The entire way in which we communicate has and will become even more cross-cultural and globally bound. So much of our present research automatically presumes it is relevant because it looks at effect A within an environment it believes is still valid. But was it ever or were we just blinded by our own jingoism?

Interestingly, I was going to comment about the negative side of this whole individualistic movement (for lack of a better term). Noting that this type of behavior can lead to isolation, which, over extended periods of time, can cause severe depression and feed unrealistic expectations around one's place in society ("I want what I want and I want it now! . . . and if it does not fit my ideals, I will just simply toss it"). Both mentalities I would consider selfish and wasteful from having our heads buried in our specialized technological world . . . and then I read your comment, Connor, about using technology as a way to distinguish yourself from others and "showcasing our individuality." That was a unique perspective I had not thought about: individualized applications/

customizations as a means to present who we are. Solid point. Ultimately, the point you make at the end regarding human interaction is key: ensuring we are passing down the importance of relationships to younger generations. —Crystal

THREE POSSIBILITIES FOR THREE-YEAR-OLDS: TOGETHER, ACTING LIKE WE'RE TOGETHER, ALONE

We're certain that we cannot be regulated, but also pretty sure that we're being tracked, and additionally very certain that we don't care. After all, what is the worst that can happen at three years old? Being tricked by a cartoon character into believing our cereal is healthy is not making the top–one hundred list of possible evils and is hardly a big deal when you are a small person fussed over by those who are pretty certain that technology is a good thing and that there's no such thing as too much of it. Technology—expressed via handheld devices . . . for now—is the answer to almost everything our parents believe. A cereal created via technology? Well, that's a different argument. What we are thinking about here is how product A, let's say, Super Fruity Cereal Snax, can be marketed/advertised/sold to small humans with the consent of those who actually have the money. Yes, yes, we know that the adults are responsible for what their balls of love and joy consume. But let's also admit that this parenting by millennials is a little less strict than it might be, a bit more forgiving than it might be, and a whole lot more wrapped up in reading than it need be. The last part might be the habit of the elites, but even average parents still have lots of information available these days from millions of "free" Web sites just hankering to pass along information.

However, that parent–small person relationship is not what we are going to spend the rest of this chapter fretting over. And yes, we will fret. The focus here is a slightly older child, one who knows the tools, uses the devices, and searches for what we will call "answers," lacking a better term for the trash that flows through the networks being used to capacity and beyond on a daily basis. I have no doubt that many of you will find what I propose in these pages straightforward silliness. That's fine. Let's just agree to withhold judgment until the end, okay?

I agree that we are definitely moving towards individualization but not at the costs of groups (societies). We are given many choices of apps that we can use depending on our individual needs. For instance, a college student may use many social networking and local restaurant apps while an older male may use more banking and sports-related apps. However, no matter what apps we use, a lot of these are the same ones that others around us use. Especially social networking apps. That is why I feel that, yes, we are moving towards individualization because of so many choices to choose from. But at the same time we are not giving up the cost of groups/societies because many of the people around us use a lot of the same apps. —Eric

Together

I guess I like this model, although I must admit I do not get a chance to enjoy it much, and, frankly, never have had the chance to enjoy it much. What we have here is an online world of actual acquaintances who actually know each other, like each other, trust other, and share lots of information with each other. Perhaps a cultural affect, individuals who value being together are rare and becoming rarer in Western societies. They were far more prevalent five hundred years ago than they are now in places like Paris, London, and even Beijing, though I suspect many would disagree with me on the last city. However, keep in mind I am not describing the cities as all having high degrees of individualism, just that all have more than they did five hundred years ago, far more.

For children between ten and fifteen years of age, this time in all cultures offers an opportunity to work with others in classrooms, later school, on athletic teams, and other "special" events. In fact, the actual terminology used by parents and friends gives away that these times are rare and, I would suggest, are getting rarer.

But let's consider what is happening in these often highly scheduled, deeply planned "group" moments. For starters, they are not what I experienced fifty-odd years ago. I love mentioning to my students that my generation is one that was more likely to receive a rock and a stick for a holiday gift rather than a computer or computer game. Group moments were rare and well planned: organized, held by a local religious group, and generally considered an "add on," not a required event. That is, it was something very special.

Playing soccer, football, baseball, or any of a wide variety of sports (lacrosse?) is a suburban gift given these days. In fact, this presumed activity for middle-income children of almost any race (which is very different than it was fifty, very white years ago) can be found in almost any major city in the United States (and, oddly enough, elsewhere—are they copying us or we them?). The children come from a widespread residential area to an organized, systematized run of fields where teams meet for practices and games. The teams themselves are composed based on age, which is actually quite silly, given that age is not much of a predictor of weight and size. But age is easy to track. Actions online are, well, anything but easy to track, predict, or, frankly, understand. This is what perhaps is the most troubling part of the tool that so many of us love: it is so easy to abuse, abuse defined as use outside what is expected. A blond, blue-eyed child who is otherwise meek and mild can be a ferocious beast online. Understanding this represents perhaps the biggest challenge we face. We use some of our senses more than others to evaluate what we think is true. Such habits may not be our best choices.

As a grandparent, I find it interesting that the parents seem at least as interested in the game and what is happening as their children. What is more interesting, though, is what happens between games or before games. Parents are talking to other parents. Their children are online "talking" to someone on a message board. The distinction is among those in their forties and those in their preteens and teens. That is roughly thirty years, the accepted boundary of a generation, at least in the Western world.

The togetherness that takes place for the parents is more traditional than what is happening with the children. For the parents, it is face to face. For the children, it is a conversation online with a known friend. Take a moment to consider the difference. We who are born in the previous century see conversation with friends as facial, within their physical presence, and complete with intonation and context. The little ones skip the entirety of those needs, relying instead on language and codes to complete the information exchange. It's not that the information for the newest crowd, the latest generation, is not still done face to face, it just seems that they equally value faceless message boards, complete with their special symbols and well-defined abbreviations.

And that is an important feature of this new knowledge exchange: symbolic language. We all know OMG and LOL and even ROTFLOL, but the list is far longer. We have a new language generally created among a handful of people, not thousands or millions. It is one of the many aspects that are attributable to the new groups that are arising within the boundaries of online groups that are actually friends versus those I will discuss shortly.

These "real" friends rely on each other for confident information sharing and a variety of elements of friendship that are uniquely created. We might call them subcultures if we really felt they had some true connection to a dominant, overarching culture. In some cases, they may, but in others, they may not. The world of belonging to the "real group" in our new generation of ten-year-olds will be defined by something other than the physical presence of members. It will, among other things, be defined by its own special language.

What else can we consider with ten-year-olds? For starters, video. No, not art school or journalism video. This will not include cameras that cost thousands but instead those that are included on their phones.

This is a massive challenge for some universities but perhaps not for many high schools (though some high schools are still struggling with the idea that their students have access to mobile phones). Universities, especially in art and journalism departments, are focused on the worlds and works of Picasso and Capa. Their newest students use their phones to communicate via video in a far rougher, less refined fashion. I must admit, the numbers are small. Willing, brave students are still few in number. Professors are hardly encouraging. The outcomes are anything but certain.

However, the use of video as a way of communicating is growing. And why not? The camera on a phone is easy enough to use. The transmission of the produced video is easy enough to carry out. The finished work is at least as communicative as the written word and perhaps a bit more effective, what with included context and intonation. And, finally, the students have two choices: they can call and talk live to several friends or pass along a video saved for sharing. Either way, the intent is communication, not a carefully crafted movie or documentary.

I admit I could be wrong here, but I believe this is what will divide real friends from the fakes of Facebook and Twitter.

> I love that we are able to personalize and individualize our phones with apps. I like that I am able to focus on my favorite apps of Trivia Crack and Instagram while my mother can adore her FB and Scrabble with friends. The individualization is what makes technology so advanced and easy, as in the old days I would have had to buy a phone with those specific games already built in them and my mother a separate phone. I agree with some comments made above that the individualization has created an antisocial environment, but I don't think that it really pushes societies back into Western culture. Yes, physically, but that is more of a personal problem of that person's personality to choose to let technology stand in the way of conversation. But, in reality, the apps let people group together and from a different society of Trivia Crack lovers. And these apps depend on other people to make them successful and continue the product, so a whole group is formed and it's not just one individual. And not all of the information a person has in apps is not just an option for someone to share. Like some third-party entries with advertisements shown on apps, I'm sure a lot of the information is recorded in a database somewhere, so the fact that we people's ideas and information can die with them if not chosen to share, I don't think is accurate. If it's shared in apps somewhere, I'm sure it's at risk to be shared with everyone. So I don't think the individualization is impacting the cost of societies. —Clarissa

Acting Like We're Together

Very little cultural exchange takes place as outlined in the previous section. Friends are usually very much like each other. We read about the ones who are not, thus making it clear that their cultural dissimilarity makes them stand out from their societies sufficient to attract attention in both. Rarity always sells and grabs the attention of those fascinated in the details. The news is in the differences, not in the similarities.

Many researchers study, with some degree of displeasure, the creation of the "fake" cultures. I suppose I'm one of those who believe that—outside the trolls who crawl through on- and offline conversations looking for prey (and maybe that's a culture in itself)—the world is made up of cultures of all types, including those strictly online. Of course, the rules are different, or should be different, for those who wish to be safe. But the term "friend" is also different and has generated its opposite, "defriend." Bottom line: the rules here must be taken into account. Let's consider them.

First, these "friends" are not friends. They do not in fact even qualify as acquaintances. They are merely individuals (maybe—they could be fake) posting a comment (again, this could be fake) about how they feel (maybe) about some event (perhaps that they witnessed—maybe) that they would like to share (possibly). Admittedly, this is shaky. The trouble is that many of the previously mentioned researchers see this shakiness as grounds for walking away from the posts on Facebook and Twitter as useless rubbish. I am willing to admit that there may be more such rubbish here than in other information exchange sites like, say, ProQuest. But nothing of interest here? No, I cannot go so far.

Second, the users are younger than the usual network user. I write some of this off to the newest of technology that drives users from one technology to another, not so much based on its features but on its sheer newness. The shifts are predictable. Such shifts are not signs that the actual activity is of no value, just that the methods used to accomplish the tasks are less than standardized and subject to the varied taste of preteens.

Third, this area of online communication is far more global than any other. Here we have the most sharing of ideas among people in China and Indiana and Japan and Queensland and Scotland. Sometimes it is through playing on the same teams in a game of war or civilization or community building. Sometimes it is playing card games with individuals in places unknown, as if that location does not matter. For many, traditional cultural aspects are not shared in this environment, or so it seems. In reality, the subtlety of cultural exchange occurs unchecked, unmarked, and unmeasured. These are impressionable individuals, each ready to adopt a cultural artifact, cultural icon, cultural belief.

Fourth, some players are actually using avatars, online characters created by users to represent themselves in various games, discussions, and events. As noted by researchers (again, check ProQuest!), the use of multiple avatars by single online entities is expanding. Thus you may be having a conversation with one hundred online users, though it is, in fact, only five. And as noted by many of the previously cited researchers, this use of "fake" characters renders the entire environment gray, unreliable, useless. Such an evaluation, it can be argued, is more revealing of the jingoism of researchers stuck in their pre-1990 culture. But such an evaluation comes from one who believes that a replicant, as presented in the move *Blade Runner*, can be argued to be as human as the human whose memories were used to create it. We have no "fake" entities to draw upon. Everything we create is reliant upon ourselves and who we actually are, no matter how seemingly distant this persona may appear to be on a daily, non-avatar-esque existence.

Bottom line: it is too easy to write off the printing press as a fad in the fifteenth century. It is too easy to consider the fashions of Paris, the food of Florence, or the thousands of other elements that became part of a culture's progress to be anything but passing fads. Even for those of us who purchased those early Macs for $4,500—you know, the ones with very little memory, RAM or otherwise, and very small screens—the idea was unavoidable. We had to move with the latest ideas, just as today's users of mass communication tools such as Twitter and Facebook must post their thoughts and emotions.

> These apps can be seen as a source of utility for every individual person, whether the person is all about social media and looking for a way to communicate on a much simpler platform than face to face. They may choose to utilize these apps in a different way than others, the different utilization of these apps can create "groups." I think we are wrong to assume we all want to be individualized or antisocial because of overusing apps or technology. It's easy to say we are in groups now based on how we use it, but I don't think we should be shamed for using what we have available to us. It's neither right nor wrong. Sure, in some cases such as defriending or having ten thousand friends [it] is unrealistic but because of the ease of social media apps, why not? Why not keep in touch with every single person you have met and call them "friends"? It's easy and you never know when you will need to get in touch with them again. We are in a fast-moving age. All we can do is try to keep up with the trillions of apps; it's no surprise that some are only stored in our short-term memory. We are moving forward and sure some people my want to stop it, but the best we can do is keep with the flow. —Cheyenne

Alone

Against the Grain by J. K. Huysmans is a book I will never forget. The desire of the main character to withdraw completely from society has been on my mind on more than one occasion. The failures that character encounters in the many attempts generate a predictable feeling of loss shared by anyone who has tried to do the same.

As I have mentioned previously, we have somewhere in the millions of blogs in which posts go up without responses, presumptively without readers. These are not diaries, as I noted earlier. These are very much notes created by those who wish to share their ideas but who have no one interested. A sort of Einstein awaiting someone to actually read his work on relativity in the thirty years after it was published in a third-rate journal.

Yet we have those who create not to share but to create for the sake of creating. These individuals are so disconnected from society that to know what others think of their work has no value. They create because they feel that what they create is so important to themselves that they cannot stop or fail. The act of writing, painting, carving, measuring, or whatever comes to them is of importance in and of itself that the need to actually ensure that anyone, such as a peer, reviews the work is a waste of time and carries with it no particular meaning or value.

What is of equal import here is that society may find the creator so rebellious, so individualistic as to fall outside the lines of acceptability, and with him or her, the works are tossed away, as well. This has been done in many cases, no doubt a vice visited upon the youth by the elders: after all, the presumption of wisdom is that it lies with age. Yet how many old fools are there compared to young?

I must share an encounter I had with a librarian a few years back after my first book contract had been signed but the tome not yet finished. She was helping me with a research task and wanted to know about my contract. I admitted I really had little knowledge about the document, if only because it had little to do with why I sought to write the book. She was shocked. Didn't I care about the royalties? No, I said, I did not. I told her that royalties were not the reason I sought to write the book (Rowman & Littlefield, don't get ideas, okay?). If no one bought the book while I lived, I guess that would be okay. I presumed they would someday. In all my years of doing research, the vast number of my works have been solo. I worked with two graduate students on a four-part anthology and a law paper with a lawyer (I was told that would be the only way the paper would ever get published: law journals are biased toward law language, go figure).

What we have today is the ability of children to spend endless hours wrapped up with themselves in their own worlds creating farms, castles, worlds. Alone. With no special awards to win, except those online. Most of the games do not call for friends near or far to play but some do. Yet none of those called in to participate are guaranteed to be humans. In fact, we have no proof that anyone we deal with online is human, with a few exceptions (those who are our actual friends).

Children count on computers and the apps that come with them for entertainment. Some invest a great deal into these games, just as some invest a great deal into their offline friendships. As noted, being online (including the use of apps) does not create bad things; it just makes existing bad things worse. Children can become mesmerized by online devices, so much so that they may forget that they are in a classroom, driving a car, sitting at a dining table. No one said that apps are not captivating. They—at least the successful ones—are very much so.

And use happens alone, at the individual level of existence. Children value this time of online gaming, even when playing a game against a brother or sister. The opportunity to play a sibling is only slightly more important than playing a game against a totally unknown person. After all, a win is win, right?

> Yeah, it seems like these apps could break apart groups, but in a way they could create new groups in the process. Look at things like Tumblr and Reddit; there are subcultures associated with them. It seems to me like I mentioned before that even though there are groups you become a part of like on Facebook, there is an element of disingenuousness to them. How much of a real connection can you have with someone over the Internet? Visual communication is a huge part of how we interact and this is absolutely lacking when you interact with people through the Web. I think one of the bigger questions that should be asked is how does this dependence on apps and smartphones affect our ability to think on our feet? If we always reference an app or look it up on our smartphone when we don't know the answer to something, then we start to lose our ability to adapt and think. My fear is that we will develop a sort of plug-and-play mentality that doesn't know how to fix anything at all. One other note would be that if you define your individuality to the choices available and these choices are driven solely by the market, then there will be a narrowing of our culture when it comes to how we define ourselves. This external force on our own individuality is already there, but this seems to be an even greater force than [it] has been in the past. At some point our online persona will no longer be our attempt at reflecting who we think we are and instead will be the leading factor in defining who we model ourselves after. It is a fine and nuanced point, but one that will make a huge difference as the generations pass. —Ryan

The certainties we face in our lives are few. One is, however, that our children will know more, face more, struggle with more, and solve more than we have. They will have to in order to survive and, yes, they will survive. Guess I am not one of those the-world-is-coming-to-an-end folks. The world is too complicated, too big, too much interwoven with a multiplicity of cultures to end. Okay, except maybe by a stray meteorite.

No, the struggle is how to reach a more peaceful, fairer, tolerant world. To that end, individualism seems not to be interested, and here we have a real challenge. Our children may not be terribly interested in war, but they may not be much interested in peace, except as it has some impact on their own activities. Apps are content neutral and by nature ethically neutral. This ought to be of more than a little concern for us, but I doubt it will be because we have no way to deal with it except through prepackaged moral beliefs, no matter what religion or political system we subscribe to.

Trouble is, our children may for a time act as if they care about a political system or a religious belief, but over time the group with which they will identify will be smaller and smaller. They are, ultimately, believers in themselves. Unless we are willing to change the way in which we model our teaching and our communication to reach the single person rather than the group, we will fail. The task is not simple, for it requires that we change the way we think about what we have come to think of as the only way anything is accomplished. But as we have learned in the past, progress has more than one path. If we have the nerve, we can take the path we have not considered necessary or viable. This path is that which our children have taken, unaware of what they are doing. Individualism is not a conscious choice any more than working within a group is unconscious. What we know for sure is that "groups" are a nice, comfortable, well-known idea that simply will not work in the future educational model or business environment. To persist and develop designs, learning tools, and other devices to extend the lives of groups is just that, a meaningless extension.

We must find a different path and adopt a different way to measure the success of those on that path.

REFERENCES

Baer, William J. 1988. "At the Turning Point: The Commission in 1978." *Journal of Public Policy and Marketing* 7: 11–20.

Bernhardt, Amy M., Cara Wilking, Mark Gottlieb, Jennifer Emond, and James D. Sargent. 2014. "Children's Reaction to Depictions of Healthy Foods in Fast-Food Television Advertisements." *Archives of Pediatrics & Adolescent Medicine* 168, no. 5: 422.

Berning, Joshua P., Rui Huang, and Adam Rabinowitz. 2014. "An Evaluation of Government and Industry Proposed Restrictions on Television Advertising of Breakfast Cereals to Children." *Journal of Consumer Policy* 37, no. 4: 507–25.

Bryant, Kristin. 2004. "Not Child's Play: Compliance with the Children's Online Privacy Rule." *University of Washington Shidler Journal of Law, Commerce & Technology* 1, no. 4.

Campbell, Angela J. 1997. "Emerging Technologies and the Law." *Gonzaga Law Review* 33, no. 311.

———. 1999. "Self-Regulation and the Media." *Federal Communications Law Journal* 51, no. 711.

Castonguay, Jessica, Christopher McKinley, and Dale Kunkel. 2013. "Health-Related Messages in Food Advertisements Targeting Children." *Health Education* 113, no. 5: 420–32.

Chalmers, Graeme. 2005. "Visual Culture Education in the 1960s ." *Art Education* 58, no. 6: 6–11.

Christakis, Dimitri A., Frederick J. Zimmerman, David L. DiGiuseppe, and Carolyn A. McCarty. 2004. "Early Television Exposure and Subsequent Attentional Problems in Children." *Pediatrics* 113, no. 4: 708–13.

Clark, Naeemah. 2004. "The Birth of an Advocacy Group: The First Six Years of Action for Children's Television." *Journalism History* 30, no. 2: 66–76.

Cox, E., R. Fellmeth, and J. Schultz. 1969. *The Nader Report on the Federal Trade Commission.* New York: R. W. Bacon.

Dietz, William H. 2013. "New Strategies to Improve Food Marketing to Children." *Health Affairs* 32, no. 9: 1652–58.

Elliott, Charlene D., Rebecca Carruthers Den Hoed, and Martin J. Conlon. 2013. "Food Branding and Young Children's Taste Preferences: A Reassessment." *Canadian Journal of Public Health* 104, no. 5: E364–68.

Fried, Ellen J. 2006. "Assessing Effectiveness of Self-Regulation: A Case Study of the Children's Advertising Unit." *Loyola of Los Angeles Law Review* 9, no. 93.

Gronbach, Ken. 2000. "Generation Y—Not Just 'Kids.'" *Direct Marketing* 63, no. 4: 36–39.

Harris, Richard A., and Sidney M. Milkis. 1989. *The Politics of Regulatory Change: A Tale of Two Agencies.* New York: Oxford.

Jackson, Kathy Merlock. 2014. "Part of a Complete Breakfast: Cereal Characters of the Baby Boom Era." *The Journal of American Culture* 37, no. 1: 97–98.

Jones, Mary Gardiner. 1988. "The Federal Trade Commission in 1968: Times of Turmoil and Response." *Journal of Public Policy and Marketing* 7: 1–9.

Karns, Jack E. 1987. "The Federal Trade Commission's Evolving Deception Policy." *University of Richmond Law Review* 22 (1987): 399–430.

Kunkel, Dale, Jessica Castonguay, Paul J. Wright, and Christopher J. McKinley. 2014. "Solution or Smokescreen? Evaluating Industry Self-Regulation of Televised Food Marketing to Children." *Communication Law and Policy* 19, no. 3: 263.

Lee, Seow Ting, and Hoang Lien Nguyen. 2013. "Explicating the Moral Responsibility of the Advertiser: TARES as an Ethical Model for Fast Food Advertising." *Journal of Mass Media Ethics* 28, no. 4: 225.

Luke, Carmen. 1990. *Constructing the Child Viewer: History of American Discourse on Television and Children, 1950–1980.* New York: Praeger.

Mikailova, Milena. 2014. "Advertising and Childhood Obesity: The Role of the Federal Government in Limiting Children's Exposure to Unhealthy Food Advertisements." *Federal Communications Law Journal* 66, no. 2: 327–56.

Opree, Suzanna J., Moniek Buijzen, Eva A. van Reijmersdal, and Patti M. Valkenburg. 2014. "Children's Advertising Exposure, Advertised Product Desire, and Materialism: A Longitudinal Study." *Communication Research* 41, no. 5: 717.

Patil, Sunil, Eleanor M. Winpenny, Marc N. Elliott, Charlene Rohr, and Ellen Nolte. 2014. "Youth Exposure to Alcohol Advertising on Television in the UK, the Netherlands and Germany." *European Journal of Public Health* 24, no. 4: 561.

Reid, Rita-Marie Cain. 2014. "Embedded Advertising to Children: A Tactic That Requires a New Regulatory Approach." *American Business Law Journal* 51, no. 4: 721.

Scarborough, P., C. Payne, C. G. Agu, A. Kaur, A. Mizdrak, M. Rayner, J. C. G. Halford, and E. Boyland. 2013. "How Important Is the Choice of the Nutrient Profile Model Used to Regulate Broadcast Advertising of Foods to Children? A Comparison Using a Targeted Data Set." *European Journal of Clinical Nutrition* 67, no. 8: 815–20.

"Scrimp on the Kids?" 2001. *Oklahoma City Journal Record.* October 18: 1.

Simon, Michele. 2006. "Food Marketing to Children and the Law: An Introduction." *Loyola of Los Angeles Law Review* 39, no. 1.

Smithers, Lisa G., John W. Lynch, and Tracy Merlin. 2014. "Industry Self-Regulation and TV Advertising of Foods to Australian Children." *Journal of Paediatrics and Child Health* 50, no. 5: 386–92.

Steiner, Robert L. 1988. "Commercial Speech and the First Amendment: Double Standards in the Regulation of Toy Advertising." *University of Cincinnati Law Review* 56, no. 1259.

Tai, Hsuan-Ting, and Shao-Shiun Chang. 2005. "The Casual Model of Internet Advertising Effectiveness." *Asia Pacific Management Review* 10, no. 1.

Thomas, Lisa, and Robert Newman. 2009. "Social Networking and Blogging: The New Legal Frontier." *The John Marshall Law School Review of Intellectual Property Law* 9, no. 500.

Verhellen, Yann, Caroline Oates, Patrick De Pelsmacker, and Nathalie Dens. 2014. "Children's Responses to Traditional versus Hybrid Advertising Formats: The Moderating Role of Persuasion Knowledge." *Journal of Consumer Policy* 37, no. 2: 235–55.

Villafranco, John E., and Andrew B. Lustigman. 2007. "Regulation of Dietary Supplement Advertising: Current Claims of Interest to the Federal Trade Commission, Food and Drug Administration and National Advertising Division." *Food and Drug Law Journal* 62, no. 709.

Villafranco, John E., and Katherine E. Riley. 2013. "So You Want to Self-Regulate? The National Advertising Division As Standard Bearer." *American Bar Association Antitrust* 27, no. 79.

Chapter Nine

Education and Porous Cultural Borders

I agree with most on this board that as a society, we are becoming greatly individualized. We are capable of customizing nearly every aspect of our lives to each individual's liking. Unfortunately, the more we are able to do so, the less grateful we become of the simplest positive aspects of life. I find the effect individualization has on groups to be quite ironic. While we students are on break and possibly hundreds or even thousands of miles apart, we have the opportunity to be a very social group despite significant physical distance separating us. However, place us all at a large table in a restaurant and half the students will be on Snapchat or Instagram with no interest in their fellow students filling his or her three-foot radius. This is an observation I too often experience and it absolutely upsets me. Technology is truly a double-edged sword. Unfortunately I value personal interactions much greater than technological advances. On a better note, the positive edge of the sword allowed me to recently share a Skype session with a good friend from Germany. I have not seen her in two years but every few months we are fortunate enough to virtually speak face to face. So at times I am very thankful for our rapid advances in technology. —Ryan

The world accepts that education is a key to longevity, peace, and improved health. The world also accepted for centuries that education was delivered via classrooms. As universities rose in popularity in the early centuries of the previous millennia, starting in Bologna and Paris, replicas sprang up in numerous cities. Professors felt that their responsibilities were shifting to include more than just teaching, as did the role of administrators, who were also shifting from just attracting customers (students) to luring the most successful teachers. To suggest that movable type changed everything might be an understatement. The creation of lower-priced, local-language texts rapidly expanded not only readership, but also the very act of individual thinking. Critical thought locked up in monastery-dominated communities was replaced, or perhaps more accurately, augmented by "free thinking" on the part of those not directly affiliated with Rome (or, frankly, Luther). Students certainly enjoyed the ability to learn from those no longer suffocated by old practices and dogmatic teaching. More and more ideas poured into a booming market eager to participate, share, and learn. And once the floodgates were opened, they could not be closed.

But this rapid growth was within a narrow slice of societies across Europe and later, the Americas. We know that this rapid rise of increased literacy was matched with the growing sense of individualism. This shift from a few famous thinkers to a panoply of intellectuals with competing ideas can easily be linked to the ability to share ideas far more easily than was the case prior to Gutenberg. It was not that great thinkers did not still attract visitors and tutors. Rather, it was that the thoughts of individuals, such as Galileo and Kepler, could be accessed at great distances by classes of individuals unfamiliar with Latin and outside the closed society of great thinkers.

This shift should sound familiar. Online education, online research, and online collaboration have opened the gates of learning to millions more potential learners. Yes, the learning rates are still slow. Getting the world education standard to rise has been more than a monumental effort ("Education Index" 2008). Politics, religion, economics, and even customs stand in the way of learning. Students in some countries, such as Kazakhstan, Uzbekistan, and other recently "freed" -stans south of Siberia, as well as quasi-new countries such as Nicaragua, Congo, Yemen, and Bhutan are facing dropping education standards amid turmoil and dictatorships. Unfortunately, most efforts to educate the peoples of these and other developing countries still rely on classrooms and other traditional structures that are very difficult to create and maintain.

Modern educational efforts in many ways face the same barriers that scholars dealt with five hundred years ago. In 1600, the ability to bypass both the secular leaders and clerical monks, and in doing so, to spread one's ideas to thousands rather than dozens must have involved a colossal effort. The impact of spreading the educator/individual's ideas to the masses was expanded at least algebraically and at a much lower per-reader cost than what was charged by the monks. That is, not only was more sharing of information possible, but the cost per user also fell, as well as the time necessary to convert thoughts into printed works. Comparatively, not only were the floodgates opened, but also the amount of information behind those floodgates had exploded. The application, for instance, of the concept of the scientific method credited to Iraqi scientist Ibn al-Haytham (*Book of Optics*, 1021), was no longer known by only a few but by thousands, possibly tens of thousands, of researchers and university students.

What was created was a product in demand—a written text for readers. It is important to remember that text had already undergone some change even in Latin, moving from a read-aloud-only form to one that could and was read in silence, a habit believed started by Augustine. The thoughts of not only the Greek philosophers, but the early pioneers of scientific methods, such as Al-Buruni, Avicenna, Grosseteste, Bacon, and others, were now available not only in their native language, but in translated works. These translations carried with them cultural cross-pollination, something we need not deal with now, but which certainly had some impact on the uptake of not only the education within the text, but the surrounding facets within the work carried forward from the previous culture.

Economics also played a major factor in the uptake of education in the centuries since 1600. Courses were available at a fraction of the cost of what they would have been—if they had actually been made accessible—centuries earlier. Europe, starting in the fifteenth century, experienced a rise in literacy rates (Buringha and Van Zanden 2009, 409–37). In fact, it was the rise in literacy that drove the demand for a printing press with movable type. This invention would deliver books at a lower cost. Once again, though rarely noted, demand preceded supply. The thirst for information, the demand for a book, a sharing of ideas would not only change the nature of science, but the nature of the forms that stored that data. After all, what preceded the book was still a book; it just looked very different, was produced very differently, and cost a great deal more money, if one could be obtained at all. What we have, starting with movable type, is a form of information that was easier to create, easier to modify, and easier to share. And ease meant a lower cost.

But it still did not reach the lowest classes. It still represented an element for the elites, at least by global standards. That is, although the landed gentry of England considered well-funded bankers nothing but the working class, anyone in the true middle class, much less those living in London's East End, considered both rich, elite snobs. Access to education was reserved to Oxford for one class and Cambridge for the other, but neither to the middle class, much less the "others."

But this is a description of one society's dealing with education. After centuries of largely descriptive, often personal discussions regarding life, the universe, and everything, we as a society are ready to get more specific on a global scale, or at least we act like we are. Our writings based on research are more detailed in their findings, more defendable by way of collected data based on observation, and unfortunately very reflective of our cultural boundaries. Our philosophies have become more diverse but are still bound by our cultural beliefs. Science would become more specialized, not simply because more literate authors were present (though that was a significant factor), but because new thinking has been demanded for centuries. In many ways, our "hard" sciences—biochemistry, medical, nanophysics, and others—are leading the way in skipping over the cultural boundaries, which still rule states like the one I reside in, denying evolution and global warming, and inspiring individuals in states around the globe to blow each other up.

> The conception of individualization steps from just that, the fact that we are individuals. I don't have the same interests as other folks and that is why the homescreens of our phones are so diverse. Is this a problem? At this point, I don't think so. It is all very logical that we move towards individualization as technology progresses and makes that possible. It is for the same reason that we all take different classes and hone different interests. The place where I believe it become dangerous is when the individual technology limits or completely cuts out the need for groups. When people no longer seek others due to enthrallment in their individual technology that gives them everything they need, it becomes a problem. It really is just something to be cognizant of at this point and be weary of for the future, because it is feasible that eventually it could matter. —Carolina

EDUCATION TODAY DEMANDS GROUPS AND EQUALITY

The givens are certainly greater than they were five hundred years ago. Yes, the moon revolves around the earth, the earth rotates around the sun, and, the sun moves through the galaxy. These accepted facts are more accepted, though by not much more than a majority, even in the United States (Fields 2014). In some places, the numbers are far worse, thus the need for education.

But with education comes change. Not many of us like change. Change is dangerous. Change is uncertain. Change is, put simply, just not a necessity, or at least that's how a majority of the planet sees it. Rather than changing things, we need to adapt ourselves to what worked for our parents. After all, it worked for them.

I spent a few years of my life (okay, I admit, too many years) in Savannah, Georgia. In the 1960s, this town was as racist as any town in Alabama, Mississippi, South Carolina, . . . well, you get the idea. It's hard to believe that it's any different today, though I know some would argue that it is. Let's just say it was better at hiding its hatred.

What I recall was the situation with education in 1965, many years after the U.S. Supreme Court had forcefully suggested that separate but equal was definitely separate but definitely not equal. High schools in Savannah leading up to 1965 were black (Johnson High) and white (Savannah High) and rarely admitted the other existed. This oddly, still racially divided education structure was driven by where people were "allowed" to live by the mortgage practices of banks—Citizens and Southern and others—which "redlined" loans for whites and blacks into acceptable neighborhoods. When busing started a few years later, I was convinced it was constructed to ensure that certain athletically gifted black teens were sent to Savannah High and certain non-Christian whites (mainly Jewish) were sent to Johnson High. I have no research to back either of these assumptions. However, Savannah High's basketball team was far better that it had been previously. However, its ninth-grade algebra class was just as weak as it had been before the busing and its history just as myopic. Nothing really changed. Except that we have added administrative layers and more pedagogic reportage. Luckily, that's not all that's happening.

Higher education has been the target of many new ideas, most about measuring, some about actually teaching. Let's skip past the politically driven measuring issue and look at the teaching. Two issues have been among the abundance of topics dealt with in our advisory, consulting, webinar worlds: groups and equality.

The first of these, groups, has led to almost every instructor including some sort of group work in their classes. Why, you might ask. That's a very good question. It's the belief that if we do not require that they work together, they will not work together, and that will be bad. Some evidence is offered that employers want group-enabled new hires. Some evidence obviously is out there that it does not matter much.

But it matters a great deal at the college level. Why, we are not sure. Why educators at universities, especially those in administrative positions, believe so strongly in group work may have a great deal to do with the evidence arising that students are coming to the university more and more individualistic than ever before. The trend is marked by the use of handheld communication devices. Students are bound to their mobile phones as their way to interface with each other and the world. In fact, the use of handhelds has led to far more dependence on apps than the Web. As pointed out by Anderson, the rise in the use of apps has at least as much to do with the preference of the device being used (Anderson and Wolff 2010). This is not a matter of the information on the Web being found useless, any more than books were found useless with the birth of the Web. Convenience simply rules.

Thus, the administrative response is to force the students to work with each other in traditional face-to-face teams. How quaint. We are in a world of online, app-driven collaboration, and all the best and brightest of our pedagogues can imagine is group work. Oh, well. Students can see this coming.

Of course, this does not mean they can see the need to take it to the next level with video communication as discussed in the previous chapter. University students are, after all, just as set in their ways as their parents. Their ways are in many ways just a little different.

As for equality, here is where things get violent. Here is where things return to the Savannah I knew in 1965. Educating women can get you beheaded. Educating children can result in much the same. Education is seen as a threat to a religion, to a political structure, to a family's cohesive nature, to a country's historical standing. Education is the center of change. One cannot occur without the other. And no matter the culture, none of the stalwarts within it like change, none embrace the setting aside of core values, and few seek leaders who wish to take them to a new, unknown place. Change is seen, in most cultures, as corrosive. It is seen, in most cultures, as a hazard to the standards that have carried the population to where it is. In many situations, the desire is to return to the known (if fictionalized) past, not to move forward to some unknown future. Even in the most vaunted free-love days of the 1960s in the United States, the call was a return to an imagined land that was before. The past always seems better than the future and certainly preferable to the present.

Yet education is today made more possible globally by apps. The spread of education does not occur in the classroom. Not with the white boards and projectors. Not with all the in-class technology. And, perhaps most of all, not with the administrative, politically driven from the top assessments. It can be argued that assessments are the last effort of politicians in places like the United States to cut back on investment in educating the masses by trying to justify lower budgets through some sort of quasi-business model applied to something that was never intended to be efficient. What is being measured is a social science. And anyone who has spent any real time in social science research (defined as not thinking that they are doing research in biology, physics, or chemistry) knows that the results are, at best, squishy. After all, the subject being studied is humans, and we all know (at least those who care to admit it) that humans are difficult to measure. For starters, they lie. Amoebas, hydrogen, and Z curves do not.

What we know for sure is that once everyone is educated, something amazing will occur. Exactly what that is, we are not sure. What we do know is that we have not the dedication to accomplish this goal. In the state in which I live, the courts and the legislature are in continual battle over how much should be spent on education. You would think that the citizens would want their children educated well. You would think that this would be reflected in the agenda of the state legislature of this and other states. It is not. The difficulty is sifting out whether the legislature's desire to cut budgets is a motive born of political philosophy or economic reality.

Of course, those who wish to learn in other places may not care much about what is happening in Plainville, Kansas. They will be logging in to MIT and Stanford, longtime providers of online educational material. They will be looking at online videos, online apps, online tools to better their thinking. They will be learning while others are arguing over the outcome of an assessment or the sum of a state education budget. Priorities are what they are, and rarely in a world of humans are they set well or correctly.

I totally agree and I've actually made the same observation multiple times. Currently you can go to any social event and see most everyone on their phones. There is little social interaction at all. In my opinion when people interact they grow closer, and this closeness is what brings forth the compassion within our society. The fact that face-to-face interaction is being lessened will, in my opinion, lead to a decline in compassion in our society. This could and probably will have terrible consequences. —Joshua

FILLING IN THE GAP: ONLINE EDUCATION

Some years ago, I was asked to help create a Web site for a new project. It had some existing artwork from a brochure created by a designer who knew Photoshop but not HTML. That happened a lot in those days. Graphic designers were great with Photoshop, and Photoshop was great with files that were terrific with use in print, like TIFFs and the like. Not many designers had much experience with GIF or JPEG files, the image files that HTML liked.

Nor were there many people who knew much about what to do with the Web in the world of marketing and advertising. I had put myself through the doctoral program as a consultant to a beverage association in Washington, D.C., and once in Chapel Hill, I helped a chemistry association get its feet on the ground Web-wise. Once I got to Manhattan, Kansas, those relationships eventually went away. I had a talent that I could use: an ability to use a new avenue of communication (the Web) with a traditional form of communication (advertising and writing). Dr. Sue Maes and a couple of other educators at Kansas State University approached me looking for some help with a new form of educational communication: the Great Plains Interactive Distance Education Alliance, GP Idea for short. The idea was simple and yet controversial: get a bunch of Big 12 universities to work together to offer degrees that individually they could not due to a lack of instructors necessary for the required courses. Sounds simple, yes? Well, it is. The difficulty (okay, one of the difficulties; there are many) is that all the courses had to be offered at the same price per credit hour. Herein lies the biggest challenge to any global cooperative and perhaps the biggest reason that few schools have joined with other schools to offer joint degrees. We will come back to this issue after describing what GP Idea and other valid online education programs actually attempt to do.

Imagine ten or so university financial officers in a room talking about how they might be able to come up with a way to charge the same amount for a course, credit hour by credit hour. Such an imaginary place is easier to conjure than to manage. Universities are each driven by their own schemes, their own budget formatting. Some of that is environmentally driven—guess what?—it costs less to live in Michigan than it does in North Carolina, and both are a great deal less expensive than California. So, it's a given that Michigan State University would cost less based on state costs than North

Carolina State, and even less than almost any college in California. Yet can we think beyond a "place" when we are considering online education? That is, having a Web site in Michigan costs roughly (or ought to) what it would in California. The Web is the great leveler of costs and views every student as an equal, which is important in finances, but even more so in taking culture into consideration.

But other factors play a part in tuition, not the least of which is state legislature support and the university's brand standing. The former is clearly on a downslide and has been for some years in most states, especially those, oddly enough, whose residents need higher education the most: the South, the Midwest. Instead, residents—generally, at least, those of Anglo-Saxon heritage—are served interesting ways in which they can pay lower taxes and their children and grandchildren can pay more in college tuition. This hardly takes calculus for legislatures and governors in states like Kansas, where the average resident is two times more likely to not have a college degree. And given the high tuition rates generated by the lack of state funding of their own universities, legislators find it increasingly easy to point to college students as members of the elite, which they increasingly are. Yes, the argument is circular, but then, what in politics is not? Consider the price of a bottle of water in Denver, New York City, Kenya, London, the deep jungle of Brazil—well, you certainly get the idea.

A university's brand—that is, its standing in the world of education, whether deserved or not—has been created over decades and does not erode easily. Most people who would qualify as potential target consumers have formed a brand image in their heads regarding places like Harvard and Yale. They have state-by-state identifications of loyalty, in many cases driven by familial relevance: mom and dad went to Ohio State University, so I want to go. Let's add one additional potential factor into the mix: undergraduate degrees have less impact than they once did. To be competitive, job candidates sometimes feel they must hold some sort of proof of advanced work, either in the form of a master's or a certificate. Certificates are growing in popularity because they can be earned entirely online.

> I believe that yes we are moving towards more individualization by using all of the apps and the fact that we have so many apps to choose from. I also believe that we are not doing this at the cost of the society or group; my reasoning for this is that most of the apps that we use are ones that will connect us with other people in some way or form. We are using similar apps as everyone around us. —Rachelle

We know one thing: education extends life. Holding some amount of higher education is almost always a good idea. So how can we, those who have this product, figure out how to spread it not only to those who do not have any degree (that would be those who are working toward an undergraduate standing) and those who have a degree, but want more. We could do something more than what I encountered meeting with a client at a religious high school in Charlotte, North Carolina, back when I worked in advertising. The director of the school took the opportunity to introduce me to his assistant who, he said, had eight (or was it nine?) degrees—all received via the U.S. Postal Service. I was encouraged to be impressed. He had papers that said he could do something. Many of today's online educational opportunities come with the same entrepreneurial feel: pay me and I will give you a paper with something on it that says you are smart. Call it the Wizard of Oz economic/educational method.

GP Idea intended something very different and started earlier than most of the questionable products offered today. Beginning with the assurance that what was being delivered was at least as quality rated as the schools offering the courses, GP Idea blends flexibility with the existing academic brands. At the time it was developed, roughly 1999, the project focused on one program: human sciences. Agreements were made among eleven universities that students enroll at any of the universities, take all classes online from any of the courses offered, at any of the universities that counted toward the degree, and pay the same tuition. Successful completion resulted in a certificate or master's degree from any of the universities involved. These universities carry a strong brand, certainly stronger than those advertised on television today.

Since the turn of this century, GP Idea has expanded and now reaches into other college campuses. Unfortunately, two colleges among a few others are not—or perhaps haven't been until very recently—very welcoming of such an online model: arts and sciences and business. Many professors in both colleges at many universities actually do offer courses online, but the universities see these courses as a way to extend their footprints, not their enrollments. That is, rather than trying to get individuals who have not been (and likely would never be) students, the universities merely consider their existing students who are already enrolled as the main targets. This degree of myopic vision almost exceeds understanding. Rather than take their product and make it available worldwide, most universities simply look for ways to be more efficient, and by doing so, to remain elite.

Professors are not hired to reach potential students outside their state, much less outside their country. The relatively few who are engaged in programs like GP Idea are focused in singular areas. Some are simply online degrees offered by a single university, thus limiting the effectiveness compared to a high-quality degree that could be created involving the top educators at a dozen universities. Bottom line: we remain focused narrowly on our own gains rather than the fate of the global community. Shortsighted? You betcha!

However, we encounter a great deal of risk when dealing with other schools that we saw as competitors until recently. Imagining that the University of North Carolina, Chapel Hill, and North Carolina University would work together to educate students scattered around the world is, thankfully, not a total dream. It is simply one that will take longer than it needs to. Yet even reports of "global universities," such as that published annually by *U.S. News & World Report*, are instead reports on universities in different countries than ours ("Best Global Universities" 2014). We do not see education as a global effort, but rather one wrapped up within a culture so tightly that we question those educated in Canada who apply for positions in the United States. Yet again any education is guaranteed to extend a student's life. So why is the educating of students so competitive that we cannot act cooperatively with each other to reach a market too large to be served by the world's universities even if they acted totally in sync with each other? What are we arguing over? In some ways, it is very much like the person at the school in Charlotte: we are confusing degrees with knowledge, and knowledge with wisdom. A degree in education may represent many things. Wisdom, it may not.

Whatever it is, our children find it useless and silly. We are focused on the comma after the second item in a series of three (you know, that Harvard thing invented by E. B. White), as if it really means anything. The students are soaking up so much more. When you are thirty, learning to read at the third-grade level is a big deal. When you are forty, learning how to use a business theory to justify an expansion proposal is a big deal. Only those who are surrounded by education, soaked up in textbooks and classes, see the littlest, most minor elements and give them importance far beyond their standing. A flawed course in advertising is far better than no advertising course in a world with little or no education regarding consumer behavior. Two advertising courses do not provide a degree in advertising. A choice from among twenty courses certainly would. In fact, providing a student the choice from among two hundred or two thousand advertising courses, along with an equal panoply of other courses—let's say fifty thousand—means each student could craft a unique degree based on the specific choices made. The resulting degrees are in the millions. That is, we have restricted our methods of teaching because we thought we had but one option. Today, we know we have millions of options if only because we have millions of possible ways of considering how to answer the questions we face. If we stop considering college as only the textbook printed this year and consider it a combination of ideas (gathered by consumers) put together (via readership pathways), we might generate a new avenue, a new option.

That's online education at its extreme: an individual choosing an individual path. Yet we faculty and administrators believe that all students should take an agreed-upon set of courses as if these twenty or so subjects carry with them some magical formula for success. The idea of students writing their own educational path, taking what they think is appropriate is, well, like a student taking calculus II before calculus I. Simply not done. Why, I remain unsure. We all agree that students should have some say in the path of their education, within the artificial bounds, rules, and prerequisites we have established for no particular reason other than we have the ability to do so. Students are provided the ability to learn within established classrooms rules (for whatever reason) with a lecture/seminar/dialogue or whatever, and the understanding that they (the students) will from time to time say something that indicates that they are paying attention and understanding some minuscule portion of what is happening.

Having cast the classroom education experience in the worst possible acceptable cast, imagining that any sane faculty person would have a reasonable argument against online education would be difficult to fathom. I could suggest that we expect sixteen-year-olds to act like adults (wielding half-ton vehicles of destruction and death). We ship off eighteen-year-olds to defend the country in the armed forces. We even let them vote. But allow them to choose a college path of education that might be intensely individualized via apps and online content? Never!

> I agree that we are headed towards individualization. I think that overall this is a good thing. As technology advances, we have the capability to be unique through technology in choosing what goes on our phones and computers. Having the opportunity to customize our technology gives individuals the ability to express themselves in new ways that had not been possible before the advance of technology. Although this can be a positive advancement, it also has a downfall. Because technology has become such a popular method of communication, a lot of relationship building relies on technology as opposed to actually being with people. Overall though I believe that the individualization is a good thing, and that it has not yet gotten to the point where it has gone too far. —Mackenzie

HOW UNIVERSITIES CAN BE SOMETHING OTHER THAN A PLACE FOR ELITES

We need not change. We are figuring out how to charge students more. We are making the argument that it is someone else's fault. We want our faculty (at least most of it) to teach and do research. Apps? We need not consider doing much more than referring to them, including them in discussions, and moving on. After all, apps were not a part of our education. How important can they be? And Asians who want more education can come to our campuses or enroll at University of Phoenix. We are what we are.

But global students now have a way to access us or at least to move themselves up the educational ladder from missing to step one. Apps will allow these current nonstudents to access educators who are willing to teach tens of thousands of students at a time. Apps will allow these currently noneducated students to share in what is known, allowing them to progress, and at some point allowing them to help their community—even if entirely unintended—to progress. What this has rendered is a new way of considering the students sitting in class: they are elites. They are the ones going to a class, in person. This will—as it always has been—remain a rare thing, something that only someone in the smallest population of the globe has the option to do. Convincing freshmen (heck, even seniors) at a state college that they are special will be quite a task, to be sure.

However, let's be clear: apps are not tools of groups. They are not built for traditional group behavior. App software enhanced individuality. When that individuality benefits the good of society, we reap the fruit: progress.

How can a university encourage online education using the tools they now have? Good question. Most faculty simply walk away: sorry, I cannot teach a hundred students, much less ten thousand, online or off. Not going to happen. And I agree with them. Using the current university pedagogical structure, it cannot reasonably be expected that a professor can both do research and teach massively online. Time restrictions make it unlikely. Political expectations make it even more unlikely: we still live in a very jingoistic world. Legislators in the United States, Germany, Italy, India, and pretty much everywhere else see their universities as tools to train students to somehow gain an edge over other countries. Education is an asset just as important—okay, maybe not quite as important—as a missile or a tank. We cannot allow country X to gain an advantage on us in the field of Y. Let's make sure our universities keep us up to speed in everything.

Of course, the problem here is that education is really a global culture cure, not a neighbor nuclear device. And here is what really matters the most: potential students do not see national borders on their handhelds using their apps. They see cultural differences (for now; more about that in the next chapter).

Culture is a roadblock. National borders are not. The latter, as discussed earlier, are ignored. The former can cause issues with transeducational exchanges, languages being the first barrier. However, the demand for education is so strong, in such demand that even not speaking or reading English is seen as only a temporary delay, especially for those who are six years old and younger. Yes, we can teach forty-year-olds to read and speak English. However, a six-year-old child absorbs language very much like a sponge.

The challenge for those delivering a course in physical science to a six-year-old (and why not?) is a possible required shift in culture. That is, just because the target student uses a handheld and accesses the education site via apps does not mean she or he is reading or understanding what is posted in a manner in which the educator hopes. This may represent the biggest barrier to adoption. We can all agree that English may be adopted as the global language (even if a majority speak something else, like a dialect of Chinese).

And we may all agree that English has some built-in challenges, such as idioms and slang not easily explained. But more important, the language itself comes in many forms, some more understandable than others.

Many of you are probably wondering what I am worried about: English as a written language is fairly easy to track. When the reader encounters an unknown word, a dictionary can be consulted, definition obtained, and reading resumed. I am not suggesting that every written book renders itself easy to understand in English: consider George Lukacs' *The Theory of the Novel*. The tome itself is short. The theory is impenetrable. Such an odd outlier in a world of far easier to follow and absorb written works is rare. In this case, however, we are not considering written works of much value moving forward—of great complexity or not. We are moving rapidly in the technology world away from the written word toward a verbal language information exchange. And here's the rub. Dialects render English a multifaceted language that can be understood in many cases but not easily understood in others. This does not refer to the language as spoken by recent immigrants. Consider English spoken by those in East End London compared to those of West Side New York City.

The barrier of dialects must be accounted for, dealt with, and resolved. The lack of dialects in portrayals of the future in movies is more than absurd but even more simply impossible. Or is it?

Can dialects be eliminated via new media, via apps? Might we not have two possible solutions to help in our move of education online: translation and transformation? The former is simply an app that transforms the spoken work of the educator from what is being said into a more basic, globally agreed-upon standard. The result is an educator who can continue to speak as she or he wishes and students who can hear as they wish (with a second translator). Of course, such devices might simply be used as they are now, with translators replaced by computers changing a foreign language into a language the listener understands. Wearing earbuds, we can all understand each other via our handhelds, using an app, of course.

Yes, there will be an app (actually several) for that.

The latter of these options, transformation, simply brings each user to an understanding of the correct dialect. Obviously this challenge is a bit more weighty than the built-in translation app. And the outcome has a far more massive impact culturally.

Let's back up for a moment and consider that I am arguing here that education may represent the most powerful engine for change than any other transformational device available. Education always results in the student being taken from point A to point B, no matter what is being taught. Even religious studies result in change.

The two outcomes outlined here provide us with two possible societal results: individualism and socialism. Obviously, the ability to maintain one's own dialect (and, possibly, one's own language) feeds into the ability to be an individual in a world of others. Having our own place with our own language may actually become more individualistic with the ability to apply an app that translates what we say into words that each person who watches can understand. This renders language as moot in the cultural mode. Of course, the question is, would it account for context? Changing one's speech to conform to a universal standard (oddly enough, everyone aboard the USS *Enterprise* spoke English—and a form of English everyone watching could understand) would result in one language, also eliminating language as a fundamentally important part of culture. Thus, no matter which way the path takes us, the existence of multiple languages is not long for this planet. We may be different from each other, but not based on language.

The elimination of language as a barrier is a key element in the globalization of universities as portals of education. If a university sees itself as less beholden to a local political structure and to a local cultural structure, it can reach out and help potential students everywhere to raise their life expectancy. If the idea of "student" comes to mean "everyone," then we have accomplished the ultimate goal of helping everyone succeed.

Early in 2015, I had a telephone conversation with Dr. Benjamin Young, a good friend with whom I had not chatted for some months. Ben is simply one of those incredibly brilliant people you—if lucky—meet and share ideas with. He is connected with many global health programs, has a great deal of research in print, and at the same time is an easy person to chat with. His latest (and, he suggested, his last) great project would be Fast Track Cities, a United Nations–backed effort to stop HIV/AIDS in thirty major cities around the globe by 2030. The conversation turned to what Dr. Nancy Maturi, one of our truly brilliant public relations professionals here at Kansas State University by way of Kenya, and I, an old advertising writer, could do to help promote the project.

The first step is to accept that this is an education project. However, rather than using the usual and quite boring ways that universities might promote it, something more dynamic, more global, more transcultural, more powerful would have to be created. Second, admit that those intended to receive the information probably do not read a daily newspaper nor watch television. If they have anything in common with each other in terms of communication devices, a handheld might be most likely.

Third, the target consumer is urban, which is a cultural element involving time, or the lack of it. What will result from the collaboration we cannot predict, but it will involve changing how the target sees the issue of HIV testing, for starters. Education is never predictable, no matter how much political committees would like to make it, no matter how much university bureaucracies would like to see it. What is predictable is its acceptability within a culture, and progress, unfortunately, is rarely a part of the equation.

Progress cannot avoid insulting the existing power structure. Perhaps the insults are perceived because so few societies are based on change but instead on stability.

Yet education lives and breathes in the world of change. Individuals are continually seeking information, looking to convert this data into knowledge, positive or negative. Education generally is seen as more on the positive side of this world of change, and the delivery of this information has in the past rested on educators and classrooms and textbooks. No more. The trouble is, unfortunately, that those seeking information need not sit in the presence of an educator in a classroom with the text. If we cannot shift the way we see education delivered, if we have a million excuses why online delivery will not work, if we continue to dig in our silly heels at apps, we will simply be sidestepped, marginalized, forgotten.

Not including us in the change has more than just the negative consequences for us. That lack of our participation also leaves education in the hands of those who either have no idea what they are doing or know exactly what they are doing (making money). The former of these are self-believers who are convinced that they know everything when they know nothing. No good. The latter of these care not whether they know anything or if their customers learn anything. They just want the credit card charge to clear. Also not so good.

We—that is, university educators—have a responsibility to drop our silly "traditions" and embrace global outreach. The politics will be difficult to overcome, but we are clever. The economics will be a challenge, but, again, we are clever. The facts are simple and the goals even easier. We have dealt with the facts. Let's consider some goals based in part on a report generated by the United Nations in 2012.

1. Every person in the world should be capable of reading at least at first-grade level by 2050.
2. Half of the world's population should have a high school education by 2050.
3. One quarter of the world's population should have a college education by 2050. ("Millennium Development Goals Report" 2012, 68)

Lofty goals? You betcha! But left to themselves, owners of handhelds (of all ages) will simply distract themselves with games rather than learning anything that will help them. And that reference to "of all ages" is important. The United Nations usually focuses on children in its studies, but what we need to keep in mind is that the world is populated by far more than children. Adults must be educated just as much as children. Harder? Yes. Necessary? Yes. In many cultures, a child cannot be smarter than the adult. Let's keep in mind that we are working within a variety of (now existing) cultures.

Within the world of universities, faculty is woefully behind. I will never forget the comment made by a faculty member of a planning committee I chaired some years ago. I had suggested that perhaps we should require our students to have laptops with them in class. I imagined the requirement today would be more flexible: "a computer device," thus covering everything from a laptop to a handheld. A fellow member of the committee complained that he could not allow students to use laptops in class because "they would be looking at porn." I suggested that if they were looking at porn, the problem had more to do with his lecture than their choices in browsing.

I also recall taking chemistry at a major engineering school in the southeast. Okay, it was Georgia Tech. The classroom/arena was filled with roughly four hundred students, or so it seemed. Could have been three hundred. Whatever it was, it was big. The lecturer down front was the chair of the department. The blackboards were filled with equations written by a graduate student and situated so that the lecturer could pull one board down after another, writing nothing, referring to one equation after the next. If you raised your hand, the chair would simply say, "Wait till lab."

Think about how that might be handled today. Questions? Post to an app-established message board during the lecture. Get a response immediately from the class-dedicated graduate student. Thus, rather than delaying the learning opportunity to the lab some days away, the answer is immediate, the clarification offered in a timely, clear fashion.

The bottom line is that we might consider the use of apps in university classrooms as a given, more so than students paying attention to lectures. The latter of these two forms of delivery is seen more and more as stale and boring, no matter how electrifying we may act. If we hang on to lectures as our mode to teach, we are very likely isolating the use of apps to elements that distract and amuse rather than educate. We must change the way we teach to embrace the way students are currently learning so that what we want them to learn is part of the package of what they will access. Short of this, we become a quaint relic of the past, much as monks are relative to publishing.

REFERENCES

Anderson, Chris, and Michael Wolff. 2010. "The Web Is Dead: Long Live the Internet." *Wired.* August 17. http://www.wired.com/2010/08/ff_webrip.

"Best Global Universities." 2014. *U.S. News & World Report.* http://www.usnews.com/education/best-global-universities.

Buringha, Eltjo, and Jan Luiten Van Zanden. 2009. "Charting the 'Rise of the West': Manuscripts and Printed Books in Europe, a Long-Term Perspective from the Sixth through Eighteenth Centuries." *The Journal of Economic History* 69, no. 2: 409–37.

"Education Index." 2008. *Wikipedia.* https://en.wikipedia.org/wiki/Education_Index.

Fields, Liz. 2014. "Quarter of Americans Convinced Sun Revolves around the Earth, Survey Says." ABC News. http://abcnews.go.com/US/quarter-americans-convinced-sun-revolves-earth-survey-finds/story?id=22542847.

"Millennium Development Goals Report." 2012. United Nations. http://www.un.org/millenniumgoals/pdf/MDG%20Report%202012.pdf.

Chapter Ten

The Future of E-advertising

Not surprisingly, it appears [that] nearly every Internet user finds advertise-ments to be a nuisance. When I am browsing the Web, I feel the advertise-ments always fail to hit the sweet spot. The ads are either completely irrelevant to my taste and browsing history or they display products nearly identical to what I was already searching. As a car enthusiast I often search for vehicles on Cars.com. Later, I will find myself on a completely unrelated Web site with advertisements for vehicles of the same make, model, and even trim level. It is so evident [that] my browsing history was given to other Web sites that the ad becomes unattractive. Rarely do I find an advertisement in the middle ground and click the link. However, there are certain cases in which I would want an app or Web site to record my browsing history to a greater extent. For me, Spotify is the best example. I find its target marketing skills to be absolutely terrible. Ninety-nine percent of the time, an advertisement for a new song or album arrives on the screen and through my headphones, it is music I wouldn't even be paid to listen to. I turn the volume down just enough to recognize when the ad is over and my music returns to playing. —Ryan

This feels like the end of the beginning or the beginning of the end. We either know exactly what we want to happen, or we are randomly taking shots and hoping something sticks. I guess I am one of those former guys, at least in terms of advertising versus journalism and public relations. Not that journal-ism and public relations are not worthy and nice additions to any society or culture. Maybe the problem circles around the lack of money for journalism, which it needs to exist, and the lack of validity for public relations, which it again needs for value. Advertising, on the other hand, has no care for validity and as for money—well, it always has and will have money. After all, every-one needed to know where the first business was, how much it cost, and all the details.

And so advertising will continue, even online. It will be studied to death
(as it is now), examined by academics convinced that they have the right
theory applied to the right product reaching the right consumer and used by
marketers to justify closing or launching new brands, believing that they can
measure accurately the reach into new or old cultures. Advertising has been
around for a very long time (longer than journalism and certainly longer than
public relations), in some ways surviving the somewhat silly analysis applied
by tenure-desperate professors looking for a rationale for what is otherwise
just a sell. In fact, as an academic field, it has been within the university
setting for less than a century. Exactly who offered the first degree in advertising at the university level is a bit of a mystery. However, in general, the
history of advertising has been written about in some detail, including what
has happened in Europe, Asia, and elsewhere.

And we have more than a few authors offering their deep thoughts regarding where advertising will take itself in the coming years, with lots of consideration regarding new technologies, either for advertising delivery or meas-
urement, and lots of consideration of how advertising will change in the
West, in the East, in some places shared by both, and even how consumers
might participate in the advertising process. Yet few suggest that advertising,
generally considered the consistently most irritating element of public conversations, will go away. It cannot leave, you see. Too many people want it.

I know; you are doubting me. And well you might, for I am suggesting
that advertising not only will continue, but it will continue boldly and handi-
ly, but in a new form with a new definition:

> Advertising is the sharing of information regarding a product or service by
> those who are most familiar with it, with those who are less familiar with it.

This particular definition presumes that the advertising in question is of value
for those seeking it, for poor advertising can be shared by those who know
little or nothing about the product or service—something we suffer through
every day watching television, especially with local companies. Advertising
in this definition has moved away from exclusively its current creator (advertising agencies and those who unfortunately act like they are an agency) to
also include others. These "others" are those who have large, often anonymous numbers and formed their opinions of the product or service either
based on their own use or the use of a friend or because they are being paid to
act like they are "regular" folks. This last category—what we now know as
public relations professionals—are simply carrying out their duties.

The true unconnected, unbiased, likely uninformed, everything-is-based-
on-a-single-trial-run user is a somewhat unique voice in a universe of potentially millions of others. This is a group not being studied except via traditional advertising technology. Of course, the presumption—an errant one at

that—is that they will respond to new forms of surveys and other data collection devices. They will not. For something else has happened to our consumers: they got smarter.

Let's start this analysis as my cohorts would by eliminating those who "do not count": roughly half of the world's population who cannot purchase sodas from machines, both due to the availability of said machines and the availability of the coins necessary to operate said machines. I guess these individuals would be simply placed on the backburner by advertising agency executives and advertising and marketing professors as "potential consumers" as if not wallowing in mud is some sort of precursor to access to markets largely defined as Western. Jingoistic? You betcha! But advertising rarely brings out the best in anyone. At its core, advertising is about convincing not only that you make the best mud, but that the potential consumer who has not tried this mud as an alternative to a pile of dead leaves is missing out on a real bonus. And did we mention we have our mud in lots of sizes and colors? And here's a coupon for 10 percent off!

So, after we have walked away from half the globe, what we have left is the target, maybe. If I make 3.5 billion of something on a regular basis that is consumed on a regular basis, then, yes, the remainder of the world's population is the potential target. If I make something less than 3.5 billion of something on a regular basis, or 3.5 billion or more on a very infrequent basis, then some targeting will need to be done.

So how do we target when our potential market is scattered within 3.5 billion somewhat different and at other times very different consumers? We start with the understanding that we know our product or service beyond the foolish "it's the best!" or other such silliness. We admit that we want to sell for more than the bloke around the corner. We admit that the way we communicate might have a real impact on the ability to sell it. And we admit that, although we tend to know more than the average bear about our product, we do not know what is important to the target consumer.

This is a story as old as the hills (and probably already mentioned in this book), but knowing that your client's piano comes with a special metal bar that preserves the soundboard is not just a big deal, it is the only deal. It is also something so accepted by the manufacturer that he can overlook it (as he did) in all the information forms provided to the advertising agency. Only in personally investigating the manufacturing of the piano was the Capo De Astro "discovered" by the advertising agency and its use during the Metropolitan's tours around the world revealed and heralded.

So that sets at rest issue number one. The client rarely knows the value of what it is selling to its target consumer, because it really doesn't understand its product or service or its real value to its target consumer.

Of course, even if the advertising agency understands the product or service and understands the real value of it to the target consumer, it has two

major challenges: what to say and where to say it. I am certain I will get
letters from art directors regarding this, but what is said these days has more
to do with ideas expressed in words than in images. Of course, being an old
copywriter, I could be viewed as fundamentally biased and a silly goose
regarding the value of words over images. I am guessing that ideas might be
more effectively transmitted through words alone than images alone.

Consider that these days, ideas are transmitted in moments, not thirty- or
sixty-second spots. Online information consumers (OIC)—I guess you might
call them bloggers or browsers or any number of things—are working at light
speed, digesting, sharing, and moving on within seconds. An idea that seems
interesting might slow this OIC, but only for a second or two longer. If this
potential consumer is to be reached, attracted, stalled, or in any other way
slowed in the trek through the information morass, the idea better stand out.
Really interesting ones hold attention. This ability to hold the attention of a
potential target consumer means a lot and is often overlooked. Simply re-
warding an advertising agency for creating an XYZ spot for a Web site, blog,
or whatever attracted lots of OICs misses the point. We are not simply
swapping out rotten, foul, generally gross guesswork conducted in print and
television for rotten, foul, generally gross guesswork conducted online, are
we?

We have the ability and thus both the responsibility and the expectation to
target the targets far more effectively. Otherwise, we are just driving more
and more target consumers to engineer methods to block, ignore, or reroute
messages to a spam catcher. That is not optimization. In fact, it is not even in
the same category. It represents an admission that the advertising agency in
charge of the task cannot target because it cannot identify, cannot understand,
and cannot communicate with the right consumer. No one said it was easy.
But if I make five hundred thousand of something that costs $100,000, I
certainly do not need an advertisement during the Super Bowl or World Cup,
thank you.

> I definitely think the Internet takes advertising way farther than it should. The
> fact that it can build off of your previous searches is almost scary in a way that
> we don't know what other information is being manipulated. This goes back to
> one of your very first questions about if we feel that our lives are being used in
> a way via the Internet that we didn't permit. There's also a step further—when
> the ads don't allow you to get past them, when you're watching those long
> videos and you're being forced to read into what the ad wants you to see, feel
> or even believe. I think it's a way of advertising that isn't done the correct
> way. —Lindsey

SOME CURRENT IDEAS DRIVEN BY CURRENT BEHAVIOR

Christopher Heine identified ten "events" or changes that he argues were significant enough to refer to as "world changing," each with its own impact. Let's consider some of what he got out of the 2015 World Mobile Congress.

- Mobile World Congress predicted that the number of mobile subscribers in the world would increase by 1 billion in the next five years to 4.6 billion.
- "Walmartville"—a city defined as all those onliners using their cellphones in the stores—would be larger than the city of San Francisco proper. Of course, what it did not include is that 1 million users represent less than one-third of one percent of all global mobile users. Oh well. Once again we are overwhelmed by thinking that a million users means something in a billion users world. In many ways, we are stuck in our thinking by our individualization: a million seems like a lot when we think of ourselves.
- Some apps grow faster than others. Line, a millennial-happy Japanese mobile game, adds 1.7 million new users every day. Again, that seems like a lot. Again, it really is not.
- Lee McCabe, global head of travel for Facebook, reports that almost four of five smartphone users have their devices within reach all but three hours a day. But then, why not? I cannot quite imagine what is happening in those three hours, but the phones are mobile, thus can go anywhere and stay with the user anywhere. This seems like a stat that at first is impressive, then fades.
- It is reported at the conference that four years ago only eight percent of the online networking site's traffic came via mobile devices. Apparently that number now stands at 50 percent. But we sensed that, right? (Heine 2015)

We know, in a way, all of what Heine reports just by looking around us. We see the shift in usage, whether among fifteen-year-olds or fifty-year-olds. We see the shift in commercialization, as movies that once were two hours on television now take two-and-a-half hours—if not more—to accommodate more overwhelmingly repeated commercials with little or no defined targets. As we can imagine, a more powerful advertising landscape with improved targeting, far more improved communication, and far more self-defined target consumers, is also an ugly one.

What are we currently doing to compensate for what some of us (who ought to know better but do not) believe is a shattered advertising world?

We—both advertising agencies and their clients—do not know what to do with commercials that are drawing smaller and smaller audiences except to run them more and more. Simply running more of the same information to the same consumers makes about as much sense as having a sale of five

hundred hamburgers to a target that can eat one or two, maybe. We are
replicating this silliness within many of our university media-planning
courses by teaching the tried-and-true idea of newspaper and television buys,
as if target consumers are still to be found reading the news on page 5 or
watching a comedy show at 7 pm (which, as noted, is a fraction of its
previous length in order to squeeze in more commercials because fewer
people watch the programs). The logic behind buying bigger ads in less-read
newspapers and more spots on less-watched television has checked out, and I
haven't even mentioned the silliness of radio advertising. We teach it because we are—okay, I admit, I have no idea why we still teach it except
habit. We do this foul planning because it is all we know. We are in com-
mand of the *Titanic* and believe if we just keep going, all will be fine.

We believe that only a few use mobile devices and that most of them are
children. We could not be more wrong. Not at some point in the future, but
right now, today, the shift has taken place and will only continue. With the
exception of most sports, what was once watched on television is rapidly
shifting to the Internet. With the exception of a few magazines and books, the
majority of what is being read is shifting online to specific apps.

I believe that what is happening today will be happening at least for the
next year, if not longer. This may be a wish more than a scientific finding.
Even those of us who might be described as innovators based on personality
evaluators like to think some things will remain constant. Trouble is, of
course, they do not. We have legislative entities desperately wishing to maintain the now: that which is predictable. That we have advertising agencies
more concerned with maintaining the brand as it was a century ago is more
regretful. If Tony the Tiger is to move more globally, then we have to think
of the product and its advertising differently. Consider that in a bit of research published by Mulhall in 2011, where it was suggested that "Advertising can be defined as any paid form of non-personal promotion transmitted
through a mass medium. The key difference between advertising and other
forms of promotion is that it is impersonal and communicates with large
numbers of people through paid media channels" (Mulhall 2011). Such a
definition reveals an out-of-touch, isn't-that-sweet connection to the real
world of advertising. Not much in common with my earlier definition of
advertising.

Also consider that in 2015, Devin Leonard in a piece for *Bloomberg
Business* suggested that Tony the Tiger's Frosted Flakes—Kellogg's leading
brand—was on a downhill slide, losing almost 5 percent in sales in one year
(Leonard 2015). Now, Tony and Kellogg must reconsider how "Great!"
things really are in a globally defined, individually created market, or a
century-old brand may fade away. Hence, there's a very good chance of
seeing a well-known brand—let's say Nike or Absolut—on a tee shirt worn
by someone who knows nothing about the brand that appears on his or her

chest. That shirt is meaningful to you. Great. To the potential new market, unlikely. Even if they knew, they cannot afford it.

Next time you're in a group (I know—that does not happen much these days or at least not as often as it once did), ask how many people watch television. Television was, not that long ago, the best example of A talking to B and getting B to consider purchasing C. The pattern of response and purchase was easy to track, easy to research, easy to measure. Group behavior, of course, helped, but so did consumer predictability. Everyone watched Ed Sullivan, Dave Letterman, and dozens of shows that ran at a particular time on a particular station. In an odd way, this represented a group response, a group behavior, a group evaluation. What you might discover from your question regarding television watching is that fewer of your friends are tuning into NBC, ABC, or CBS. Set aside sports (and that is a separate issue for advertising) and entertainment of any kind can be had for less money, at a more convenient time, and on almost any device. Entertainment becomes a tool available when the viewer wants to watch it, not when the producer wants to show it. This may make more of a difference in time. Bottom line: advertisers can no longer count on when a particular show is being watched and that used to be important. After all, soap operas or telenovelas were shown during the day when housewives were home doing—among other home-keeping activities—the laundry. That was a long time ago (the 1950s through the 1970s), but the shift away from this type of commercial in a particular time of day, connected to a type of programming broadcast at a particular time of day, lasted for at least the first sixty years of television. It has changed radically in the past five years. What your friends will say will surprise you.

It wasn't that long ago that I wrote about the advertising writing of the Creative Revolution and its heroes, Ogilvy, Burnett, and Bernbach. They were writers. They created imagery and pushed it to consumers (and won). This creative era as it was referred to was a misnomer. Nothing that was offered did much more than offer something that had not been done before. It was very much like the evolution of music from the Duke to Ella to Diana. The continuum was predictable from those who preceded Ogilvy to those who would follow. In all instances, the players were key: the art director combining with the copywriter was the magic. Even recently with the addition of a third "planner" type, the ideas were self-generated with all the intent in the world to push, shove, force the target consumer to swallow the pitch whole. It is no longer, though it remains taught that way in universities due to the certainty that someone wants it taught as it was. Maybe advertising presents that challenge on a regular basis: change ultimately is presented by the consumer, routed through creative, only to end up back with the consumer.

The idea that creative generated the idea—the X Factor or whatever special name an agency gave to what it was doing—made it possible to charge
for what was otherwise the consumer's idea. This global behavior of misap-
propriation is perhaps the one commonality shared by all advertising agencies.

The sole challenge for the advertising agency creative team is segmented:
they must create a spot no longer associated with a time of day; one that is
not boring, not pushy, not obnoxious; and, most of all, one that is actually on
target. It should be a spot that the target consumer wants to watch. It should
be a spot that answers questions that consumers have already formed in their
heads. It should be a spot that fulfills the self-identified needs of the consumers, even if the details are blurry or poorly defined.

Easier said than done.

> I wouldn't exactly use the word "worse" when describing advertising on the
> Internet. Compared to advertising with the current TV and radio system, it is a
> lot more advanced, which can be annoying but useful. For example, I was
> looking to buy a new pair of boots a few weeks ago. After looking on a site
> and returning to my Facebook page, my page was filled with advertisements
> for boots. I actually clicked a link where I ended up ordering my boots from.
> But, I got the ads for a week because I wasn't really searching [for] anything
> else, and it was just going off of my computer cookies. I found it annoying. I
> see how it may seem manipulative, but in the end, I got what I wanted, as well
> as the advertisement of the business. They were able to target their specific
> consumer who they knew would be interested in their product. It's scary, yes,
> in the big picture. But if people are that afraid, clearing their cookies and
> history files will make [for] a lot less specific advertisements. It takes work on
> the consumer side, as well, if you don't want to be as seen as a "manipulated
> target" or don't want to see ads related to you, annoying or not. But the amount
> of advertisements that are being put on Web pages is getting very annoying.
> Five years ago, advertisements were only on the sidebar of a page. Now, on
> Facebook, they are between your newsfeed of friends. Sometimes it's hard to
> differentiate between a friend's posting and an ad, which can get touchy with
> FCC violations and codes. So that does make my experience a little less
> enjoyable than before, but companies have to make their money some way.
> And like most people, we will put up with the ads for free social sites and less
> upgrades. —Clarissa

SOME NEW IDEAS DRIVEN BY CURRENT BEHAVIOR

Some years ago the idea sprang up that readers could direct the pathway of a
story within a single book by choosing the next step. I tried it a couple of
times. Not sure it is still offered much. It was a real spiffy deal for a while. It
left me with the feeling that I never did anything that defined how I thought
the story might end. I just chose from a series of acceptable (and offered)

options. By doing so, I determined whether Jane found her true love or if Andrew decided his father was wrong. It was never much beyond the predictable, though it was marketed as a story whose outcome was within my control.

I have always been the not-very-nice professor because I expected my students to write, especially those who wanted to move into public relations (do not ask me why). My superiors received all manner of reports that I expected too much, was "fuzzy" on expectations, and was just mean and nasty. I imagine change is not welcome anywhere, whether among undergraduates or department administrators (but that story can be told another day). Bottom line: the way we do advertising has to change; advertising and its impact will be defined by the consumer whether we like that or not.

The problem in advertising is that we have many of the old guard who think television commercials are king. We have just as many creative directors who want more video-thinking pros than they do consumer response–thinking pros. Agencies still think media planning when they should be thinking consumer planning. They are still thinking *push* when the demand that we all switch to *pull* happened years ago.

Why? It cannot be a lack of engineering. The technology has been available. The ability to create groundbreaking new ideas delivered in newly created platforms has been in our backyard for years. What is the barrier? What has always been the barrier has remained immovable (at least at the individual level, as we have discussed): fear. Hofstede refers to and globally measures fear as "uncertainty avoidance." There is no culture that does not feature some degree of this. More important, no individual—independent of his or her culture—does not exhibit some abiding concern that the cliff will fail, the board will break, the bridge will fall. What will determine the success of an advertising campaign that needs an edge is the degree to which the creative director is willing to tune into that specific edge demanded by the target consumer. If the product is dull, low-priced, simplistic, then the commercial required by the target consumer need be only similarly interesting and unique (perhaps bears selling toilet paper will do). If the need is for something more rare, like a certain automobile or a special perfume, then creative had better rely on something more than a full-page advertisement in a fashion magazine. Anyone can do that. Anyone can read that. Anyone can ignore that.

So, oddly enough, I have been asked to teach media planning for the first time in my sixteen years at the university. What an opportunity to change the way of teaching a course that probably requires the most change. What will we do this fall? Probably start with the impact of media on information sharing and the forms within which it can be offered. Will we be using the old software that shows how to predict the costs of running an ad on television, in a newspaper, and on radio? Nope, I don't believe that makes much difference. What I have discovered is that media use is very much in the hands of the user, the consumer, not the agency media buyer. You can create the most beautiful, most persuasive, most provocative commercial ever ima-gined and have it unwatched by the target consumer.

> The Internet has helped advertising companies advance to another level in manipulating our society into thinking, feeling, and doing some of the craziest things, in my opinion. With the Internet's help, advertising companies can see whatever we look at, buy, and search, while surfing the Web. For example, I shopped for all kinds of presents during cyber Monday, and the very next day I get on Facebook, and I'm getting ads thrown in my face about "similar presents I might like." It was kind of shocking how quickly the Internet picks up on things we look at and then compiles advertisements that are similar to the things we already have and enjoy. Can't blame them, though; it's smart and it gets the job done. And, no, it's not helping me at all; it's more annoying than anything else. I don't really think advertisements are made to help, they exist to sell and make money. The invasion of my privacy and the tracking of my search history is in no way worth the recommendation of a new color watch "I may like." Tracking my search history helps them know more about the demographic they are striving for, I guess, but I don't care to be a part of their research project and projectile advertisements. —Ashlynn

NONTRADITIONAL GETS EVEN MORE NONTRADITIONAL

I must admit that in my nontraditional advertising class I have the hardest time getting the vast majority of students to think nontraditionally. Coupons and billboards seem to be what they expect will satisfy class expectations. I have taught this course several times in the last few years, and each time the complaints are that the course was not what the student expected. Oh, well—change is rarely accepted where we learn what will be needed, rather, it is what we once needed. The past is a friend. The future, who knows? Kinda scary. Most students are like most agencies: they like to curl up with certain-ty and leave risk and new ideas outside.

   In some ways, that nicely describes new nontraditional advertising. Big risk taking can often result in a major failure. Having a client willing to take part in the risk taking is more than just a signoff: defending a failure requires a willingness to explain that what might have happened justified taking the chance. Of course, if the damage is too great, everyone faces the music. Thus, we are going to look at what can only be described as a couple of risk-of-being-fired campaigns. They will give us a very good idea of others that are being offered globally, shared globally, and reacted to globally.

   Go to YouTube and type "Aguilera," "perfume," "Guy Dayan," and "im-age." One of the choices is "Christina Aguilera Perfume Promotion (unedit-ed)" at https://www.youtube.com/watch?v=YtYUgVXxhN4. Watch it. What you get is the commercial that appeals to people not interested in the perfume. Maybe some who are not interested in Christina Aguilera. Maybe some who find the approach inappropriate. But all of this is okay because, for whatever reason, more than a million bottles were sold with no traditional ads—this represents a more direct conversation with the target.

The idea was simple: if you want people to buy something, especially perfume, give them a sample. The perfume could have been on scent tabs placed anywhere. Instead, the advertising agency involved, Mizbala, based in Tel Aviv, and its creative director, Guy Dayan, imagined the perfume, one created for Aguilera, placed on coat hangers. A scented bit of cardboard hung from each coat hanger. In some cities, like Milan, the hangers were a bit more elegant. But in all cases, the cost was minimal and the communication so effective between those who saw the hangers and those who received the images via Facebook, Twitter, and other channels. The thought here was simple: gain consumer interest. Certainly many would take pictures and share with those with no interest in the perfume, but a lot would be interested. So many were interested that they went to nearby stores and checked out the product's actual smell (which, of course, did not come through on the postings).

The success was overwhelming. Millions of bottles sold for relatively little advertising investment. Yes, another advertisement could be purchased in *Who Cares Fashion Magazine*. But the intent was a bargain first: the product was of interest. Not your usual perfume commercial. In this case, the consumer and the product itself filled the field. This advertisement was clearly information (I guess I would have called this advertising in the past) and was clearly shared with others.

I say I guess about what this would have been called in the past because we have always had to pass along information. But we have always had information that provoked trial. Here the information regarding the product was generated by the consumer, and I doubt we can call these consumers "leaders": they just happened to be on a sidewalk in front of some coat hangers.

Saatchi & Saatchi, New Zealand

Okay, so you have this movie to promote. You can do the usual television spot that almost everyone will watch and remember very little about. Or you can use an elemental part of the film, in this case blood, to make the ad not only memorable, but shareable. In sharing parlance, this one is a you-can't-wait-to-show-Joe image. And here's the great thing about advertising in the second decade of the second millennium: where it takes place is not the issue. In this case, the billboard was posted in New Zealand. Who cares? The idea was so strong and the desire so present to share this powerful image that it went global almost instantly.

Why? Because the idea itself was so unique, so ultimately shareable that it had to be sent. Even more interesting was the likelihood that those interested in *Kill Bill: Volume 1* would want to share a billboard promoting *Kill Bill: Volume 2*. The ability to gather and share the information reinforced the information itself as even more valid and valuable. You cannot expect more. You cannot wish for more.

What the creative director hopes to attain, what the media strategy director hopes to create, what the advertising agency president hopes to attain is a consumer-adopted, consumer-driven, consumer-blessed campaign that looks and feels like anything but an advertising campaign. We do not push; we do not convince; we do not sell. We show. And wait.

In so many ways the outcome of a singular, somewhat out-of-the-way locale event becomes a global message. Again, let's presume it sold ten million bottles. The total amounts to less than one-third of we have defined as the purchasing world population. Again, it requires little to succeed in a world of billions when the target is in the millions. That is, assuming the product is reasonably appealing.

Of course, if your product is not quite up to snuff, the new consumer information transfer network will only out you sooner and more effectively than ever before. Compounding this is the certainty that without some form of cosmic intervention, the product in question shall remain dead forever. Consumers have a way of doing that.

> Internet advertising can be annoying, but so can almost any type of advertising. While it can be a little unsettling to know that companies are tracking your Internet history, at least they are taking the time to build a profile on you and advertise products that you are more likely to be interested in, rather than just random commercials that you simply tune out. —Ross

CONSUMER DEATH BLOGS

It's happened a few times during my time at a university: a faculty member finds him- or herself on the wrong side of the faculty and the students and does not make it past the first five years. Is it fair? No. Is it always necessary? No. Could it be avoided? Yes.

The problem usually starts in one area and builds without sufficient correction. That is, the problem was minor but wasn't addressed in a timely way. Of course, if the problem is known, it could be addressed. If not, the result can be more secretive and vicious.

Oddly enough, some products face the same troubles. Rather than face a problem (that is, admit it and move forward), we see the full array of Kübler-

Ross's stages of grief, including denial. Rarely—whether you are BP Oil, Toyota, or Exxon-Mobil—does this work. In the past, the press delivered scalding criticism of these three. Of course, given the small numbers of consumers who actually watch the news, read newspapers, or in any other way keep up with what is happening, ignoring a disaster (such as Exxon and the *Valdez*) has never really amounted to that much damage. Exxon-Mobil trades just fine on Wall Street, thank you.

But we have a new system of information sharing that oddly but predictably loves bad news more than good news, or so it seems (Easaw 2010, 253–64; Hansen, Arvidsson, Nielsen, Colleoni, and Etter 2011, 35–43; Lamont 2005, 1217; Soroka 2006, 372–85; Xiong and Bharadwaj 2013, 706–24). Maybe we, as humans, have always loved gossiping bad news more than sharing good news. It's a given that bad news dominates the evening news—no matter how much we wish it didn't, and no matter how often we wish it would run "happy news." Bottom line: we want to know about bad news. Consider that forty thousand people die every year on highways. Consider that these deaths rarely get much more that a thirty-second spot on the local news. However, were two hundred people to people to die in a plane crash (and yes, I have lost a friend in a plane crash), the news coverage would last at least a week. I have had friends die in car accidents and in plane crashes. Not sure why one is more newsworthy than the other.

The trouble with seeking to block the bad news these days versus, say, fifty years ago is that back then it was possible for the chatter to fall away after a day or two by a moving-on-to-the-next-disaster news crew. After all, in 1970, we were always facing a new disaster, scandal, you-name-it. Today, online, the world and the "societies" within it act a bit differently. First, scandals are part of the big menu of sharing that itself can last months. Second, additional "information" can be added that is or is not true. Third, names are named, unlike traditional news, which might withhold names until legal issues are resolved. This gets spicy, driving more readership, images, and storytelling. We live forever—at least online—in a world of possible scandalizing information sharing by those who have adopted the idea that the world of reality (and, thus, real harm) ends with the send button.

Okay, what does this mean?

If harm does not exist, neither does real benefit. But consumers who believe their lives will be changed by switching their toilet paper are few and far between. The creative age of the 1960s (and 1970s, a bit) is over and might be referred to these days as the BS era. We live in a sort of quasi-reality where hyperreality about all products can be found, including false information, false reviews, and totally made-up information, so in-depth, so seemingly real that no researching consumers/academics are even aware that they are being misled.

Yes, I am suggesting what I am suggesting. Not only will it be next to impossible to verify advertising, it will be next to impossible to verify research. Consider that researchers are bombarded on a weekly basis with fake, thrown-together "academic conferences" intended to generate dollars in applications. Consider that dozens of these so-called academic conferences are held every year by people wanting to make money. I "presented" at one these only to find that the only people who attended the conference were those who presented at the conference. Hey, I like Cambridge, England, as much as anyone; however, that was a waste of money and time.

SMASH-UPS, LIES, AND DAMAGED BRANDS

Consider that for the first time in commercial history, what I just described in the field of academic research can occur equally in the advertising of products and services. We have turned over the evaluation of the message to the consumer, asking the consumer to investigate questionable claims, verify issues raised, act as a reasonable individual relying on solid information. What this represents is a lot to ask of a population that is largely uneducated and that intends, oddly enough, to remain that way.

The term "uneducated" does not suggest that they cannot use mobile devices. Such tools are made for ten-year-olds, not sage philosophers. In fact, users have their own languages, their own symbols. Language, too bound by dictionaries during the past five centuries, is skipping ahead, freely adding words from other languages. Part of the mix is the quasi-advertising messages being shared globally. As is so often the case, critics stand back and note that English has not overwhelmed the existence of other languages, as if it was trying and has ceased its campaign. The fact that it will is a given, like it or not. But to assume it will sound anything like it does today is short-sighted and silly. English in fifty years will be as different from English today as English today is from English in 1615 (roughly around the end of the time of the great vowel shift). What may happen, though, is that English may actually be freed from dictionaries and defined by an ever-changing, ever-shifting online environment that creates words as needed.

Amid all of this will be those with an abiding interest in defining elements of our society, mainly for those with some desire to purchase and acquire. We wish that honesty ruled the day. Of course, it does not. We in advertising are ruled first by the need to sell. An honest advertiser is admired, but one with a happy client is much more likely to be fed, clothed, and housed. Honesty and client happiness are not always peaceful cohabitants. So it has been that some fudging has taken place. No, we cannot scientifically suggest that happiness exists in a beverage bottle or that a vehicle honestly stands for the United States, or that a hotel, airline, or restaurant will in any particular way change, satisfy, or make a customer a better person. Shirts are shirts, and a perfume is just a perfume.

Few people know this more than those acting online, especially the three types that reside there today: the honest critic, the paid critic, and the rotten, secretive critic. The first of these tries to offer only their best thoughts in a forthright way. They generally offer suggestions for improvement, are rarely just critical, and are famous for talking up the scenery if the rest of the play is lacking. The quality of the honest critic varies, as does the quality of the honest creator. We have no special academic degree that guarantees with any certainty that what is being offered as a critical assessment is any more accurate coming from a person with a doctorate, a master's, or a person on the street. Universities would argue to the contrary, but doctorates mean only that the holder has done what is necessary to hold a doctorate, nothing more. A critic working for the *New York Times*, by the same reasoning, has no more power of reasoning or criticism than a Plain Joe wandering the streets of Omaha. Of course, some of us grant one more power than the other. It is our human nature to believe that somehow the thoughts of the New York critic are more insightful, more useful, more accurate than those of Plain Joe.

This has always baffled me. Why do we hand over our thoughts, our rationales, our best abilities to sift the good from the bad to someone we have never met, briefly read, hardly know? Do they really know more than your best friend? Can they really advise you better than your spouse? It is a puzzlement. Your friends are certainly more honest, at least as far as you know. That is, the critic from the soon-to-be-gone *New York Times* may be an honest type, but then again, times are tough. Maybe a few bucks are passing the transom. Who knows? Doubt enters the picture, yes? But why? Are we by nature dishonest?

Perhaps, if we are personally less than truthful ourselves. I am sure that Macbeth or Hamlet had something to say regarding this, but let's just agree that the purer our own selves, the purer we see the selves of others, sometimes to our own detriment. Postings on blogs are often presumed by others in a few ways: the post will be believed, as posted, by the person doing the posting; the person doing the posting is a real person; and the thoughts of the poster are honestly represented. None of this may be the case.

In some ways the issue is that of a smile. Precisely what the smile actually means is not a certainty. We have presumed that anyone posting who seems honest, is honest, and therefore should be believed. Trouble is, of course, that this poster may be very much like our type three, which we will discuss later.

But before we discuss the evil ones, let's examine what may be, for certain, the only "honest" poster. The paid critic is a wonder. Here we have someone who openly admits to being compensated by the sponsor to defend, compliment, and provide a bounty of flowers for the corporation based on the belief that the rewards are deserved. This person, usually a professional, has used personal beliefs and chosen to make an argument. This is where we would like to think advertising professionals reside. They believe that what they are selling is of value, is helpful, is a good thing.

Now I know this will generate pushback from those who believe the advertising professional does not have a card to play in the game of product validity. The argument here is about representing those companies who make products that are known to shorten lives—cigarettes being the leader.

But consider the issue as a subject on a message board. Does it matter now that we have a poster who clearly states affiliation with R. J. Reynolds or who proclaims he is just John J. Jones, but is being paid by the cigarette manufacturer to post? The third category of posters are those who would, for a variety of reasons—none of them honest or reasonable—lie about their identity, that they are being paid, or that they are in any other way affiliated with a "side" in the discussion. This secret poster corrodes the entire system, rendering the entire communication process questionable. With little certainty that the person posting is anyone but a paid voice, no one can be trusted. Thus, what could be a useful exchange of ideas would be rendered a sham. After all, who can trust a system that has paid liars posting nothing but lies?

Unfortunately, the system does not rely on trust. Instead, belief rules the day. Readers tend to believe what they already believe. Few eurekas! are ever created by posting, if only because few readers go to sites that are likely to generate ideas foreign to what they already believe. Hence the problem for advertisers. Anyone can (and does) say anything they want about any brand. Not much can be done. The use of the online world of blogs and message boards requires constant attention, if only to know and counter the lies placed there. No one suggested technology was only a good idea.

> I believe that the Internet's advertising schemes has both its positives and negatives. On the positive side of things, I have allowed my Safari browser to allow certain advertisements to appear to my previously browsed items on Amazon and other Web sites, and then on the side of a certain Web site, it will have items similar to what I browse. So in other words, it all appeals to me based on what I have looked at on shopping Web sites, which is quite nice. It is good because it is not some random advertisement, such as on Youtube, and it at least gets me to look at the product that is presented. I do not feel manipulated by the fact that it knows what I have browsed, because I know there are all kinds of way it is tracking me, so it might as [well] be of use to me. On the negative side of Internet advertising are the pointless and forceful ads of Pandora and YouTube. Hardly ever have I watched or even listened to their advertisements, since they are forced upon me and are inconvenient. I will usually turn the volume down or do something else while they are playing. I contemplate even looking up a YouTube video due to the fact that I know I will be stuck watching some pointless video about something I don't care about. So while the personal ads are a plus to advertising, the forced videos

and activities are a big negative and are probably only going to get worse. — Connor

SOME LEAD, SOME FOLLOW

One message, one consumer, one product delivered at the right time and in the right place. The silver bullet is on the horizon. We are considering what 100 percent consumer-appropriate advertising will mean to future brand adoption. This goes far beyond what we discussed in a previous chapter. As we watch the differences between cultures disappear, we face three (at least) possibilities: pseudo-cultures created by advertising to heighten product appeal; universal values that will differentiate one product from another; and/or global marketing structures that will suppress local identity.

If I sell perfume, don't I want to suggest that the brand comes from Paris? Do not some consumer goods just belong in some places? Wines from France and the Napa Valley? Skiing in Colorado and the Alps? Adventure in places where you are not? I will never forget a poster created, I presume in Athens, Georgia, in a move against Clemson, a longtime competitor. The poster contained a young man bearing ski gear, bent over a pair of skis on his feet. Surrounding him were cattle. Across the bottom of the poster? "Ski at Clemson."

The romance of connecting a product or service to a particular place is part of the argument for why it's an appropriate choice. That the product is made in New Jersey or London's East End is neither important nor the kind of thing you want to make a big deal out of, if only because consumers can hardly be expected to hold positive thoughts about such places.

Cut to the chase: you are selling an orange to someone not in Florida, but you want them to think the orange came from Florida, even if it came from Brazil. Or do you? Orange growers in Florida certainly want you to want oranges from Florida. They do not even want you to consider oranges grown in Texas or California. But do consumers really care? A good orange is a good orange, whether it comes from Texas, Florida, or Brazil.

Now imagine if this all takes place on a blog. How can an advertising agency use the locale, ignore the locale, or focus on other attributes to sell the orange? If I am selling a car made in Canada and Mexico, but sold in the United States under a U.S. flag, is that the best idea I have? Is it an honest idea? Is it an idea that would be outed on a blog site and used to call me a series of not very nice words, however appropriate they might be? More than anything else, can I not come up with a better, stronger, more relevant idea why a vehicle should be purchased from me? It cannot be that no other idea is possible. It is very possible that no other idea is searched for and found.

We have confused technology with consumer thinking. We are thinking that all we need to do is place the idea in front of consumers and—stupid as they are—they will purchase the item featured. If the market is local, that might work for a while. After all, how many cars can you sell in Omaha? But if the market is global, suddenly the possibilities of gains and losses are in the multimillions. Even in Omaha, as the information transfer shifts more fully online, less reliant on e-mail, and on to mobile devices with global apps, consumers will be getting wise, wiser than they are now. Risk appearing manipulating. Risk appearing price gauging. Risk being liars. The coming world of apps provides a simple way for consumers to develop a way to talk about you and your company, what you are trying to do, what offers you are making, and what is the real deal, none of which you have the chance to stop, modify, or amend. A thirty-second spot on WNEB is not going to work. A post on your Web site is not going to work. You will be forced to deal with the world of apps and second-by-second conversations by thousands, maybe millions, of commentators, some with no real interest in visiting Nebraska or even the United States.

The days of advertisers being the talkers and consumers being the listeners are gone. Globalism has made everyone a participant in a discussion that is about your product or service. Apps have made it possible for everyone to be in the mix easily and cheaply. So what does your advertising agency do for you? It keeps you honest, deals with liars, counters accusations, and, more than anything else, it does all of this on the same battlefield where it's happening. Good advertising of the future will not be about convincing the consumer that you are better than you are, but that everything about you is true. No one suggests that you can cure cancer (unless you can) or climb mountains (unless you can). Truth is not just a good idea, it will be the only defendable idea. Anything short of that will be stripped down and revealed.

Advertising's future strength will be its willingness to be truthful. Anything less is an exercise in futility that undoubtedly will be the subject of a blog. The message will be honest, it will match the product or service, and it will reach the targeted consumer. Reaching that target will continue to be the biggest challenge of any campaign that involves both the media planner and the creative team. And, of course, the elephant: social media.

REFERENCES

Easaw, Joshy. 2010. "It's All 'Bad' News! Voters' Perception of Macroeconomic Policy Competence." *Public Choice* 145, no. 1–2: 253–64.

Hansen, Lars Kai, Adam Arvidsson, Finn Aarup Nielsen, Elanor Colleoni, and Michael Etter. 2011. "Good Friends, Bad News—Affect and Virality in Twitter." *Future Information Technology Communications in Computer and Information Science* 185: 35–43.

Heine, Christopher. 2015. "Ten Mind-Boggling Stats from 2015 World Mobile Congress." *Adweek*. March 5. http://www.adweek.com/news/technology/10-mind-boggling-stats-mobile-world-congress-163290.

Lamont, Monica. 2005. "Text Messaging and Breaking Bad News." *British Medical Journal* 330, no. 7501: 1217.

Leonard, Devin. 2015. "Who Killed Tony the Tiger?" *Bloomberg Business.* February 26. http://www.bloomberg.com/news/features/2015-02-26/for-kellogg-cereal-sales-recovery-may-be-lost-hope.

Mulhall, Katherine. 2011. "Kellogg's Marketing Mix." *Kellogg's Market Research.* http://www.academia.edu/5882182/Kelloggs_Market_Research.

Soroka, Stuart N. 2006. "Good News and Bad News: Asymmetric Responses to Economic Information." *The Journal of Politics* 68, no. 2: 372–85.

Xiong, Guiyang, and Sundar Bharadwaj. 2013. "Asymmetric Roles of Advertising and Marketing Capability in Financial Returns to News: Turning Bad into Good and Good into Great." *Journal of Marketing Research* 50, no. 6: 706–24.

Chapter Eleven

One World Agency

Governments and Advertising, States and Consumerism

There is no doubt that advertising plays on our emotions to catch our attention, and to persuade us to purchase. Research has shown that the emotional appeal is much stronger than the rational, and so this is a key factor that drives advertising creativity. It is also what is sometimes referred to as 'subliminal seduction.' I think the Internet just made it more affective. This I don't feel is a crime or that crucial. For someone like me who gets very impatient and frustrated with this random advertisement, I subscribe to premium apps where I have a little more control. Plus Internet users have to realize that all these various media on the Internet do not fund themselves to just serve you for free: those 'annoying' ads and placements do. Same goes to the other medias of communication like TV, radio, newspapers, except for the fact that since newspapers are not free like TV and radio, you tend to have a little more control as to look over ads except if you already find it interesting. —Tosan

LIFE, THE UNIVERSE, AND WHAT'S AHEAD

I imagine you, the reader, think I should have some big conclusions. After all, I have written a couple of hundred pages, given more than a few hours of thought, and certainly reveal a real commitment to the subject. Why not get big headlines and a spot on CNN, as Friedman does with his conclusions and beliefs? After all, as long as I make my prognostications twenty or more years out, I should be safely gone from this dimension before I am proved wrong.

Any "conclusions" I suggest would be just that, guesses. If we can agree on that without feeling cheated, then we have a deal. Yes, I feel strongly about some outcomes that may come to pass in each area we have examined:

advertising, apps, and culture. We will start with the last first, if only because it is perhaps the easiest to predict. Evidence abounds, trends are more obvious, and subjects readily available to back up whatever research efforts are offered by a faculty person in a journal, a writer in a book, or a graduate student in a class.

So what I am proposing or perhaps offering to you is my sense of what will happen in some undefined future. We all think that we have a pretty good idea about what will happen in the future regarding some things, usually the most obvious. What remains uncertain are those in the world of ideas: the uncertainty about how Frank will react to a new type of app or Juan to a new style in clothing or Ali to a new advertising stunt. We are desperate to feel that what will happen will both be safe and predictable, and, in most ways, safe *because* it is predictable.

But new media has changed the rules. Predictability is a less-sought-for attribute to life for many (individualists) who seek to make their otherwise rather boring lives somewhat interesting. After all, we cannot all paraglide off West Coast cliffs, can we? We need something that makes what we are doing seemingly ours, special, unique, shareable: a no-one-will-believe-this sort of thing that we can post and wait for largely meaningless, but still momentarily thrilling, postings from people we barely or do not know at all.

The world today hints that we care less and less about others but act more and more as if we care about others. A dead giveaway: creating organizations to do things that the average human should be doing indicates that the average human is not doing those things—too bad! We care more about ourselves but act as if we care for others, posting to thousands of total strangers. We defend our cultures while quickly adopting others. This may be the most humorous of all. We are nationalistically "us first!" but we are culturally "come see the Buddhist monks!" as if nothing rubs off, as if no culture is traded back and forth.

Let's consider what we have learned in brief.

Culture: It's a Happy Day!

The sharing of culture is the mission of dozens, if not hundreds, of nonprofits. They believe that by sharing cultures, we will all understand each better, peace will grow, and the world will be a better, happier place (and, by the way, so does Coca-Cola, but more on that later). Here's the bottom line on sharing: an average is created. If we all in the room share, then we will at some point all have the same, right? If we all in the world share all of our cultural attributes, we will soon all have the same cultural attributes. Without getting too terribly technical, the total sharing will result in the disappearance of something we call "culture," which exists only as a difference between one and another. No difference, no cultures.

I know, this will never happen. After all, look at West Virginia and San Diego. But I can assure you that these two geographic areas are far more like each other in 2015 than they were in 1915 or 1965. And in 2065, they will be very, very like each other. How can I be so sure? Maybe it's the mass media that evolved into a very personal media that is still mass and still carries and still receives culture. I could bury you with lots of researchers who are publishing lots of stuff about this (hey, check it out: it's very deep and very cool), but you could just take my word for it. Cultures are not growing apart: they are growing together. And as they grow together, they grow alike.

Does everyone like this? Of course not. Change is not a welcome feature for more than two-thirds of the planet's population. But it is of some interest to note that that number was some time ago much higher. We are growing more comfortable with change, more familiar with change. It also helps that change does not always mean the loss of life or home, though for some, the resistance to change does.

Change is allowed in some areas before others, for males before females, for elites versus the uneducated. Change is a cultural enemy for many and a cultural improvement for fewer others. The risk associated with taking that paraglide off the cliffs of the West Coast of the United States can be used in many ways as a descriptor of how cultures are modified by exposure to new ideas, new fashions, new directions.

Change is more than it seems, even more than just turning left rather than right. It requires the person, the individual, to make a choice that is unique for him- or herself, though millions of others may have made that same choice. Nothing softens the change from white being a dangerous color (as it is in some cultures) to black being the preferred new dangerous color. This may seem so minor, so childish, yet the basis of what constitutes culture is the uniqueness of each culture as compared to another. The use of a color is certainly one that is easy to follow.

For example, white. Were I a copywriter at a big Western advertising agency, I might not know that the concept of white being "pure and good" does not extend to a culture that makes up roughly a third of the world and more than that in active modern consumers. In fact, to the overall cultures that we lump together and call "Chinese," white is seen as an evil color.

You have a problem, yes? You want to think global in your campaign and yet you cannot get past step one, the color.

I suppose the good news is that the culture of colors will change and that it's likely that white will come to be a "good" tone. This presumes the "victory" of one culture over another, if that is the way you think about these things. Sometimes it is discontinuing the use of a specific color. Consider McDonald's new store design. Are the colors the same as they have always been, or are only two, yellow and black, stressed? Without much discussion here in this culture, does this color change work better elsewhere, and does

McDonald's feel pretty certain that someone eating a Big Mac in Beijing will likely have the same in New York City? If so, let's make sure that the consumer can find the store easily, with consistent colors. And, by the way, who needs that much red?

We defend our countries, we defend our states, we defend our school districts. Want to witness some exciting debates? Hang out in a county meeting about the closure of one high school and the resulting shift of students to another, previously considered a rival, high school. Yes, it gets hot.

But discussions about culture in that same county are rare. It seems a given that those in Plainville, Kansas, will act like those in that small-ville ought to act. They should dress the same, speak alike, and prefer similarly accepted items. After all, fifty years ago, they did. But do they today? As I mentioned earlier, walking down the street in Plainville in 2002 or 2003 and hearing the latest rap song blasting out of a passing pickup truck was not only not expected, it would not have been expected in the suburbs of Kansas City, two hundred miles east. It was a shock at the time, but placed within a cultural matrix, it becomes one of those spikes that demands attention. Had I known better, I might have flagged down the driver for a conversation.

Yes, culture is changing, and yes, it seems to be moving toward what might be best described as Western culture. But maybe we should consider the elements involved, if only because some elements of culture seem to be changing faster than others. And since we mentioned music just now, consider how rap and more modern music, mostly created in New York, Los Angeles, Detroit, and London, are being picked up and "localized," as if they had been created in Beijing, New Delhi, and Rio. These obvious copies are being included as part of the culture as if they are somehow different from their Western parents. They are not. But the artists involved cannot first state, "what I will now sing is a rough copy of a Western song by LL Cool J," any more than country singers in the United States can admit that their music is now more rock-and-roll than it was fifty years ago. The push and pull of cultural differences occurs both outside and inside cultures. We cannot expect it to remain constant, though we wish hard that it would.

Perhaps the most insidious element of the culture change overtaking places like China, India, the rest of Asia, and elsewhere is individualism. The cultural grounding of these cultures is a belief in the group, in the family, in the community. The Western individual exists as a separate, independent individual acting alone based on information self-gathered, self-assessed, self-relied upon as accurate. The actual method of validation is terribly flawed, as are those that are used within the family, so we do not measure a difference between the two by the degree of accuracy.

Perhaps the main difference is the actual actions in the gathering of information. Whereas at some time in the past, the gathering was more of a group activity, it is now individual. Value placed on its accuracy is wholly left to the individual. Oddly, we might think that today's individual might deal with the issues that follow along after a failure. Not this generation. That may be the curse or benefit carried forward by the next generation, but even in the most advanced Western culture, the failing individual has some group to fall back on.

This is getting too psychological. Bottom line: individualism and risk are the most important personal attributes that push cultures forward and toward each other.

Advertising's Just Fine, Thank You!

Yes, I teach in a journalism school. No, we are not doing so well. Few midsized schools are doing well, nor are they likely to do well. But that's another tale. Bottom line: advertising as a sequence is still in great demand. We get few, if any, requests from newspapers or television stations (are there still radio stations?) for interns or new graduates, outside of people to sell, before they give up and move on. Agencies are always looking.

Advertising itself is always looking. It's flexible, moldable, easy to turn, shift, and redirect. It's not married to many "standards" (much less to ethics). It has no hard and fast beliefs about what consumers will read, watch, or listen to. Want to watch TV? Okay, we will create commercials. Want to watch online stuff that kinda looks like television? We will figure out how to advertise to that. Want to watch that program, read that book, listen to that song without an advertisement sticking itself into the activity? Hmmm. . . . That will be a hard one. But we'll figure it out.

What advertising is "figuring out" today is the most massive change in its existence since 1960 and the Creative Revolution. The change here is who controls what. The "who" changes from the agency to the consumer. The "what" is the message. Let's be clear: the agency still controls the message. It still controls what is said, how it is said, and for whom the message is intended. The agency simply does not control when the message is read or on what device. These two elements never were much of a concern in the past: agencies knew that the commercial would be in the second pod after the opening of the *Ed Sullivan Show*. Pretty easy to also count on the entire family to watch on a black-and-white in the living room. In the 1980s, the family broke up a bit, with each member having his or her own set to watch more than three channels (welcome cable!), usually in his or her own room. A step toward individualization. But the time was the time. The agency said *Days of Our Lives* was at 1 pm ET, and every housewife (yes, in those days many women were called that) knew it.

Profiling the programs shown and matching commercials to the shows was much like a fish, a barrel, and a gun. Yes, we made media an entire course in the curriculum of advertising, but over the years, software took over the planning so much that the actual act of media buying become little more than punching buttons (gee, sounds a lot like life on the stock market, yes?).

The life of advertising today is using media to answer questions, not to push "the one and only answer." We live in a fully mature global market. Half the world is a growing market, presuming we, the elites, do not want them to continue working for less than $2 a day. But the growth that occurs will likely be within a cultural structure already in place that encourages individual choices and options.

Global campaigns can occur only in something like the oddity of a Coca-Cola or Nike spot when consumers read the same and think similarly. What does this mean? That individualism must grow more before we can declare that we have a global market? Risk must allow for more trials before new items are allowed into newly opening "safety and certainty first" markets to more mundane Western commodities. When will these two events occur? Good question. If I were to guess, ten years. Maybe sooner. Maybe a little later. But it will happen. It kinda depends on something else, which I'll discuss next.

What advertising must face is a consumer who seems smarter by virtue of her or his control of media, who appears more willful by his or her lack of desire to perform complete research (at least for a large slice of the population) in order to become really smart, and who acts impatient for no reason other than he or she can. Nothing reveals that impatience more than the way consumers treat apps.

Who Needs Anyone Else?

Now I offer some ideas about culture and advertising in the near future. Let's add the real game changer: apps. Somehow a definition of apps leaves out the real impact of these little, seemingly harmless programs, usually games. What do we know about them? They are fast. They are usually free (to start with). They are usually built by someone in California (but not as much as they once were). They are usually, for lack of a better way to put it, fun, even if educational, helpful, and all that. They are fun. And they are so Western, so individual. Even in games where you think you are playing with other people-driven characters, you could be playing with computer-generated "flawed-to-seem-human-like" characters. We have billions of these devices with billions more on the way. And, again, they are so Western in language, style, ethics, and any other cultural mode you want to consider that during that moment of use, all other cultures are suppressed.

What is late to be realized by international agencies (maybe—it could be that they are aware and keeping it to themselves) is the ability of consumers to completely control media and thus to be able to control what advertising they will be exposed to. The evolving, obvious new model would be apps specifically created to deliver information sought by consumers. The "mass" part of media will disappear in its old definition. Although many readers will be using apps, each user will define what he or she is looking for. If the information is not what they seek, they will call it "advertising." If the information answers the questions they have, they will deem it of value and almost dictionary-like in its quality and reliability. The result will be hundreds of billions of apps created to answer every possible question in the style required by every consumer.

Yes, this could be pushback on the adoption of a global culture, though the rationale for such an event does not rest solely on advertising.

Let's all agree on one reality: this planet is finite. What can happen is finite, what options are contained within the physical bounds of this world. Still, many possible outcomes present themselves. I am not so bold as the futurists like those I have cited in this book. I bow to them and read every work they offer. But I am a culturist. I look at a particular subject that is hard to follow, hard to predict, almost impossible to assess. I admire when others try. I wonder if it's a shortcoming in me that overstresses the irrationality of the population, the unpredictable nature of the herds, the frequency of the unreliability of the subjects.

Ah, humans!

Index

Absolut, 13, 15–16, 109

ad stack, 16

advertising: animation in, 163–165; apps'
effect on, 151, 157, 224; changing
approaches to, 207; children and,
162–165, 169; consumers' creation of,
137–138; credibility of, 150, 212, 216;
defined, 200, 204; electronic (e-),
199–216; as entertainment, 34; false or
deceptive, 166, 167, 211; and global
culture, 94–95, 215–216; groups
created by, 137; history of, 1;
information-centered, 4, 5, 6, 7;
nontraditional, 208–210; online (see
also Web-based), 139–140; open to
individual interpretations, 11, 12, 13,
14, 15, 19; payment methods for, 35,
36; persistence of, 199–200; predictions
concerning, 223–224; print, 6;
regulation of, 166–168; research
conducted for, 14; on social media, 18,
38; television-based, 1–22; and timing,
134–135; Web-based (see also online),
30, 31–39

advertising agencies: commissions of, 18;
conservatism of, 34, 155, 204, 207,
208; fundamental challenges for, 39,
201, 206; information and its
dissemination in control of, 132, 165,
223; research as focus of, 14; responses
of, to new media, 151, 155, 157, 206,
224; responses of, to television, 20–21;
and truthfulness, 216

AdWords, 33

agencies. *See* advertising agencies

Aguilera, Christina, 208–209

Al-Buruni, 183

Allan, G., 78

aloneness, 175–176

Amazon.com, 60–63, 141–144, 145, 146

Anacin, 4, 5

Anderson, Chris, 39, 104, 115, 143, 153

Anderson, Thomas C., 77–78

Angry Birds, 40, 41, 74, 87

animation, in advertising, 163–165

anime, 73

anonymity, 81

AOL, 16, 72

Apple 1984 commercial, 10

apps, 39–42; antisocial character of,
40–42; and atheism, 111; brand
adoption driven by, xiii, 95, 125,
129–131; catalogs and, 124, 125;
consumer-oriented, 39, 129–133, 216,
225; control of, 117–118, 119; and
credibility, 112–113, 116; cultural
aspect of, 132–133; defined, 70–71; and
education, 112–113, 186, 191, 196;
effect of, on advertising, 151, 157, 224;
and entertainment, 72, 205; and experts,
111; functionalities of, xiii; and global
culture, 86–87, 93–97; individualism

About the Author

Thomas H. P. Gould is professor of communications and head of the Advertising Sequence at the A. Q. Miller School of Journalism and Mass Communications at Kansas State University. He spent his graduate years in North Carolina, first in Charlotte, then in Chapel Hill. With his position at Kansas State, it is the first time Gould has spent more than ten years in any one place, and, frankly, Kansas has overtaken his previous loving memory of Paris, France, where he spent some of his childhood. He finds Kansas irresistible, especially when there is a chance to take occasional trips elsewhere.

CPSIA information can be obtained at www.ICGtesting.com
Printed in the USA
BVOW02*1827120216

436531BV00001B/1/P